Unholy Grails

A New Road to Wealth

NICK RADGE

RADGE
PUBLISHING

First published in Australia in 2012 by Radge Publishing

Radge Publishing
PO Box 721 Noosa Heads QLD 4567 Australia. www.radgepublishing.com

National Library of Australia Cataloguing-in-Publication entry (hbk)
Author: Radge, Nick, 1967-
Title: Unholy grails : a new road to wealth / Nick Radge.
ISBN: 9780980871210 (hbk.)
Subjects: Investments.
Stocks.
Finance, Personal.
Dewey Number: 332.6322

Typeset in Book Antiqua 11/15
Typesetting by: Master Page Design

Cover design: Photografica Creative Solutions
Cover image: ©Carlos Gotay Martínez

Printed in Australia by Griffin Press

"If you challenge the conventional wisdom, you will find ways to do things better than they are currently done."

Michael Lewis

For Hannah, Zach and Holly

Always my favourites.

Contents

Important Information

This book may contain advice that has been prepared by Reef Capital Coaching (AFSL 288200). Being general advice it does not take into account your objectives, financial situation or needs. Before acting on this general advice you should therefore consider the appropriateness of the advice in regard to your situation. We recommend you obtain financial, legal and taxation advice before making any financial investment decisions.

This material has been prepared based on information believed to be accurate at the time of publication. Subsequent changes in circumstances may occur at any time and may impact the accuracy of the information.

Past results are not a reliable indication of future performance.

All results are considered to be hypothetical unless otherwise specified. Hypothetical performance results have many inherent limitations. Unlike an actual performance record, simulated results do not represent actual trading. Also, since the trades have not actually been executed, the results may have under- or over- compensated for the impact, if any, of certain market factors, such as lack of liquidity.

Acknowledgements

Any worthy project has to be supported by friends and family, and this book is no exception. Primarily my thanks go to Trish for not only encouraging me to keep moving forward with this project but also playing the roles of editor, publisher, wife, mother and #1 supporter. You are my true soul mate.

A special thanks to Craig Fisher from The Chartist and Brett Winton from www.AmiBrokercoding.com who have tirelessly put up with my selfish persistence to take these ideas and put them into computer code.

My gratitude to Richard Dale from Norgate Investor Services for supplying quality data and talking me through the intricacies of its use.

Thanks to John and Kris Rowland, Michael Harrison and Scott Goddard, all of whom have critiqued various ideas in this book and helped point me in the right direction.

Specific thanks to some online forum members: katarapko42, The Phantom, Cookie, oztrader, Stevo, bingk6, N40K, zipzap, GlennR and thetrendfollower.

I am also truly grateful to the many colleagues I have worked with over the years, the numerous supportive clients and other users of my online community who continue to inspire, grow and offer honest opinion and feedback where required on all things trading and investing. Like market cycles, our worlds have converged and diverged over the years, yet with each small meeting I gain more useful insights from you all.

Preface

Investing manifests itself in different ways for different people – one person's prized strategy may cause another investor to shake their head in disbelief. We do, after all, swim in our own pool of personal logic. If it were any other way the market would not be the market as we know it and opportunities would not abound as they currently do. This book details one way, rather than the only way. It goes against almost everything that your stockbroker, financial planner, accountant and your fund manager will ever tell you. It will detail a road less travelled; it is a compilation of objective and practical strategies for the active investor that goes against traditional thinking.

In that mould Richard 'Dick' Fosbury is someone who knows a little about the road less travelled.

As a young athlete he had trouble mastering the standard high jump using the textbook scissor technique. The traditional western roll and straddle were also styles that he simply didn't get. During a school meet at Grants Pass in 1963, he improvised and went over the bar backwards – literally; physically upside down from every other competitor in the field.

It had never been done before.

It had never been seen before.

His coach told him to "stop goofing around."[1]

Coaches from other schools complained to the judges that what

---

1 *Portland Tribune*, "From Flop to smashing high jump success", Kerry Eggers, July 23, 2008

he was doing was not legal.

He was called an idiot and one news reporter suggested he looked like a "fish flopping in a boat"[2], hence the term 'flop'.

A Dr J. T. O'Hanlan of Waynesboro, VA, questioned the safety of the style in an article to the *Virginia Medical Monthly* suggesting that young jumpers were "...liable to suffer severe vertebral damage"[3].

Even the U.S. athletic team coach Payton Jordan commented that "... an entire generation of high jumpers could be wiped out because they all will have broken necks."[4]

But then Dick Fosbury won Gold at the 1968 Olympics.

He set a new Olympic and American record that day and eventually entered the National Track and Field Hall of Fame.

Just four years later, during the Munich Olympics in 1972, 70% of competitors used the now-famed Fosbury Flop. During the period 1972 through 2000, some 94.5% of Olympic medallists used the Flop and it is now considered the industry standard technique for high jump[5].

Going against the herd is extremely difficult. It suggests you're out of step with the rest of the world. It encourages criticism from those that are unable, or unwilling, to open their minds to other possibilities.

The contents of this book are actually nothing new, although only practiced by a quiet few; indeed the broad concepts can be traced back to the 1800s[6]. Those that do successfully use these concepts are still considered fringe dwellers. Even with evidence to the contrary they are dismissed by the herd and deemed long-tail aberrations that will eventually fail.

Unholy Grails is designed for investors requiring a hard-wired yet robust strategy that has been statistically and robustly proven on past data before directly committing funds to the market. It is for investors wanting to move away from 'Buy & Hold' and a refuge from sustained bear market events. The goal is to offer an alternative to traditional investment methods; many would argue the 2008

---

2 As reported by a Medford newspaper
3 *Sports Illustrated*, "Being backwards gets results" Roy Blount Jnr, February 10, 1969
4 Source: Hickok Sports Biographies
5 Source: Wikipedia
6 *The Great Metropolis, Vol II* by James Grant, 1838.

stock market decline, when global markets and capital managed by fund managers dropped up to 50%, demonstrated exactly why a robust and historically proven alternative is desperately needed.

Conversely this book is not for advanced systems traders looking for sophisticated quantitative methods and statistical theorem, nor is it for investors wanting to encompass fundamental ratios or forecasting techniques; there are enough Buffettt books on the market to keep several generations busy.

There is very little that is new in the world of trading and investing. When it comes to developing investment strategies of any type we tend to borrow bits and pieces, ideas and rituals from those we come into contact with. In some cases it may simply be a small part of a strategy, such as an entry mechanism read about in a book or on the net, adapted to suit our own personality. In some situations, such as John Rowland's TechTrader, it's a complete strategy that has been in the public arena for a number of years and successfully implemented by numerous retail investors. The world is full of strategies that get bandied about freely in the press, on investing and trading forums and in various magazines and books. But do they really work? This book is not about recreating the wheel. It's about taking some of the commonly referred to strategies and putting them to the test so we can better understand what they can and, perhaps more importantly, what they can't do.

Some of these strategies are dubbed 'back of envelope' because they are simple to understand and use. Others are a little more complex and require some basic off-the-shelf software to operate. However, either way, the goal is to limit the cost of implementation in both time and money spent. You do not need a financial planner or stockbroker to beat the market. You need fresh ideas that offer proof-of-concept. Not only are these ideas being presented for thoughtful consideration, they have been robustly tested using historical data to ensure they stand a chance of working into the future.

That said, any amount of testing, hypotheses and conclusions are not exact science. Indeed the stock market is not an exact science. It's a game of probabilities in an ever-evolving world of human emotion. Within the realms of what is offered here one must be cognizant that past results are not indicative of future performance and that some of these ideas, indeed possibly all of these strategies, may not be appropriate for your own circumstances. It is highly recommended that if you intend to follow through with any of the methods presented that you complete a full assessment of the risks and merits of doing so or seek the advice of a qualified person to advise you.

I was unwittingly introduced to momentum investing in 1985, so this book is based on 26 years of my first hand in-market practical experience. My goal is to provide investors with a new direction, especially people looking for something a little different to what is usually touted. It is designed to offer a sensible basis upon which to make sound investment decisions, reduce exposure and protect against risk.

Even so, regardless of how good a strategy is, you should be warned that success can only come from confidence, consistency, discipline and patience. Whilst the foundations of profitability in this game are very easy to grasp and teachable, it's these four psychological attributes that account for the majority of investors and traders failing to follow through or falling short of their expectations. These foundations are explainable, but they can be difficult to implement consistently over the longer term.

1. Confidence
2. Consistency
3. Discipline
4. Patience

Remember these.

Add to these foundations some rules for success, yet if you can't or won't follow these rules they will not be of any use to you.

Rules you can't or won't follow are of no use.

The secret of success is so simple it's usually discarded as exactly that—too simple. People tend to gravitate toward complex solutions when usually a simple solution will work just as well and in some cases, better. Several decades of direct market experience during varied and adverse conditions prove this beyond doubt.

To be a successful investor or trader you must:

- Find a strategy that works
- Validate it
- Do it

This book is designed to deliver the first two of these core attributes in a succinct manner, then guide you to gain confidence in doing the third.

The journey is worth it.

Nick Radge
Noosa Heads

SECTION 1
Laying the Foundation

Momentum Investing

Momentum investing is a form of active investing. Active investing refers to making specific investments with the goal of outperforming a benchmark. In most instances active investors attempt to predict or forecast various market anomalies in order to create a return greater than that benchmark. For the vast majority of fund managers and analysts these forecasts are based on micro and macro fundamental inputs, various financial metrics as well as qualitative traits such as management experience. Much of what is practiced by 'the big end of town' tends to be subjective and commonly accepted as investing in a traditional manner.

The opposite of active investing would be a 'Buy & Hold' strategy: an investor or fund manager purchases a stock based on perceived value or a desire to hold a particular product, then sticks the paperwork in the bottom drawer and forgets about it. The goal is for the stock price to increase over time and for the investor to receive regular dividends.

The definition of active investing is important because much academic research purports that active investing is a pointless pursuit and that over time nobody can beat the benchmark[7]. Indeed, if the mandate of the average fund manager is to remain 80% invested and charge higher fees, then it certainly does become a difficult task to outperform any type of benchmark, at least over the longer term and with consistency.

Yet, by definition, rather than predict or forecast in advance, what if active investing meant moderating your exposure as markets naturally oscillate up and down? When prices start to move higher you increase market exposure to 100% and conversely when prices start heading lower you decrease market exposure to 0%. This could be deemed active investing in its purest form: choosing when to be involved in the market, how much to invest and when to sit out of the market and wait for conditions to improve.

Moderating exposure is a form of momentum investing and is a subset of active investing. Momentum investing refers to buying securities that have shown higher returns over recent history compared to the broader underlying market or, for sophisticated investors, also short selling securities that have underperformed over the same period and attempt to balance their market exposure accordingly. There are many performance measures to define momentum including price-to-earnings growth, price-to-book ratios, dividend yields and relative strength, to name just a few. This book does not deal with any of these.

The goal of an active investor is to grow capital, pure and simple. To achieve this goal requires two very simple, yet logical, performance drivers:

1. Be fully invested in stocks exhibiting upside momentum during sustained bullish trends, and
2. Defend and revert to cash, 100% if necessary, during sustained bearish trends[8].

---

7 "Luck, Skill and Investment Performance" – Cornell (2009)
"Luck versus Skill in the Cross Section of Mutual Fund Returns" – Fama and French (2009)

8 In late 2008 all short selling was banned in Australia for a period of time meaning that a momentum strategy based on short selling weak stocks would not have been viable. If the rules of the game are changed during these episodes then there is no point relying on a 'short selling' strategy to be useful in the future. For the average person in the street, reverting to cash is simple, easy to achieve and above all extremely useful.

The first driver is, on the surface, quite logical. You need to be invested when the market is rising to produce a return. However, buying stocks that are not moving in lockstep with the broader market can dilute performance based on a simple and surprisingly robust premise that a stock in motion will tend to stay in motion. It means buying stocks that are already going up. This thought process is counterintuitive and probably why it's still not accepted by the herd. Most people want to buy something cheap and sell after it rises, not buy something that has already risen and sell it higher still.

Empirical evidence suggests a stock exhibiting downside momentum, i.e. a stock getting cheaper in price, has a higher probability of continuing to travel lower—a stock in motion tends to stay in motion. In order to make a profit you must sell an asset at a higher price from which you bought it, so buying something that's heading down, and has a high probability of continuing to travel lower, goes against that goal. In his outstanding book, *What Works on Wall Street,* James O'Shaughnessey found evidence that if you bought 10% of the large cap stocks that had experienced the biggest price drops over the previous 12 months, your account would have declined over the following 12 months.

To test the theory I asked the computer to buy all current and delisted stocks on the ASX as they made a new yearly low and then again as they made a new yearly high. What is the probability of the stock continuing to move lower or continuing to move higher after a certain holding period?

In Figure 1 below, the upper line shows that a stock making a 250 day low has a 52% chance of continuing lower over the next 20 days and continues to have a 51% chance of being lower after 300 days. However, buying a stock making a 250 day high has a 47% chance of being lower after 20 days yet just 37% of being lower after 300 days. At 300 days the edge of buying a stock exhibiting strength versus a stock exhibiting weakness is significant at 15%.

FIGURE 1: Probability of Loss after *n*-days

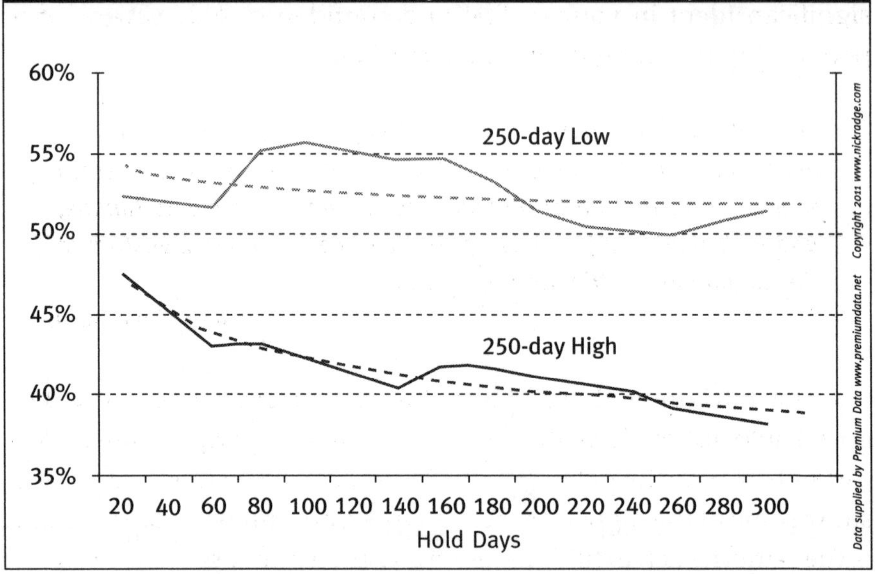

Figure 1: Probability of loss after holding a position for n-days.

That is not to say that you would base a complete investment strategy on the simple premise of buying weakness, although many investors would be guilty of having bought a stock simply because it was priced lower than what it had traded previously at some stage in their investing career: the myth that what goes down must come back up, or anchoring one's opinion on a past price level. Buying weakness is like standing in front of a moving vehicle. Sometimes it will stop but most of the time you'll get run over and suffer varying degrees of injury. In some instances, as in the Tech crash and in the Global Financial Crisis (GFC), there may be times you won't be able to get back up again.

The second driver of performance is defending capital during sustained adverse market conditions. Many so-called 'investment grade' companies now face new challenges, including declining economic and business conditions, that can materially impact future earnings. In most instances, such as we saw in 2008, these changed conditions only become apparent after price has declined by a substantial amount. An intrinsic part of this defensive exercise is to avoid stocks that plunge into the abyss. During 2008 we witnessed many companies drop from very high levels into default and bankruptcy. Just having one or two of these stocks can put a significant dent in your capital and confidence. 2008 saw a lot of people stop investing in the stock market.

> *"It would be simple to run down the list of hundreds of stocks which, in my time, have been considered gilt-edge investments, and which today are worth little or nothing. Thus, great investments tumble, and with them the fortunes of so-called conservative investors in the continuous distribution of wealth."*
>
> **Jesse Livermore**[9]

The intriguing thing about this is that every company that goes bankrupt exhibits the same price pattern—with almost 100% certainty. Know the pattern to avoid the abyss. The following charts show some of the higher profile collapses, although the salient point is the pattern each exhibit before the company delists:

FIGURE 2: HIH Insurance

Figure 2: HIH Insurance Ltd, June 1992—January 2001.

9 *Reminiscences of a Stock Operator*; Edwin Lefèvre; 1994, Wiley Investment Classics

FIGURE 3: Babcock & Brown

Figure 3: Babcock and Brown, October 2004—November 2009.

FIGURE 4: OneTel Limited

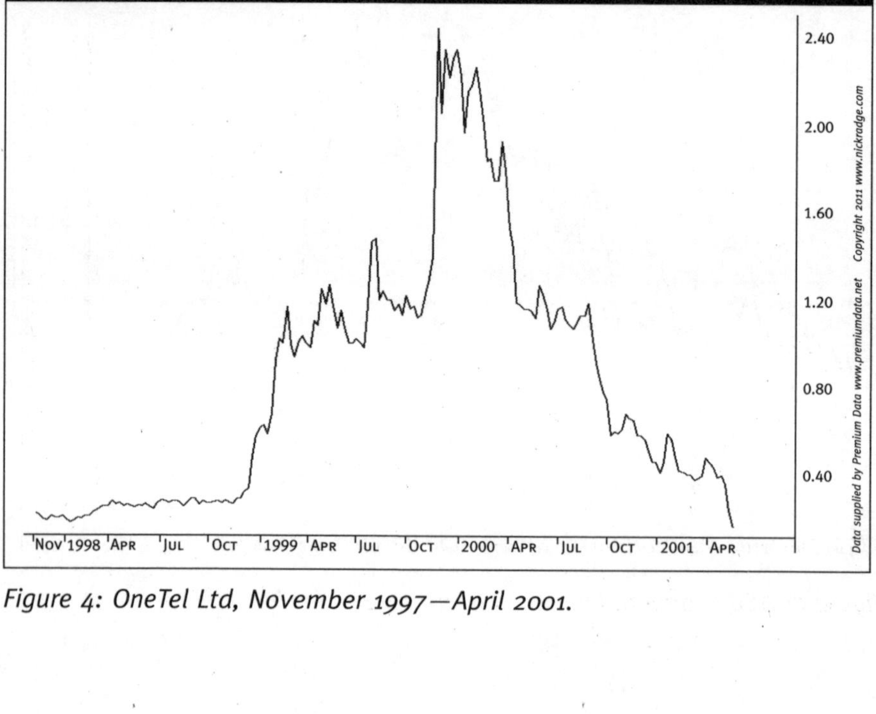

Figure 4: OneTel Ltd, November 1997—April 2001.

FIGURE 5: Great Southern Limited

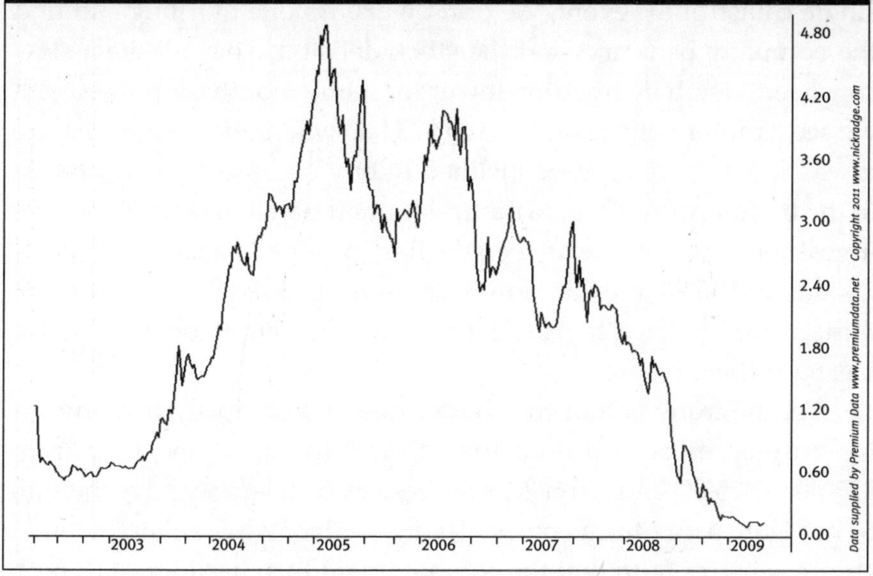

Figure 5: Great Southern Ltd, January 2002—April 2009.

FIGURE 6: ABC Learning

Figure 6: ABC Learning, June 2003—July 2008.

The common trait is that their downfall is not an overnight or single catastrophic event. We don't wake up one morning and find the company bankrupt and the stock delisted. They all die a slow consistent death by trending lower for many months, if not years. If we see a motor vehicle on sale for $25,000 when several months ago it was $35,000, we're more inclined to buy because we're anchored to the higher price. This is a natural human trait and is what induces investors to buy stocks as they decline in price. If a stock was once trading at $35.00 and can now be bought for $25.00, it is natural to think it can go back to $35.00, based on the simple premise that it has been there before.

Yet the irony is that the share price of a company heading for bankruptcy must also drop from $35.00 to $25.00 and then from $25.00 to $15.00, and so on. Most investors believe they have the skill to navigate away from companies in trouble, while others retain a strong sense of faith that the company will turn itself around. Both situations are a recipe for disaster.

Not all companies go into administration, but there are many instances where a company will lose its value and stay down for very long periods of time. Holding onto an underperforming asset, especially if it was purchased at an inopportune time, in the hope that someday it may return to its former glory will dramatically dilute returns.

The following chart shows a stock that has been falling for a long time and remains in a downward tailspin. Broker Consensus Opinion[10] points to numerous analysts recommending this stock as a BUY or OUTPERFORM and have been doing so for the many months. For a long term holder of the stock it will require a miracle to recoup these losses, assuming it can ever turn higher.

10 Source: Thompson Reuters

FIGURE 7: Billabong International

Figure 7: Billabong International, September 2003—May 2011.

There are many examples that were, and still are, considered safe investments. On a dividend adjusted basis, QBE Insurance (QBE) topped out at $28.30 in September 2007. Four years later it remains sub-$15.00. Macquarie Group (MQG) topped out at $79.00 only to now be trading closer to $20.00. Harvey Norman (HVN) used to trade circa $7.00 and is now $2.00. How long will it be (if ever) before these stocks return to former highs so investors locked in at higher levels can get back to a breakeven proposition? They may be safe stocks but if purchased at the wrong time they can lead to extreme drag on portfolio performance.

An active momentum investor will automatically avoid these types of stocks which is a key driver in delivering outperformance.

Being fully invested when the market is rising and reverting to cash during a sustained bear market is not about predicting or timing the market. It's about reacting to the *current* market trend and then positioning oneself accordingly. We don't take a position because we *think* a stock will travel higher or because we've *valued* a stock at a higher price (a form of prediction), but because it *is* travelling higher.

By the end of this book you will grasp the critical distinction between predicting and reacting.

As we can't predict the future we can therefore never know whether the current market trend will continue or whether it will reverse. We can never know if the stock will travel from A to B and we can certainly never know if, or when, a stock will meet a predicted future valuation price. We don't need to know, or predict, the future. What we need to do is react when a trend, either up or down, has been established and we need to do so in a methodical, repeatable fashion. Methodical means eliminating emotion from the decision-making process and working to a predefined plan that has been proven to work using historical simulations. Repeatable is a strategy that we can continue to use over and over into the future knowing it is reliable and will deliver on our goals.

By refraining from predicting and instead reacting to current events in a methodical and repeatable way, we are able to add significant value to our investments over the longer term.

Becoming a Hitch-Hiker

There are many ways to measure momentum, such as Price-to-Book Ratio, Price-to-Cash flow, Earnings Growth and others. But ultimately we are judged by the difference between our purchase price and our sale price, or the current mark-to-market price if a position remains open. Therefore the heart of a pure momentum strategy is solely price action. Indeed, the heart of any strategy, regardless of how much you want to dress it up, is price.

> *"The price is the verdict. Follow it or perish."* **Michael Covel**[11]

Catching price momentum is like a hitch-hiker catching a ride. A hitch-hiker solicits a ride by standing at the edge of the road, thumb out while facing the oncoming traffic. When looking to capture a ride, hitch-hikers don't know which car will stop or how far a ride will take them should a driver offer a lift. A hitch-hiker simply goes with the flow but will only join a ride that is heading in the right direction.

---

11 www.trendfollowing.com

Likewise a momentum investor will tend to stand aligned with oncoming price action ready to buy as prices are rising and ready to exit when prices start falling. A momentum investor has no idea which stock will offer the next ride or how far the ride will take them. A momentum investor, like a hitch-hiker, simply goes with the flow of the market: fully invested as the market rises in a sustained up-trend and reverting to cash in a sustained bear trend.

FIGURE 8: Riding a Market Wave

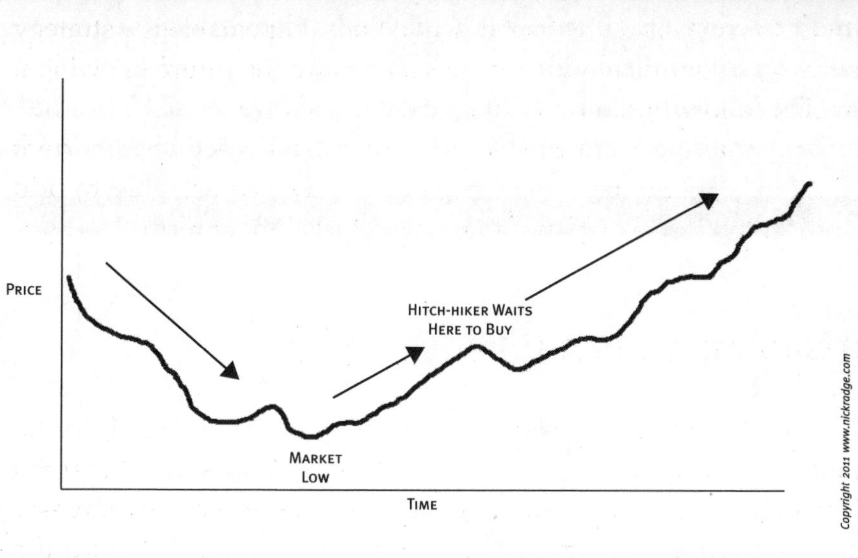

Figure 8: A hitch-hiker catches a market wave only after a low is made.

Nick's Top Tips

It is just as important to know when to be involved in the market as it is to know when to be sitting on the sideline, waiting in cash. A good defence goes hand in hand with a good offense. Staying in cash as the market declines ensures faster recovery to new equity highs and is easier to manage psychologically.

A common misconception is that a momentum investing strategy 'buys high, sells low'. Sceptics suggest that momentum investors are more likely to buy when everyone else is buying and sell when everyone else is selling, rather than follow the traditional laws that govern value investing whereby one 'buys fear and sells greed'. This is inaccurate. By definition, what exactly is high? What is low? Regardless of the type of investor you are, reality suggests we can never predict the absolute high or low, nor buy or sell the absolute high or low. An investor can try to guess (or predict) when a high or low is achieved but a momentum investor will wait for confirmation.

The following chart of Iluka Resources shows the stock in a clear range spanning several years. Is the price considered high or low?

FIGURE 9

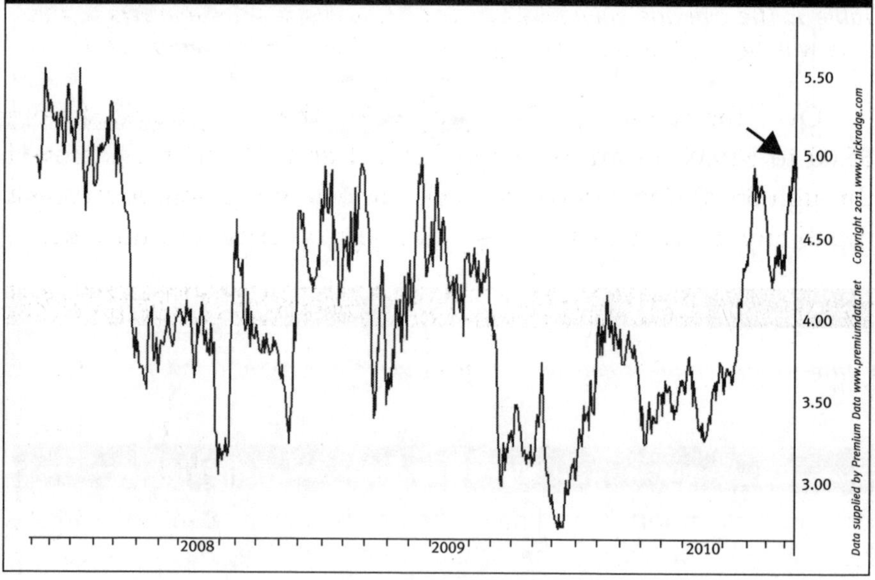

Figure 9: Iluka Resources appears to be trading toward the top end of a range that had been in place for several years.

The following table shows various opinions expressed by analysts at the general time Iluka Resources was trading in this range. The average valuation by these analysts is about $0.27 higher than the current price. One could argue that at this point they consider the stock fully priced.

Date	Broker	Target Price
17 May 2010	RBS Australia	$4.53
30 June 2010	Deutsche Bank	$5.10
5 July 2010	Citi	$6.30
8 July 2010	BA-Merrill Lynch	$6.01
13 July 2010	JP Morgan	$5.26
21 July 2010	Macquarie	$4.00
21 July 2010	UBS	$5.70

Table 1: The average valuation by some of Australia's top analysts at this time was $5.27. (Source—Australian Broker Call www.fnarena.com)

Over the following 12-month period the stock traveled from $5.00 to $19.00 in an extremely clean trend. When price moved through $5.00 it never looked back—it just kept going. Awaiting a dip to buy the weakness would have been a very costly mistake.

FIGURE 10

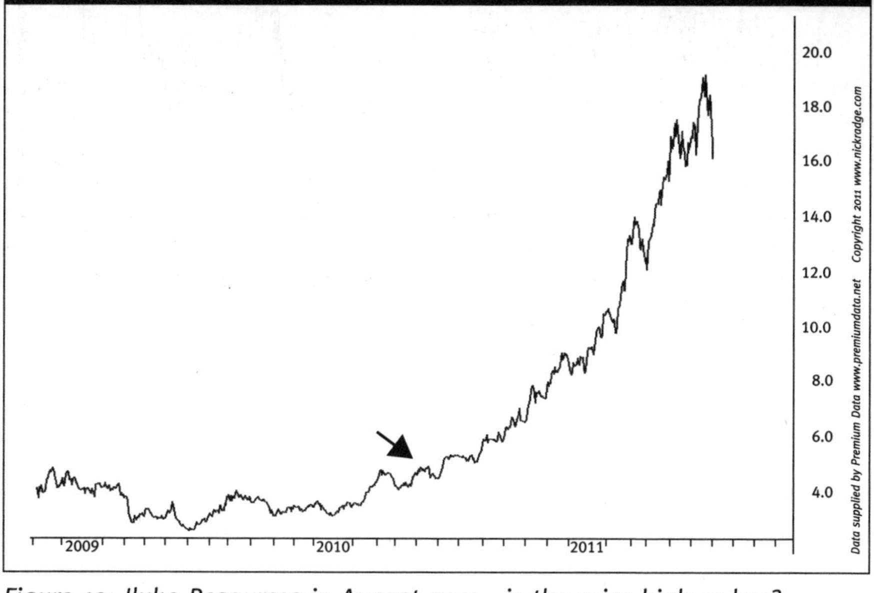

Figure 10: Iluka Resources in August 2011—is the price high or low?

Traditional logic says we need to buy into weakness usually with the intent of purchasing a quality asset at a cheap price and well below its valuation. Doing so, however, creates unknowns, specifically:

1. Will the stock continue to travel lower?
2. If so, how far lower will it go?
3. How long before weakness reverses and prices start to rise?

We have already discussed the risks of these unknowns yet they remain the acceptable call to action by the herd.

On the other hand a momentum investor removes these unknowns by waiting for strength to return before entering. The following diagram shows how both types of investor have essentially bought in the same general region yet the momentum investor is less susceptible to the three traits above.

FIGURE 11

Figure 11: A value investor buys into weakness. A momentum investor awaits strength before buying.

Not every stock will trend all of the time, but there are generally enough stocks trending some of the time to present opportunities. In certain market conditions these rides, or trends, will be very long and extremely rewarding. In other market conditions they may be short and non-rewarding. The following table shows a history of broad market trends where the average uptrend lasts 3x the average downtrend, and the average upside gain is 3.5x the average decline.

BULL MARKETS			
Start Date	**End Date**	**Time (days)**	**Gain**
Jul-82	Sep-87	1888	421%
Nov-87	Sep-89	670	55%
Jan-91	Nov-91	304	42%
Nov-92	Feb-94	457	73%
Nov-94	Sep-97	1035	54%
Oct-97	Feb-02	1585	56%
Mar-03	Nov-07	1710	158%
Mar-09	Apr-11	763	64%
	Average	1052	115%

BEAR MARKETS			
Start Date	**End Date**	**Time (days)**	**Loss**
Nov-80	Jul-82	607	-41%
Sep-87	Nov-87	61	-50%
Sep-89	Jan-91	487	-33%
Nov-91	Nov-92	366	-20%
Feb-94	Nov-94	273	-23%
Sep-97	Oct-97	30	-21%
Feb-02	Mar-03	392	-23%
Nov-07	Mar-09	486	-55%
Apr-11	?		-24%
	Average	338	-32%

Data supplied by Premium Data www.premiumdata.net   Copyright 2011 www.nickradge.com

Table 2: Thirty years of stock market trends in the All Ordinaries Index

A momentum investor will take the good with the bad knowing that, over time, the good outweighs the bad by a significant margin due to the creation of a positive expectancy. Whilst momentum investing works reasonably well most of the time, like any strategy, investment or asset class, it will have periods where performance is lacklustre. It is important to stress that during these times the strategy is not broken and needn't be discarded. This is a beginner's trap. We'll talk more about this in the coming sections.

The vast array of traditional investment strategies rely on picking the right stocks, or at least the right sector in which the stocks sit. A momentum investor on the other hand does not pick the stock, but rather the stock picks the momentum investor. The stock must start trending higher before it becomes a buying candidate, as is shown in Figure 11. An extrapolation of this is that a momentum investor need not predict the next hot sector, because stocks in a sector that is moving will automatically rise to the top and be presented as a new trend opportunity.

A momentum investor does not rely on picking the right individual stocks per se to generate profit. It's the underlying strategy that generates the profit. We actually don't mind what stocks are held, what they do as businesses, the fundamentals, the financial metrics or what the stock's future outlook is. These are all simple by-products of the underlying strategy itself. An investor using a momentum strategy creates what is known as an edge, or a positive expectancy, and it's this edge that is a generator of profits. Rather than focus on selecting the next great stock or sector, a momentum investor's sole focus is replicating their edge over the longer term.

Why Profits Are Generated

To someone expecting profit generation to aggregate from complexity, what follows here may seem too simplistic. In my view nothing could be further from the truth. Keith Campbell is Principal at Campbell & Company, a $4.9 billion fund with a 30 year annualized return exceeding 14.5% after fees[12]. In his book, *Trend Following,* Michael Covel quotes Campbell on simplicity:

> *"Everything we do we could do on the back of an envelope with a pencil."*

The more you can intimately understand, which Keith Campbell does, and explain why profits are generated, why you have an edge, the less historical testing and validation techniques are required and the more comfortable you will be applying your strategy.

You do not need to understand all the different tools employed by successful investors to make investment decisions—far from it. We can easily dispel the myth that there is some 'secret' to success. For example, if we were to select twenty of the most successful fund managers, place them in a room together and ask them to explain how they make their investment decisions they will each have different styles, different criteria, different position management processes and different risk management techniques. Yet they are all successful.

If these twenty investors are successful yet all use different tools, then the tools being used are not the common denominator in the success equation. The tools they use, their valuation techniques, their metrics and models, are all a crutch or process for triggering participation in the market; nothing more.

The actual profitability comes from something else.

Success in the share market comes from understanding how the underlying mathematical principles behind trading and investing work.

> *"There is no such thing as luck. It is all mathematics."*
>
> **Nico Zographos**

In simple technical terms that means understanding how and why you have an edge. An edge is not the method of buying and selling to generate a profit. An edge is not how far a stock is trading below its intrinsic value, nor is it related to future growth prospects,

---

12 www.campbell.com

predicting the next hot sector or any other financial or qualitative metric. An edge is the mathematical outcome of the buying and selling process. All successful investors create a positive edge. Unsuccessful investors have a negative edge. It's important to know how to create that positive edge over the longer term. Once you can create that edge, all you need to do is apply it consistently.

There are three factors to consider when determining if your edge will be a success:

1. How much you win when you win
2. How much you lose when you lose
3. How often you win

We can combine 1 and 2 and call the resultant number the win/loss ratio.

George Soros has winning and losing trades. He is a Global Macro investor and he also generates these same statistics. Warren Buffettt, arguably the world's greatest investor, has good trades and bad trades. He too would generate these same three statistics. Keith Campbell, with a 30 year track record, will too. Any trader or investor of any calibre, regardless of how they operate in the market, will generate these figures.

Let's consider an example: if Jane makes 10 transactions over a period of time we can calculate these three factors and understand her profitability.

If 5 of her transactions are winning propositions and 5 are losing, you may assume that Jane isn't much of an investor with a win rate of just 50%. That kind of strike rate within society would be deemed close to failure. But if we knew that each loss Jane sustained was limited to $1000, yet each profit she made averaged $3000, then all of a sudden Jane is a very profitable investor.

Her win/loss ratio is 3:1 and we can calculate her profit by:
(5 x $3000) – (5 x $1000) = $10,000

If Jane can generate 20 transactions a year instead of 10, she becomes twice as profitable albeit still with a success rate of just 50%. This 'mediocre' success rate is not so mediocre after all.

The momentum investor cannot know how far a stock will rise. Nobody can know, with any certainty or any consistency, how far a stock will travel, either up or down. However, there are two things that a momentum investor can do to increase their mathematical edge:

1. Allow the stock to continue to rise and, like a hitch-hiker, get off the trend only when it reverses, and
2. Control any loss incurred if the stock reverses immediately after the initial entry.

This is exactly how Jane managed the above example. She limited her losses to $1000 yet allowed her profits to grow to an average of $3000, enabling her win/loss ratio to rise above 1:1.

Jane created her positive edge simply by cutting her losing positions yet allowing her winning positions to run. We haven't discussed why Jane bought those stocks or the tools she used to determine why she should buy them. Those factors or tools simply do not matter. Remember, they are deemed 'comfort' items only. Had she not created that mathematical edge in the first place she would be a loser. Period.

FIGURE 12: P&L Stock Price

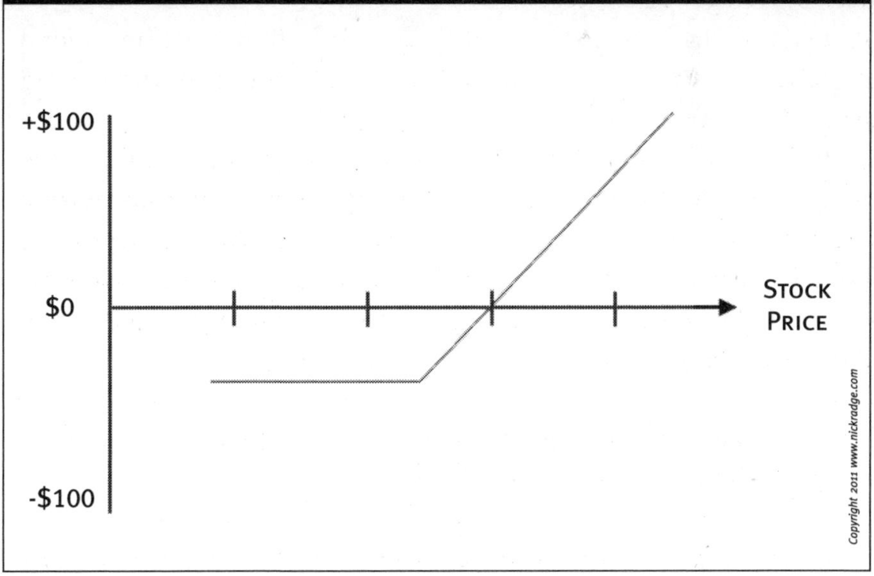

Figure 12: The expiry profile of a long call option.

The simple premise of cutting losses and allowing profits to grow is likened to buying a call option. The buyer of a call option has limited loss and theoretically unlimited profit potential. The expiry payoff diagram for a long option shows an initial limited loss on declining price, yet a steady climb in profitability as price rises.

A momentum investor however does not pay an upfront premium like an option buyer does. The cost incurred by following trends will be the difference between the purchase price and the initial stop-loss price should a trend not occur. The major element contributing to the strategy's profitability, or edge, is that this cost is limited at all times by exiting a losing position rather than waiting and hoping that it will come good.

Another way of showing this relationship between winners and losses is plotting the distribution of completed trades. The following diagram shows a set of losing trades in a tight formation to the left of the 0% point on the distribution curve. Note that all trades fall between -40% and 0%. However, the right side, showing all profitable trades, continues to plot well beyond the +40%, indeed we can see considerable trades out to +100% and then a scattering of 'outlier' trades extending as far as +230%. This distribution is known as Positive Skew.

FIGURE 13: Positive Skew Profile

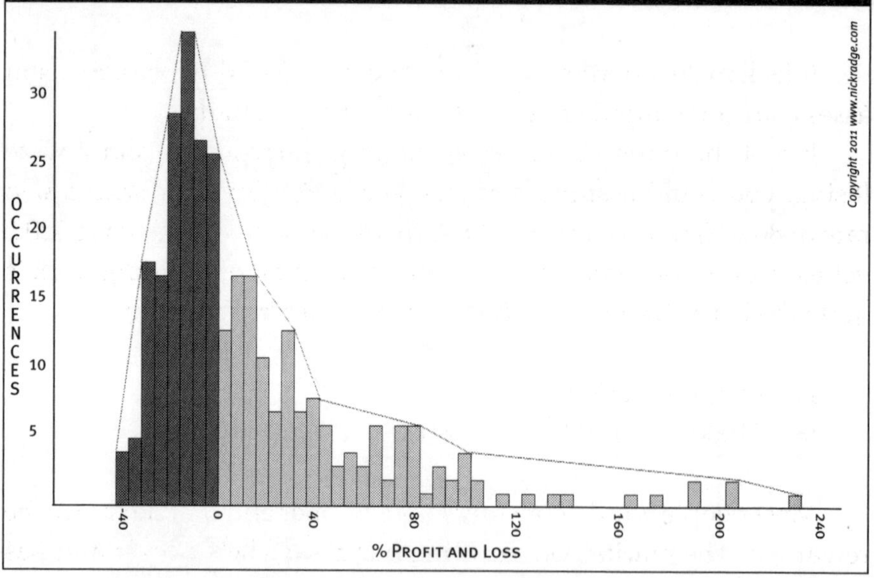

Figure 13: A distribution of trade outcomes. The 'tail' to the right is known as a Positive Skew.

Out of the 273 trades plotted on this distribution diagram just 129 (47.25%) are winners but those that win are, on average, over five times larger than the losses. This is, mathematically, an extremely profitable strategy.

The larger that win/loss ratio grows, the higher your profitability will be and the less important the win rate becomes. Unfortunately the win rate is where most novices, and indeed many experienced market professionals, come unstuck. It is human nature to think that a high winning percentage of transactions equates to higher profits, yet, as these examples show, nothing could be further from the truth.

The issue we have is that our society naturally rewards those who do well. High School students with the best marks become eligible for the better university degrees. A better university degree enables better job prospects and potentially a higher income in the workforce and therefore potential for a higher standard of living.

Unfortunately when it comes to the markets the same is not always true. In fact pursuing that same logic in the market can cause severe frustration and disappointment. An investor who makes ten trades and gets eight correct can mathematically still lose.

An edge is the outcome, the mathematical outcome, of the buying and selling process.

If Jack makes 10 transactions over a period of time we can again assess our three inputs to understand his profitability.

If 8 of the transactions were winning propositions and 2 were losing, you could assume that Jack was a gun investor with a win rate of 80%. But if we knew that each loss Jack sustained was $5000, yet each profit he made averaged $1000, then all of a sudden Jack is quite the loser even though he has 80% of his trades 'right'.

His win/loss ratio is 1:5.
(8 x $1000) – (2 x $5000) = -$2,000

Most people would consider Jack a winner and that he should be rewarded. The market, on the other hand, says he's a loser and has quite rightly removed cash from his pocket. We haven't discussed how or why Jack bought the stocks he did. It doesn't matter what tools he used. He allowed his average loss to become so much larger than his average win that he turned his high win rate, and his foray into the stock market, into a losing business proposition.

People like Jack, who pursue a higher winning percentage of trades, are more prone to disappointment and frustration because the search for the high winning strategy in pursuit of higher profits is never ending.

What Jack fails to understand is the basic mathematics behind success and failure. How much you win when you win and how much you lose when you lose is far more important than how often you win. Jack achieved an 80% win rate by waiting and hoping for any bad positions to come good again. When faced with a relatively small profit he will tend to grab it prematurely to satisfy his need to be right. Unfortunately the longer you play this game the more you learn that some positions will never come good which is why so many people lost so much money during the GFC.

In my 2006 book, *Adaptive Analysis for Australian Stocks,*[13] I introduced the concept of the Expectancy Curve which is now reproduced by many others.

The Expectancy Curve shows an important yet consistent relationship between the winning percentage and the win/loss ratio; moreover it shows the point at which a strategy will move from a losing proposition to a profitable proposition. It must be understood that these two statistics move in a converse manner: when one moves higher, the other moves lower. An investor wanting a higher percentage win rate will forego a high win/loss ratio.

Nick's Top Tips
Sports men and women of all calibre go through cycles of being in form and out of form. When it comes to investment strategies the same holds true. Feeling out of form? Step back, reconsider your routine and frame of mind and when you are ready, restart. Patience. Tenacity. Discipline.

13 Wrightbooks, John Wiley & Sons Australia, Ltd

FIGURE 14

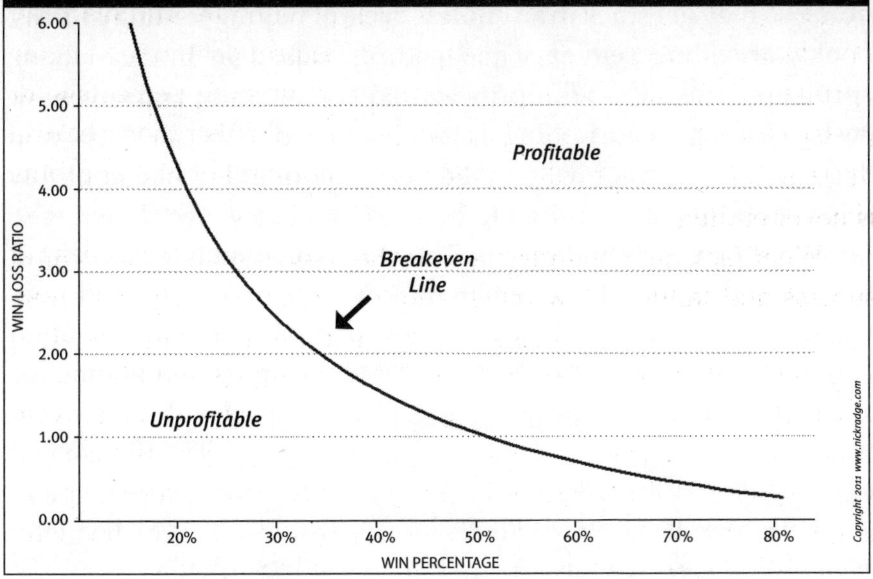

Figure 14: The Expectancy Curve plots the win/loss ratio against the percentage of winning trades.

In 25 years of practical investing and trading I have come to understand that you have two simple choices:

1. Accept a high win/loss ratio at the expense of a higher winning percentage, or
2. Pursue a high winning percentage strategy at the expense of a high win/loss ratio.

Although it's logical to desire both, you can't. They rarely co-exist, at least not with any robustness to suggest they will consistently do so in the future. If you see a high win percentage coupled with a high win/loss ratio, be very wary.

Faced with these two choices we need to decide which will most likely offer up the higher profits. What comes as a surprise to most retail investors (except you, having just read the explanation above) is that the answer is (1)—a high win/loss ratio and a low winning percentage.

More importantly the natural desire for a higher winning percentage induces investors to continue searching for strategies that win a great deal more often, thus offering a high win rate. In doing so they get stuck in an endless cycle of buying trading courses, books, attending seminars and getting sucked in by fast-talking spruikers. This all adds up to wasted opportunity and excessive costs. There is no such thing as the 'perfect edge' because it would suggest being correct 100% of the time. Not only is that completely impossible, it's not required to be successful, as we've shown with Jane's 50% win rate and profits. The more you search for the higher win rate the worse off you will tend to be.

> *"Ours is not to say what should be, but to analyze and exploit what is."*
>
> **Calvin Coolidge[14]**

I recently received an email from a gentleman who has been searching for 10 years for a strategy that offers a higher than 80% success rate. So far he has failed to find it. He is frustrated, disillusioned and has basically wasted 10 years of good investment time.

I have the answer for him, with a strategy that has a 79% winning rate:

1. Buy a portfolio of 20 stocks that are making a new yearly low
2. If any of those stocks drop 50% from point of purchase, exit and replace with another making a new yearly low
3. Exit any position that shows a 10% profit

As is usually the case with higher winning systems, it works well until it doesn't. As can be seen with the following equity curve this strategy, with a 79% success rate, suffered a 70% decline in capital during the GFC. The user gets his desired almost 80% win rate, along with a very expensive lesson.

---

14 President USA, 1923–1929

FIGURE 15

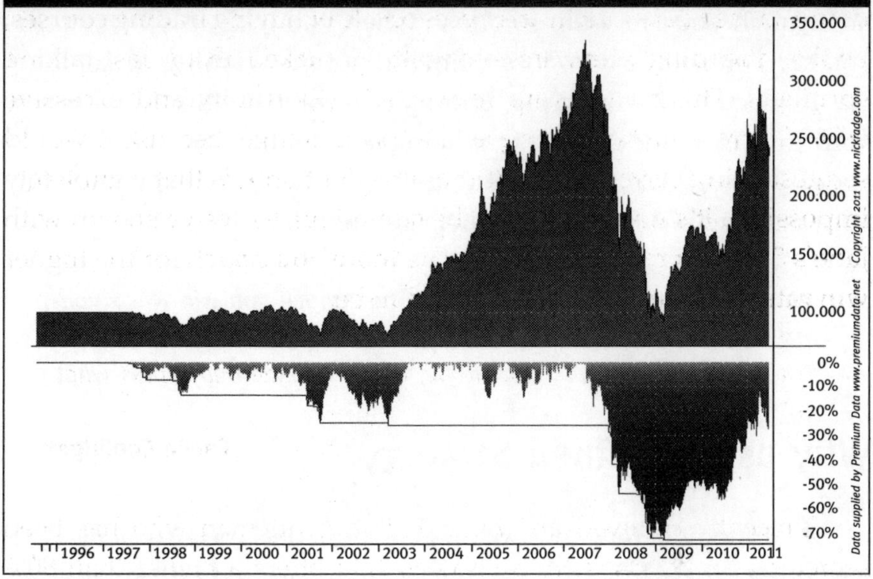

Figure 15: A strategy with a 79% winning rate does not necessarily equate to a smooth equity curve.

If you cannot predict the future then there is no point being convinced that you, through research or skill, can achieve a high winning percentage of transactions. The market will give you whatever it will give you. You have no say in the outcome of any particular transaction. By all means you can attempt to 'time' the market and only invest in times that are perceived to be beneficial, but again timing is a form of prediction and tends to be a futile exercise. Let's use the great Warren Buffettt and his foray into ConocoPhillips (COP) during 2008 as an example:

> *"...I bought a large amount of ConocoPhillips stock when oil and gas prices were near their peak. I in no way anticipated the dramatic fall in energy prices that occurred in the last half of the year. Even if prices should rise, moreover, the terrible timing of my purchase has cost Berkshire several billion dollars."*[15]

Accept that you cannot predict the future, that you can't time the market and also accept that you cannot control the market.

---

15 Letter to Berkshire Hathaway Shareholders, 2008

However, you can control how much you win when you win and how much you are willing to lose when you lose. In other words, you can control the win/loss ratio, but not the winning percentage.

In Section 2—Example Strategies—we test this hypotheses. Your goal is to understand that being successful in this game is not about a secret, it's solely about the underlying mathematics. Put your ego and old-fashioned beliefs behind you.

Successful investing comes down to how much you win when you win and how much you lose when you lose.

Why use a Defined Strategy

A strategy refers to a plan of action designed to achieve a particular goal. In our case the goal is profitability. However, when investing, our plan is more than just generating a profit. It involves an element of research, an understanding of the required mathematical edge, some kind of entry trigger, an exit criteria and an on-going position management technique. Importantly the plan should also encompass our own psychological strengths and weaknesses—human emotion is, after all, a key roadblock between success and failure.

There are various types of investment plans:

- Discretionary
- Rule Based Discretionary
- Systematic

Discretionary refers to using various and ever-changing inputs for entering, exiting and managing positions, including making judgment calls. The inputs tend to be subjective with instinct playing a major part. Successful proponents of this style tend to rely on right brain skills rather than left brain analytical skills. They argue the human brain is better able to process information and can adapt to ever-changing market conditions at a much faster rate than other more rigid methods. A simplistic example would be a trader noticing an increase in the demand for a stock within the market depth screen and initiating a long position thinking the stock is being supported by buyers.

Rule Based Discretionary investing is a plan with pre-set criteria that need to be met before a position is entered as well as some predefined rules for managing and exiting. If these rules cannot be programmed into a computer then we classify the strategy as discretionary. An example would be an investor that required a company's Price/Earnings ratio to be below 14 combined with 3 years of earnings growth and that the stock be in the resource sector. If and when these criteria are met, the investor takes a position.

A Systematic approach, on the other hand, encompasses a set of rules that can be hard wired into a computer and by doing so allows us to back-test the strategy on historical data. If done correctly, we can gain valuable insights into not only the viability of the strategy, but also how the journey to profitability is made. Using a systematic approach to buy, sell and manage positions ensures nothing is left to chance, specifically leaving our emotions out of the decision making process, especially during critical points of market activity or personal performance. Understanding what the strategy can and can't do before it's applied with real money can remove a significant amount of angst for investors. The benefits of a systematic approach include:

1. A map of how the strategy has performed in the past and therefore a better indication of how it may perform in the future.
2. An understanding of what the strategy can and can't do, as well as understanding what the journey to successful implementation entails.
3. Removal of emotion from the decision making process.
4. Set guidelines which enable the strategy to be replicated in the future without discretion or deviation.
5. Time each day to implement tends to be lower as technical analysis software such as AmiBroker can be programmed to 'spit out' the required orders and automatically manage positions.

The type of strategy implemented will depend very much on the personality of the user but in my experience there is a transition from beginner to experienced that tends to move from discretionary to systematic and from short term to longer term. Whilst it's always difficult to accurately project the future rate of return of an investment it's just as important to understand the risks of taking on that investment. We should have some idea of the potential downsides of a strategy as well as ensuring the risk of ruin is as close to zero as possible.

Portfolio Construction

There are many ways to build a portfolio and there are many ways to measure and manage risk. Whilst we could extend our discussion into advanced portfolio theory and management it really detracts from the key messages of the book which are simplicity and robustness. For the average retail investor the use of hedging or other portfolio tools are complex to understand, usually very expensive to facilitate and, more often than not, aren't overly effective over the longer term. Sticking with vanilla techniques will tend to get the job done adequately and substantially lower the added stress that comes with managing hedge positions.

Using an active investment strategy will automatically enable us to establish positions when broader market trends are running higher and revert to cash when these trends are running lower. This automatic moderating of exposure relieves much of the tension and guesswork surrounding the best time to be invested and the best time to take defensive action.

There are two effective ways to build a portfolio and ensure its robustness and simplicity are kept in check. To do this we need to decide (a) how many positions to open, and (b) which universe of stocks to trade.

The first question, 'how many positions to open', is probably the most important because it can involve sample bias or position variability, which is an error involving the number of stocks chosen to trade. In its purest form it can't be avoided because in certain market conditions almost all investment strategies will generate more opportunities than one has capital to trade.

For example, a strategy that generates 100 consecutive signals in 100 consecutive days will have 81 different permutations of a 20 stock portfolio. However, a strategy that generates 30 signals in the same period has just 11 permutations of the same 20 stock portfolio. The higher the level of permutations the more variance of returns and the more the real time results could diverge from historical testing if the strategy is not robust. As a rule of thumb, the more simplistic the strategy the more prone to sample bias it will be and therefore the more likely returns will vary considerably in the future.

This error can be extrapolated further by suggesting a differing quantity of positions be allocated to different capital amounts. If we suggest a $100,000 account takes 20 positions, yet a $30,000 account only takes 10 positions, then the smaller account will be at a distinct disadvantage to the larger because its sample of possible permutations will increase. Over a 30 trade period the 20 position portfolio has 11 different permutations possible yet the 10 position portfolio has 21. The incidence of diverging from the historical test results has almost doubled simply by choosing to trade a smaller portfolio size.

There is no specific right/wrong answer to this question but there are two definitive conclusions:

1. Simplistic strategies are more prone to position variability.
2. The same number of positions should be used regardless of the capital allocated to the strategy.

Experience shows, and the most conventional view[16] is, that using 20 positions, regardless of capital allocation, tends to offer the best risk-adjusted return relative to time taken to implement and manage the portfolio. Addressing and arguing the risks of terminal wealth dispersion[17] are not as strong in our case mainly because we're recycling positions on a consistent basis and not reliant on a single outstanding performer.

The second consideration is defining a specific universe of stocks to trade. A universe represents a group of candidates to which we will apply our strategy; however, experience again suggests that candidates should fit within the same broad risk boundaries unless

---

16 Most famously in *A Random Walk Down Wall Street*, Burton Malkiel, 1996
17 The range of possible values of a portfolio at some future date, usually retirement.

your intention is to have a diversified portfolio. Trading highly speculative stocks and conservative stocks together will offer some diversification but ultimately it will degrade performance and more seriously could be incompatible with your risk tolerance. Trading a universe of stocks of the same breed, such as all blue chip or all small-cap, will keep volatility in check, or at least offer an understanding of likely portfolio volatility.

Here is a simple yet robust example of how to match risk tolerance and universe:

Risk Tolerance	Universe	Return Profile	
		CAGR	MaxDD
Conservative	ASX1 to ASX100	12%—15%	-13%
Growth Orientated	ASX101 to ASX300	15%—22%	-19%
Aggressive	› ASX300*	20%—30%	-25%
			*ensure liquidity is adequate

Table 3: Trading a specific universe can help manage risk and portfolio volatility.

Using this 'pigeon hole' approach a conservative investor, for example, will have less signals due to a smaller and less volatile universe of stocks, will tend to hold a higher percentage of cash and would benefit from higher dividend and interest income. Dividends are considered 'icing on the cake' rather than being a core part of the strategy. A higher growth investor, on the other hand, will trade a larger and more volatile universe of stocks meaning less cash holdings and limited dividend income.

A word on using sector specific universes: a core philosophy of active investing is ensuring we do not predict. If you attempt to 'anticipate' which sector will be the next best performer you run the risk of falling into the prediction trap. In reality the best performing sector, or the constituents that make up that sector, will naturally float to the surface as momentum increases.

Lastly the other benefit of running multiple positions is that risk is also managed on an individual holding basis. With 20 positions the risk per individual stock is a maximum of 5% of the full portfolio value. If we assume an exit point set at 20% from entry then risk per trade is just 1% of portfolio capital. There can be some very complex methods for allocating capital to specific trades and whilst some of these are extremely beneficial for short term trading, they can also be detrimental to equity-specific investing. Using a portfolio broken up into 20 equal sizes is a very robust way to manage risk without diluting returns.

Monte Carlo Simulations

There are two important factors to consider when simulating investment strategies on historical data. Firstly, it's not an exact science and the future will not look exactly like the past, although if simulations are done correctly, the future will look something like the past. When simulating a strategy using historical data on a single back-test run it's impossible to know whether the result generated from that single run is average, above average or below. If the results from a single run are above average we may have heightened expectations for our strategy and become disillusioned quickly when it fails to perform according to the test results. On the other hand, we may discard a perfectly good strategy if the single run doesn't appear to meet our goals.

Position variability is the situation where possible outcomes are skewed when presented with 20 opportunities but we can only take 10 due to capital constraints. Whilst we can never know ahead of time which will be the best possible combination of trades to take, we would like to know the range of possible outcomes.

Monte Carlo simulations ask the question, "What if the past had been slightly different?" It allows us to view a range of possible outcomes and statistical probabilities which in turn gives us a better expectation of what may occur in the future.

In layman terms it's like giving the strategy to 5000 individuals and asking them to come back in 10 years' time to collate their results. For various reasons a range or distribution of statistics will be presented. Some people will ignore system signals at times due to personal biases; others may not take signals if they go on annual leave or become emotionally detached from the longer term goals. Position variability means that different people might choose to take different signals. By collating the 5000 sample results we gain an insight into the variability of the strategy and can therefore make a better informed decision than that of a single run back-test.

Not all technical analysis software is capable of running Monte Carlo simulations. AmiBroker was used to run all simulations in this text[18].

The following diagram is a simplistic example using a random number generator. It essentially shows the results of 10 separate investors using the same strategy over 500 transactions, yet note how their respective equity curves deviate slightly during the test period. In the real world this deviation can be due to numerous factors so Monte Carlo simulations attempt to map the probable distribution of broad outcomes rather than rely on a single outcome.

FIGURE 16

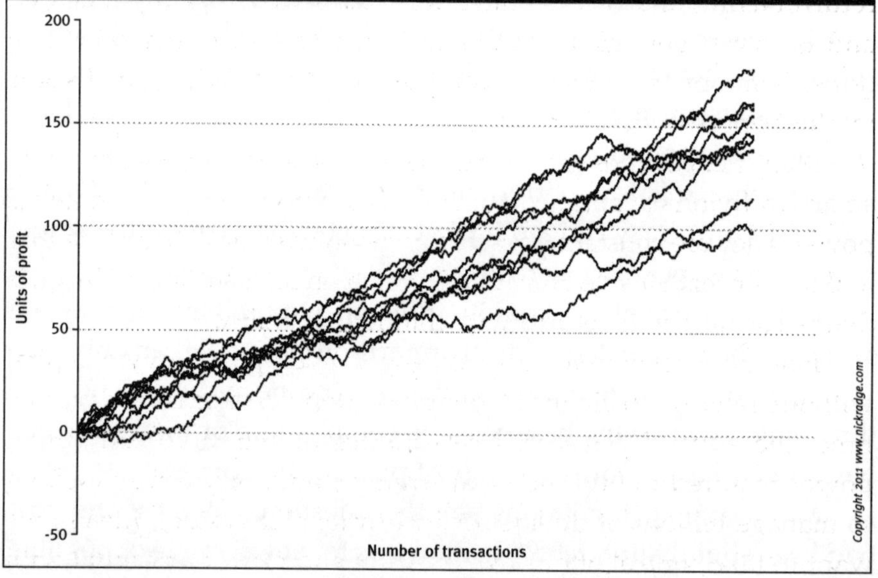

Figure 16: Ten possible equity curve outcomes generated by the same strategy.

---

18 www.AmiBrokercoding.com provides coding assistance.

Basic Performance Measures

"What makes a good strategy?" isn't as straightforward as we'd like to think. There are three core tenets to measuring performance – the three R's:

Return
Risk
Reliability

Ideally everyone wants a strategy that makes an exceptional return, has minimal risk, has minimal volatility, is easily implemented and is robust enough to be useful in the future. Easier said than done. Some of these factors don't go hand-in-hand; indeed some totally oppose each other.

Many hedge funds strive for these attributes, employing extremely smart individuals and exhausting large amounts of computing power. They are constantly researching and tweaking their strategies looking for that elusive Holy Grail, which on an institutional level, is defined as moderate returns with minimal volatility.

However, retail investors wanting to manage their own capital without relying on financial planners, don't necessarily have the time, the advanced research capabilities or the large computing power required to find the ideal strategy, but nor are they looking to manage billions of dollars for institutional investors. Ideally we want to take control of our own destiny and grow our capital with confidence and preferably return a little better than the average fund manager. Confidence comes from understanding what can and can't occur with the strategy and confidence comes from understanding the journey that needs to be travelled to achieve our goals.

Section Two outlines and tests eight different momentum strategies. To compare the performance of each strategy we use a number of performance measures.

Compound Annual Growth Rate (CAGR)

The CAGR is a pro forma number that tells you what an investment yields on an annually compounded basis. It essentially provides a 'smoothed' rate of return. Whilst CAGR is the best measure to compare two investments it does not necessarily compare the inherent risks of those two investments. As investment returns tend to be volatile, using a smoothed annual return can give the illusion of a steady rate of return when in fact the truth could be quite different.

Maximum Drawdown (maxDD)

Maximum Drawdown measures the maximum depth of an equity peak to an equity trough. If account capital falls from $100,000 to $80,000 at any time during the investment period, we can conclude that the drawdown is -20%. If this is the largest percentage decline in equity then we define it as the Maximum Drawdown. All strategies will have equity declines of some degree during their life. When simulating strategies we need to be cognizant of not only how bad that equity decline could get but also how long it takes for the strategy to recover. In the ideal situation we'd like equity declines to be minimal and recovery quick.

Equity Curve/Underwater Equity Curve

An equity curve gives a visual representation of the growth of equity over a set period of time, and can offer a quick reference guide on how the journey to the terminal value was achieved. Ideally the smoother the slope of the equity curve, the better the strategy. The upper half of the following chart shows the growth of $100,000 since January 1997.

The lower half of the chart is called an Underwater Equity Curve and is a visual representation of the time and depth of drawdowns. It offers the investor a more pessimistic view with the degree of equity decline shown as a percentage on the y-axis.

FIGURE 17

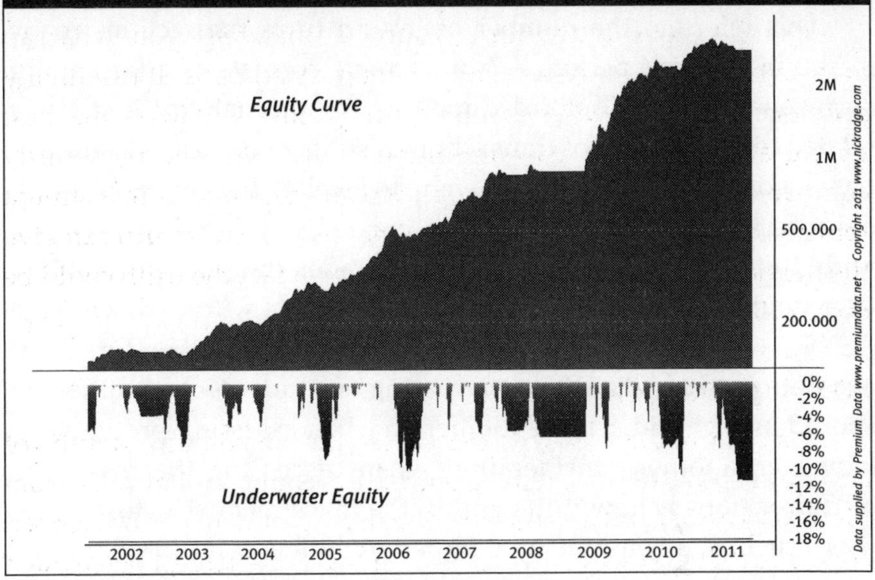

Figure 17: Growth of $100,000 is shown in the upper half of the page. The lower half shows the negative equity declines.

Market Exposure

This measures how often the investor will be invested, or exposed to the market during any given period of time. A Buy & Hold investor will have 100% exposure and therefore be required to endure all market events, both good and bad, during the investment period. The goal of a momentum investor is to be exposed to positive market events, such as bull markets, and less to negative market events, such as bear markets. An investor with a 50% market exposure that achieves the same return as an investor with a 100% exposure is using capital a lot more conservatively.

Win/Loss Ratio

Sometimes known as the Payoff Ratio, it's calculated by dividing the average win by the average loss. As a momentum investor looking to capture longer trends our goal is achieving a higher number; 2.0 is considered good, 3.0 or higher is excellent.

Number of Transactions

This refers to the number of 'round turn' transactions made in the investment period. A 'round turn' consists of a buy and a corresponding sell. A third dimension of profitability is directly related to the number of transactions a strategy makes. If a strategy has a positive edge then we want to exploit that edge as much as possible. Remember that Jane created a positive expectancy with 10 trades. If she could make 20 trades then her profitability also doubles. Using a small universe of stocks, for example the ASX50, will limit the number of transactions and therefore limit absolute profitability. When comparing one universe to another we should also consider trade frequency when assessing profitability. However, another consideration when discussing the frequency of transactions is how it fits within the investment structure being used, such as a Self-Managed Superannuation Fund (SMSF). As a rule of thumb, generating more than fifty transactions a year may be considered running a business and therefore deemed inappropriate by the tax office[19]. Other structures, such as companies or trusts, have no transaction limitations.

MAR[20] Ratio

Perhaps the easiest risk-adjusted performance measure for the layman is dividing the Compounded Annual Growth Return (CAGR) by the Maximum Drawdown (maxDD). This ratio offers a more robust guide to risk-adjusted return. Using Commonwealth Bank (CBA) as an example, it has a 10-year annualised return of 11.8%[21] yet during the GFC its share price dropped from $61.87 to a dividend adjusted low of $27.82, or -55%. Its CAR/maxDD, or MAR, is therefore 0.21. The higher this ratio the better and a reading over 0.50 is good and over 1.0 is considered excellent.

---

19 You should seek independent advice from your accountant or tax agent.
20 Developed by Managed Account Reports. Source: www.marhedge.com
21 Source: Huntleys' Investment Information Pty. Limited

Time Window Analysis

Sometimes referred to as 'Rolling Returns' this analysis is a different way to look at how a strategy has performed over various time frames. It attempts to answer the question, "How long do I need to be invested to gain 100% probability of profit?" Investment returns are usually stated as a calendar year-on-year which assumes you were invested on January 1st each year. By looking at rolling windows we're attempting to minimise start-date dependency by calculating a monthly return for the previous *n*-months, where *n* equals different time windows. A rolling 12 month return chart, for example, demonstrates the annual return over 12 periods in the track record—highlighting year over year performance for January 2009 to December 2009, February 2009 to January 2010, March 2009 to February 2010 and so on.

The following table shows that an investment in example Strategy-1 has a 65% chance of being profitable in any 6 month period of time. As time moves on and the rolling window increases, the probability of success eventually gets to 100% at 30 months.

	6-month	12-month	18-month	24-month	30-month
XAOA	73.4%	79.8%	79.6%	79.4%	79.3%
Strategy-1	65.0%	79.7%	86.4%	95.5%	100.0%

Table 4: Time Window Analysis allows us to understand the probability of profit over various periods of time.

If an investor in this strategy is unwilling to leave funds invested for 30 months, there is a chance they may not make a profit. When assessing an appropriate strategy the investor must be willing to commit for a commensurate period of time to achieve profit certainty or risk being disappointed. Unfortunately for most investors they neither know how long this period will be or they lack the patience to endure the required time.

Another way to view Rolling Returns is by plotting the actual window return over the life of the investment period. The following chart shows a profitable investment strategy with a CAGR of almost 17% but in this example we have broken the return into 6-monthly chunks and plotted each combination in 1 month intervals. It can be seen that in any 6 month period there is certainly a randomness of return. You could be making +10% to +15% or losing -5% depending on which 6 month window you choose.

FIGURE 18

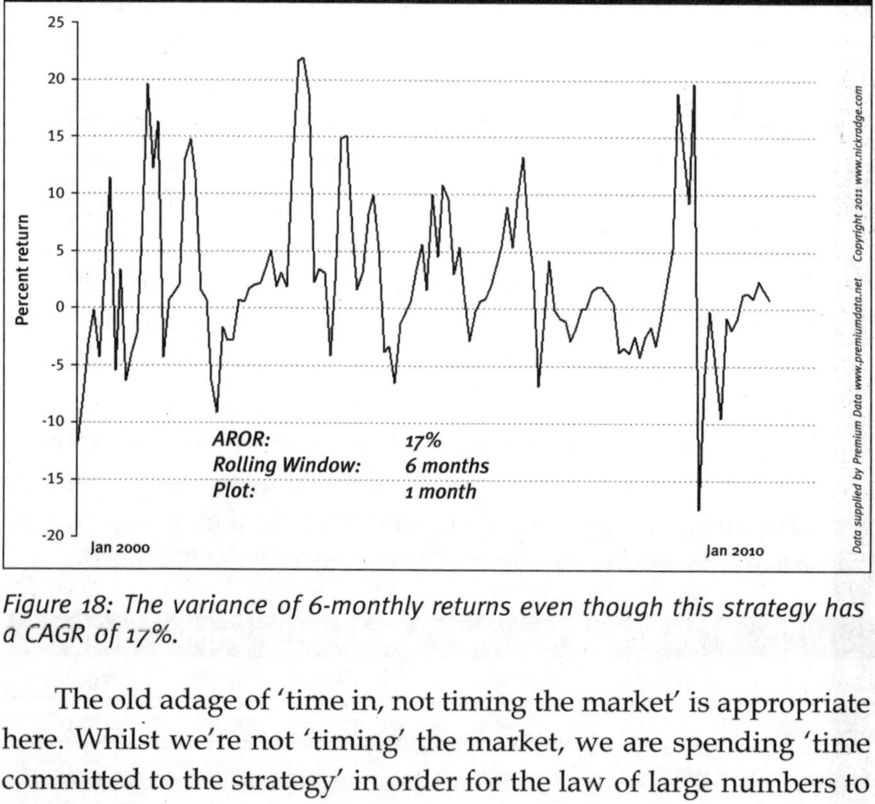

Figure 18: The variance of 6-monthly returns even though this strategy has a CAGR of 17%.

The old adage of 'time in, not timing the market' is appropriate here. Whilst we're not 'timing' the market, we are spending 'time committed to the strategy' in order for the law of large numbers to do its work.

Monthly Profit Table

This allows us to see a month-to-month breakdown of returns using a single run simulation. A summary of year end return is also tabulated as is the average monthly return (see opposite page).

Year	Jan	Feb	Mar	Apr	May	Jun	Jul	Aug	Sep	Oct	Nov	Dec	Yr%
1997	n/a	n/a	-0.2%	0.1%	0.4%	4.2%	-0.3%	-3.4%	7.9%	-10.9%	0.3%	1.1%	**-1.9%**
1998	0.3%	0.9%	1.9%	0.7%	-2.2%	0.3%	2.5%	-5.8%	2.1%	1.6%	3.8%	3.6%	**9.6%**
1999	3.6%	-6.7%	2.1%	-0.3%	-2.4%	-2.7%	-1.4%	0.7%	-1.7%	1.2%	2.4%	1.1%	**-4.6%**
2000	0.7%	11.0%	10.4%	-10.6%	-4.0%	6.2%	1.9%	7.7%	-4.7%	-2.3%	3.9%	-0.8%	**18.5%**
2001	3.2%	-1.9%	-7.7%	5.7%	3.2%	1.2%	2.2%	0.1%	-7.0%	5.3%	0.9%	2.7%	**7.1%**
2002	1.5%	4.5%	-1.3%	1.3%	6.0%	-5.8%	-5.5%	3.3%	-3.2%	-0.1%	2.5%	1.8%	**4.1%**
2003	-0.5%	-0.1%	5.8%	4.3%	5.1%	5.5%	2.4%	7.1%	6.9%	1.3%	-3.6%	4.4%	**45.5%**
2004	-1.5%	7.7%	-0.1%	-5.1%	3.1%	3.3%	3.9%	-0.1%	2.5%	8.1	8.1%	4.7%	**39.4%**
2005	1.7%	9.1%	-1.3%	-8.2%	-0.4%	4.3%	9.6%	4.4%	6.2%	-4.7%	3.6%	-0.7%	**24.6%**
2006	2.3%	-1.0%	14.0%	6.7%	-5.1%	4.3%	4.7%	2.3%	6.8%	10.1%	8.0%	10.3%	**83.2%**
2007	1.3%	-3.8%	8.5%	5.3%	9.5%	7.7%	-3.3%	-3.8%	10.3%	14.0%	-12.3%	5.6%	**42.1%**
2008	-13.8%	3.0%	-10.9%	11.0%	23.2%	-13.5%	-14.8%	-10.5%	-11.8%	-12.0%	-3.1%	4.0%	**-44.2%**
2009	-3.5%	4.3%	22.1%	2.5%	6.9%	2.3%	12.6%	22.9%	11.4%	-4.6%	9.8%	-2.9%	**115.6%**
2010	-16.0%	5.8%	10.7%	-2.4%	-8.5%	-5.5%	16.6%	-0.1%	12.8%	4.6%	3.0%	22.1%	**43.5%**
2011	-7.6%	0.1%	1.0%	-1.9%	-2.2%	-14.5%	n/a	n/a	n/a	n/a	n/a	n/a	**-23.4%**
Avg	**-1.9%**	**2.2%**	**3.7%**	**0.6%**	**2.2%**	**-0.2%**	**2.2%**	**1.8%**	**2.8%**	**0.8%**	**1.9%**	**4.1%**	

Table 5: A monthly breakdown of annual returns offers further insights of strategy performance.

Annual Standard Deviation

Standard Deviation shows the volatility of the strategy's annual returns. The higher the deviation, the broader the possible return outcomes, both upside and downside. Ideally the lower the number the more stable portfolio returns will be. The current Standard Deviation of annual returns for the All Ordinaries Accumulation Index (XAOA), used as our benchmark, is 18.88%.

Sharpe Ratio[22]

The Sharpe Ratio is a risk-adjusted measure of return that is often used to evaluate the performance of a portfolio. The ratio attempts to compare the performance of one portfolio to another portfolio by making an adjustment for risk. The Sharpe Ratio is calculated by subtracting the risk-free rate—such as Australian 90-day Bank Bill Rate—from the portfolio return and dividing the result by the standard deviation of the annualized returns.

For example, if Strategy-A returns 20% while Strategy-B returns 15%, it would appear that Strategy-A is the better choice. However, if Strategy-A takes larger risks and has higher volatility than Strategy-B, then Strategy-B will be shown to have a better risk-adjusted return.

In theory, the higher the Sharpe Ratio the better the investor is being served. However, there are two major failings with this measure which is why I don't consider it overly beneficial for use in this book. Firstly, it penalizes a strategy that has high upside volatility which, for an everyday investor, is a good thing. The types of strategies to be discussed in Section 2 all exhibit high upside volatility and will therefore tend to generate low Sharpe Ratios. The second failing is that readings are accentuated by strategies that don't have normal distributions of returns, specifically complex derivative style investments. The most famous example was Long Term Capital Management, the infamous billion dollar hedge fund that imploded in 1998, which had an extraordinary Sharpe Ratio of 4.35 and in hindsight was obviously too good to be true.

As a benchmark we will use the All Ordinaries Accumulation

---

22 Developed by William Forsyth Sharpe in 1966 and revised in 1994

Index (XAOA) which has a Sharpe ratio of 0.204, and a risk-free rate of return of 5%.

Scatter Plot

A Scatter Plot is used to plot two variables, in this case the Total Return generated by each strategy coupled with the Maximum Drawdown. By plotting 1000 individual simulations we can gain a strong visual representation of the robustness of the approach, specifically the tighter the cluster of returns the higher the future reliability of the strategy. We all aspire to achieving the highest return with the lowest possible pain threshold, yet if the distribution of possibilities is broad then robustness is diluted. Whilst the Standard Deviation of returns can offer a mathematical estimation, using the Scatter Plot greatly enhances the visual evidence of such.

The following example shows an extremely tight cluster of possible outcomes around the mean, suggesting strong reliability.

FIGURE 19

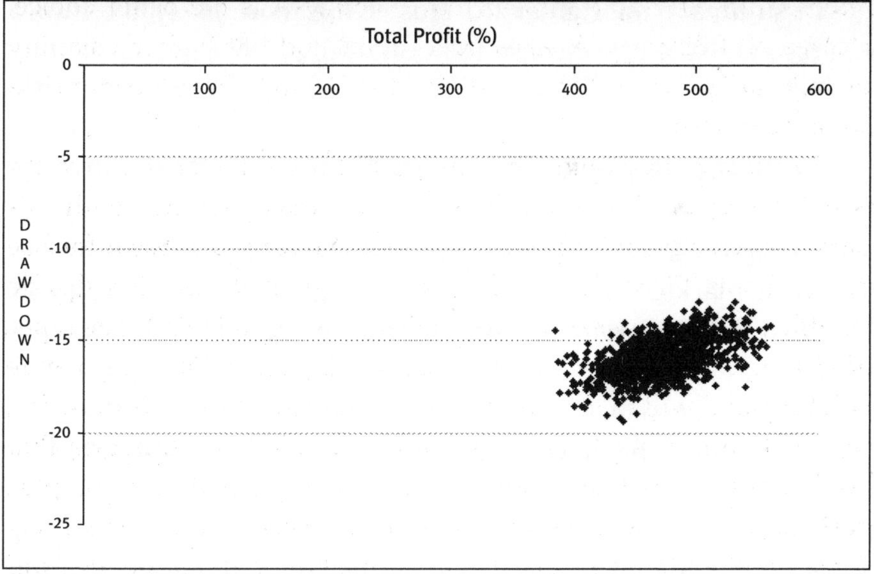

Figure 19: A Scatter Plot showing total percentage profit and maximum drawdown together.

However, the example on the next page, has a broad distribution or wider cluster around the mean, so future reliability will be hit and miss and therefore robustness could be questioned.

FIGURE 20

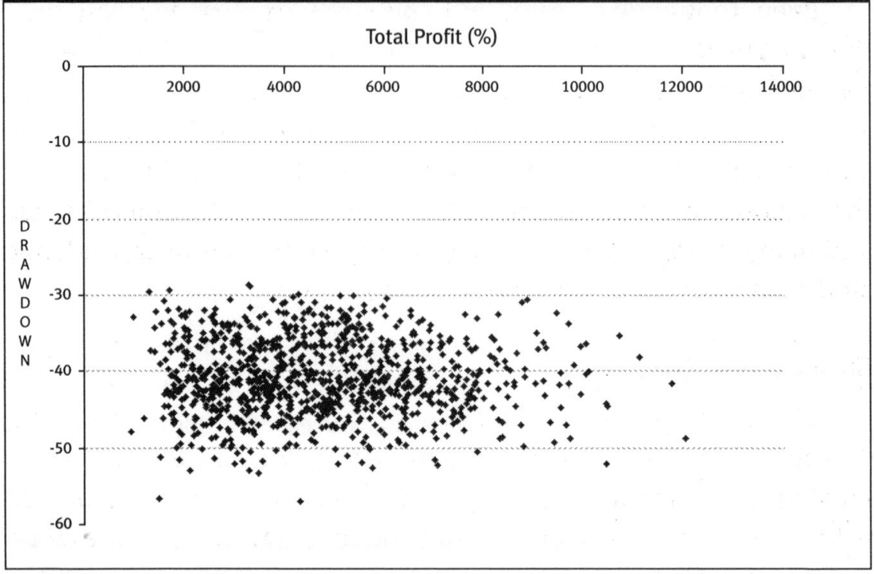

Figure 20: This Scatter Plot clearly shows the dispersion of possible outcomes.

In summary the tighter the cluster the more likely the future will resemble the historical simulation results.

Known Issues—A Common Sense Approach

As much as we want concrete answers when investing in the stock market we need to be cognizant that it's not an exact science and that variability and uncertainty play a major role. In a marketplace environment where change is constant there can never be anything concrete, at least not anything that repeats itself exactly like the past. We therefore need to live, learn and operate within an environment of uncertainty and the best way to do this is by using probabilities rather than relying on absolute certainties.

With this in mind we also need to evaluate the testing process itself and not just the end result. Ultimately if the testing process is flawed then any outcome will also be erroneous. It is important to remember that testing is simply a means to an end, and not the end itself. Our goal is to understand the good and the bad of the strategy but in doing so we need to be assured that rigorous testing processes have been adhered to.

Even though we test our hypotheses as best we can with the current information we have, there will always be scope for rebuttal to some degree. Academics are great at coming to various conclusions about risks, rewards and various outcomes, yet we don't need to look far to see how perfect theory gets thrown out the window once tested in reality. This is where common sense and many years of direct market experience prevail over academic studies. Known issues and possible solutions include:

Survivorship Bias

This is a very serious issue when testing trading and investing strategies and one that comes down to a very simple question: 'Over what universe should I base my simulations on?' Survivorship Bias is the mistake of overlooking elements of the strategy that existed in the past but now do not. It can refer to individual stocks such as HIH Insurance (HIH), OneTel (ONE) and ABC Learning (ABS), and the many other high fliers that used to be considered major players in the market and that now no longer exist. Survivorship Bias can also refer to being reliant on a single element of the strategy that could very easily change in the future and therefore degrade the strategy. A good example would be a strategy that relies on high volatility, such as option writing. If volatility declines over extended periods then the premium received by an option writer declines considerably, possibly to the point where the strategy reward is not commensurate to the risk being taken. A third example is when a trader becomes an expert in a single market or a single stock and that market changes or that stock is merged or removed.

In finance the classic example of Survivorship Bias, known as Type 1 Bias, is following a specific index. An index, such as the ASX200, is made up of those companies that 'have survived' and not gone into administration, been merged with others or taken over. Those that do not survive are simply discarded from the index and replaced with a new one. Over the longer term this swap skews the index in an upward bias and is unrepresentative of real world returns. (Not coincidentally long term charts of indices are often shown in the foyers of stockbrokers' offices although the reference to survivorship error is not mentioned.)

Another example of Survivorship Bias, Type 2 Bias, involves including companies in the simulation that did not meet membership requirements until more recently. In Australia we have several major indices: the ASX20, 50, 100, 200, 300, Small Ordinaries and All Ordinaries. The constituents of these indices change on a regular basis so when we test one of these indices today it will not be representative of the same constituent list of 10 years ago, or even 12 months ago in some circumstances.

The impact on Type 1 and Type 2 Bias will tend to overestimate the performance of the simulations, more so when those simulation results are compared to an index.

As constituent lists from the past cannot yet be replicated by data providers it is difficult to get accurate insights on portfolio returns when anchoring to a specific constituent list based on an index. Indeed prior to 1999 many constituent lists did not exist in their current formats. To overcome this problem as much as possible we will look at a broader range of stocks rather than a tighter constituent list such as the ASX100.

With regard to Type 1 Bias, where stocks have been delisted due to a company going into administration or as a result of a merger or acquisition, the appropriate data needs to be used in the simulation universe. In this case we will assume the cash component was realised by exiting the position at the last traded price. In reality this would be a manual decision and the last traded price may differ slightly from the actual receipted price. In order to use these stocks a purpose created postdictive error needs to be added to the computer code, meaning we look into the future to determine an appropriate exit price. For the purpose of this exercise if a stock does not trade for 100 calendar days it will be deemed to be delisted and an exit triggered at the last traded price.

Dividends

Data for our simulations have been adjusted for dividends.

Capital Adjustments

A company may choose to raise funds or reinvest in itself using a variety of tools commonly referred to as capital adjustments. These tools vary depending on circumstances and can include:

- Rights issues
- Buybacks
- Bonus dividends
- New issues & placements
- Bonuses
- Splits

These capital adjustments will tend to create unintended gaps in the price data which in turn may distort simulated results. We have therefore adjusted all data to ensure smooth pricing although an actual account may still suffer in certain circumstances if a capital adjustment was not taken up.

This chart shows Fortescue Metals Group (FMG) unadjusted data after a 10:1 share split. Note the massive gap in price which in real terms did not occur.

FIGURE 21

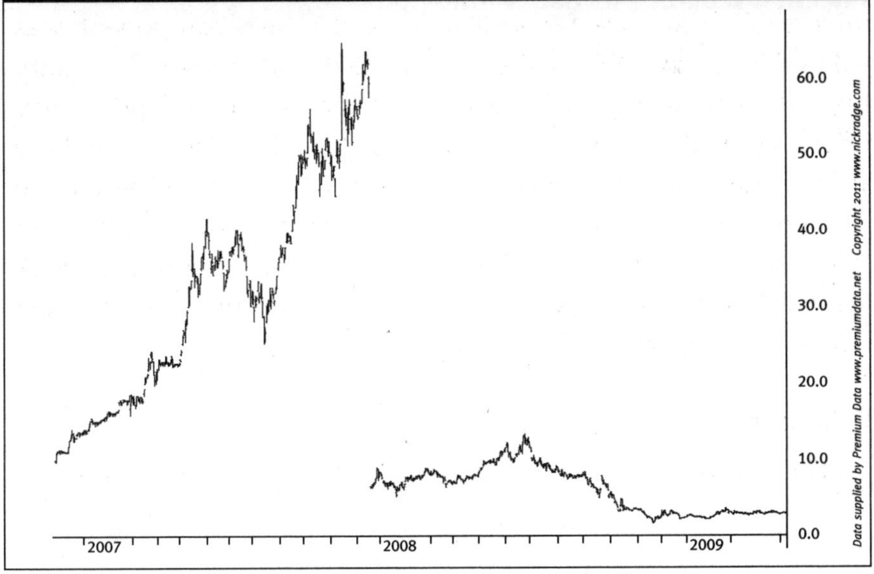

Figure 21: Poor data quality will cause large price discrepancies such as this and will also impact on simulation results.

The next chart shows the exact same period of time but the data has been adjusted. This is the real share price activity that all shareholders would have been exposed to.

FIGURE 22

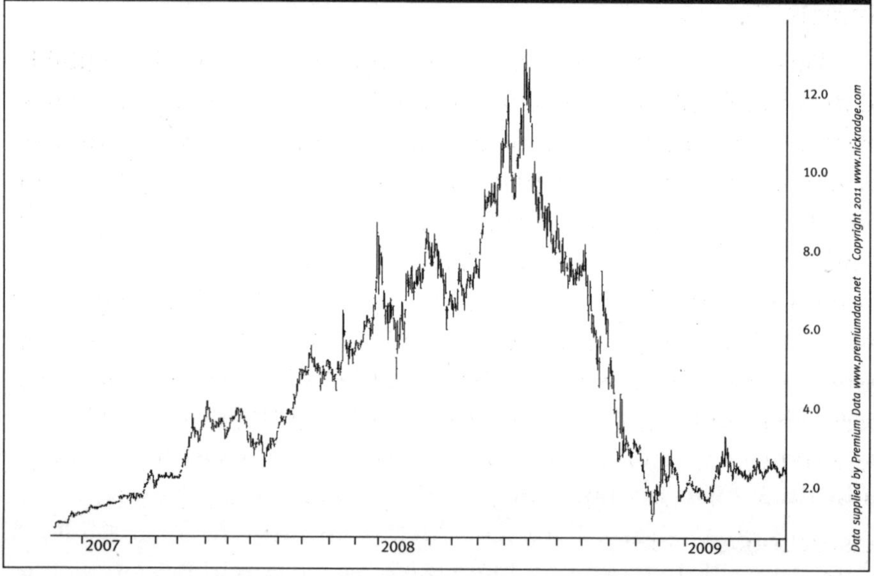

Figure 22: Correct data adjustments remove discrepancies and ensure correct simulation results.

Selection Bias or Position Variability

Simplistic strategies that generate too many buy signals at any given time could fall foul to position variability; that is, being reliant on a small sub-set of the total possible events. For example, say ten investors are following a basic strategy that offers 20 signals on any particular day, chances are each of those ten investors will end the day with different portfolio constituents. In certain circumstances, involving robust, well-tested strategies and defined universes, this may not present too many issues over the longer term, although there still needs to be a point at which limited discretion takes place. The less discretion in the decision making process, the more likely the simulated results can be replicated in reality. Conversely a strategy that produces many triggers, and therefore many potential portfolios, yet produces a tight cluster of returns, is ideal. It means the system is robust and the tight cluster of outcomes defines the robustness. To overcome position variance we will use robust strategies without optimisation and will test with Monte Carlo simulations to ensure we have a broader view of the full distribution of possible outcomes.

Sample Bias

This is an error that occurs when not enough data is available to draw a robust statistical conclusion. The risk of relying on results from a very small sample of transactions or universe of possible symbols is that one will cause an under- or over-representation of possible outcomes. When simulating investment strategies we often tend toward an under-representation of what is actually possible in the real world and avoid the inevitable Black Swan events. An example would be a strategy that generates very few signals over extended periods of time or where simulations have been run on a very small universe of stocks, such as the ASX100. Agreeably the ASX100 contains a certain type of stock, but when testing a robust strategy we'd like to see a wider profile of performance attributes to ensure robustness.

Commissions and Slippage

Commissions are an extremely important part of simulating strategy performance. The higher the frequency of trading or conversely the lower the holding time of positions, the more important commissions become. In our testing sequence we will use a basic commission structure of 0.25% or minimum $29.95, whichever is the larger amount. This is a standard rate for any investor using a broker's internet platform although in many instances investors can secure lower rates than these.

Slippage, or 'skid' as it's sometimes known, refers to the difference between the theoretical price and the real price achieved in the market. Slippage becomes less of a cost as the investment time horizon increases, but certainly for short term trading it can be a significant cost and drag on an account and must be accounted for when conducting historical testing. Slippage costs can also be influenced by certain order types. For example a 'stop loss' order will tend to increase slippage and is very difficult to accurately assess in simulations especially when liquidity fluctuates. On the other hand, a 'market on open' order which utilizes the open auction VWAP[23], recognised as the most liquid part of the day, will greatly limit the amount of slippage and therefore be a more accurate proxy when used in simulations.

Compensating for slippage can be done in various ways. A fixed dollar or percentage value can be added to the cost of doing the trade, although this tends to be arbitrary, especially if knowledge of the market or instrument being traded is limited or non-existent. Secondly, as mentioned above, entering and exiting positions during the opening auction can greatly reduce slippage, plus it ensures a much more realistic expectation because the opening price can always be secured. Lastly, when entering a position, ask the computer to always buy at the high of the day so as to achieve the worst possible price of that day. When exiting, ask the computer to sell at the low of the day to ensure the worst possible price of that day. In the real world it is unlikely that this would occur that often, but if you wish to be extremely conservative then using this technique in your simulations will ensure you fully account for slippage[24].

For years I have used the next day's opening price using the VWAP in real time trading without issue and therefore believe it's the best option for our testing purposes.

Liquidity

The traded volume, or turnover, of a stock is an often-overlooked aspect of strategy simulations. Substantial risk occurs during times of crisis when positions need to be exited quickly. It is important for all universe constituents to have reasonable liquidity, or traded volume, in order for exits to be executed as required. A key reason Long Term Capital Management imploded in 1998, and why so much damage was inflicted during the GFC, was due to the trading of illiquid markets or markets that became illiquid under duress.

Another consideration when using simulations is that results that compound over long periods of time require larger holdings

---

23 Volume Weighted Average Price

24 For advanced users we are purposely creating a postdictive error meaning we are looking into the future to generate a buy or sell price on past data. In the real world this would not occur and it will not impact negatively on results, indeed real time results could only be increased.

to facilitate the growing capital allocation. Sometimes this becomes disproportionate to the actual stock available to trade in the real market. A simulation may suggest a transaction in stock XYZ was 660,000 shares yet on the day of execution the stock only traded 500,000 in total.

Obviously in reality you would have been unable to transact the volume and therefore the simulations will be inaccurate. We can never know what future liquidity will be, but avoiding stocks that are naturally illiquid will help in making simulations more accurate for the real world. This book will only use stocks where the 7-day average volume exceeds 500,000 shares traded or the 7-day average turnover exceeds $500,000. Any stocks that fail to meet these criteria are automatically excluded.

Test Universe

With knowledge of the issues listed above we need to select a universe of stocks from which to run our simulations. To do this with reasonable robustness we will select all securities from the current All Ordinaries Index (XAO) which contains the top 500 Australian stocks by market capitalisation. This universe contains many different types of stocks, from big blue chips right down to smaller developing companies. It doesn't contain tiny speculative stocks but there are enough varying personalities in this top 500 to ensure we get a good spread of price activity.

However, as mentioned previously, this current list only contains stocks that have 'survived' and does not contain stocks that have been delisted. If we ignore stocks that have not survived the results we generate could be overly optimistic and skew simulation returns higher than what may occur in reality. To circumnavigate Survivorship Bias we will also add the complete delisted stock universe back to January 1997[25], including all stocks that have gone into administration as well as those delisted due to merger or acquisition.

In summary our test universe will contain a total of 1847 securities and will therefore provide a fair idea of how the strategies have fared over the years without giving too much bias to a single sector or index.

---

25 Data provided by Premium Data www.premiumdata.net

Our simulations will run from 1st January 1997 to 30th June 2011. This period encompasses a wide variety of major 'price shock' events such as:

- 1997 Asian currency crisis
- 2000 Tech crash
- 2001 September 11
- 2002/03 Bear market
- 2007/08 Global Financial Crisis

It should be noted that our selected universe contains stocks that offer a variety of personality traits. Lower capitalised stocks tend to trend better yet exhibit more volatility than major capitalised stocks. One can show with relative ease that certain types of strategies will perform better on certain types of stocks, or stocks that exhibit certain traits. The importance of robustness though cannot be overlooked when allocating a specific strategy to a specific universe of stocks. It is better to accept 'reasonably good' performance over the entire universe rather than hunting for 'outstanding performance' on a small sub-section of the universe.

Optimisation

A key philosophy of mine is that all trading methods should be simple in design, construction and usability. The more complex a strategy, the more problems that can arise and the less understanding the user has about how and why profits are generated.

In an attempt to find the perfect solution a trader or investor can optimise these parameter settings, that is, attempt to find the best input value from a set of alternatives in order to maximize profits and/or minimize risk. The major concern is that the personality of the market as a whole, and all constituents within the market, tend to change over time. The optimal input variable from the past may not be the best for the future because the personality of the instrument may change. Too much optimisation leads to curve fitting, meaning there is a high probability that the strategy only works on the sample test data and not future data.

It is more fruitful to have a robust strategy with minimal degrees of freedom that works reasonably well most of the time rather than a strategy that has been optimised to work spectacularly well just some of the time. This however doesn't bode well for aspiring investors and for some so-called professionals, who, being human, prefer perfection all of the time. There is a school of thought that every strategy is doomed to fail at some stage. That line of thinking is wrong. A strategy that has been optimised or built with data mining is more likely to fail than a robust strategy designed around strong market foundations, specifically trends. The market has always trended. Stock markets trend because of investor fear, greed and expectation. Human emotion is a constant.

I have never subscribed to the implementation of optimisation and am extremely wary of data mining techniques that are so widely used by sell-side vendors. The over-use of optimisation and/or data mining is solely designed to show outstanding yet unlikely performance, usually in order to sell a product. Whilst the strategies in this book could be optimized for better performance for future robustness they have intentionally been kept as simple as possible.

SECTION 2
Example Strategies

Introduction

It is my strong belief that you can manage your own capital and beat traditional stock market investment methods without the need to digest reams of market data, financial ratios and attempting to predict future events (which are inevitably unpredictable). Investors would also like to outperform a Buy & Hold portfolio and, for that matter, so would the majority of fund managers. Therefore our goal is to create specific rules that have been proven to work and that eliminate looking at too many variables that inevitably make decision making difficult, if not impossible. To do this we abide by a simple principle:

> *Absorb what is useful,*
> *Discard what is not,*
> *Add what is uniquely your own.*
>
> **Bruce Lee**

Sceptics will argue that in order to generate positive returns you must use fundamental variables and ratios, you must intrinsically understand the businesses you're investing in as well as the economy and that you should not time the market. Whilst this may be the case for the majority, and it may make you feel comfortable with your decision making process, it's not the essential element for success that we've been sold on. Section 3 will conclusively prove that we do not need to know what a company does in order to generate positive returns.

But firstly we look at simulated yet practical examples of objective rule-based strategies that are designed to capture intermediate-term trends, specifically trends that last 6—12 months or that may extend longer in certain market conditions. Our goal is to investigate strategies that may provide better risk-adjusted returns than those traditionally accepted by the majority. More importantly we are looking at strategies that can be readily replicated, are objective rather than subjective and do not use discretion.

For comparative purposes we will use the All Ordinaries Accumulation Index (XAOA) as a benchmark. The XAOA is made up of the largest 500 'surviving' companies defined by market capitalisation and includes the reinvestment of dividend income. We would expect a Buy & Hold investor to see a return profile similar to the XAOA, indeed the vast majority of Australian fund managers offer a very similar return profile.

Nick's Top Tips

Forget the accuracy of your stock picks. The key to success is creating a positive expectancy by allowing profits to far outweigh any losses.

Our strategy simulations will adhere to the following criteria:

Test Platform	AmiBroker v5.30 Professional Edition
Data Provider	Premium Data
Test Period	January 1 1997—June 30 2011
Universe	Current All Ordinaries Index (XAO) constituents PLUS all delisted stocks
Start Capital	$100,000
Position Sizing	20 equal weighted positions of 5%
Dividends	Yes
Commissions	0.25% or minimum $29.95
Margin	Nil
Interest Rate	Nil
Corporate Actions	Data proportionately back adjusted
Liquidity	7-day average must exceed 500,000 shares traded
Turnover	7-day average must exceed $500,000

Table 6: To ensure an equal playing field to test our strategies we use a core set of criteria.

Software plays an important role in running these simulations and to some extent makes ongoing signal generation and trade management a much easier task. There are many different software packages on the market costing upward of $300 and it's not necessarily true that the more expensive packages will be more proficient. We have used AmiBroker as our main simulation platform and have confirmed signals and performance using TradeStation. It is important that people new to systematic testing check signals and rules to ensure the coding is correct[26].

New Yearly Highs

Outline

There is a quote attributed to Einstein, "Everything should be as simple as possible, but not simpler," and the simplest way to determine a strong trend is when a stock makes a new yearly

26 For coding assistance see www.AmiBrokercoding.com

high. A rational view suggests that a stock making a new yearly high can only be in an uptrend and conversely a stock making a new yearly low can only be in a downtrend. Buying a stock making a new yearly high is an objective way to ensure we're joining an uptrend. If a stock makes a new yearly low it is considered to be in a downtrend and it is therefore time to exit. However, unlike many fundamental-based strategies buying new yearly highs is counter-intuitive to most people, if not completely absurd; why buy something today that is more expensive than it has been for the last year? As discussed in Section 1, trends tend to persist in the direction they're currently travelling, either up or down. Therefore, if a stock makes a new yearly high, it is likely to continue going higher and vice versa.

Research by George and Hwang published in the *Journal of Finance*[27] shows that the closer a stock's current price is to its 52-week high, the stronger that stock's performance in the subsequent period. They conclude that "*...price levels are more important determinants of momentum effects than are past price changes*". In subsequent work they also found an industry level 52-week high effect which was even more pronounced.

An added benefit of this strategy is that most daily financial publications include 52-week high and low data, meaning it's a strategy that can be easily employed with minimal expense and expertise.

To put this theory to the test we will use daily data to avoid unwanted price gaps that could occur on an intra-week basis. We measure a yearly high using the last 250 days of data (there are approximately 250 trading days in a year). When price closes at a new 250-day high we buy on the next day's open. We exit the position on the next open after the stock closes below its 250 day low.

The following chart of Commonwealth Bank (CBA) from 2008 through 2011 shows price bound by the 250-day high and the 250-day low. In August 2009 price moves and closes through the 250-day high triggering a buy signal. The trend continues for a small distance before faltering and falling back into a range. Finally price falls back through the 250-day low in August 2011 triggering an exit.

---

27 *Journal of Finance*, Vol. LIX No.5, October 2004

FIGURE 23

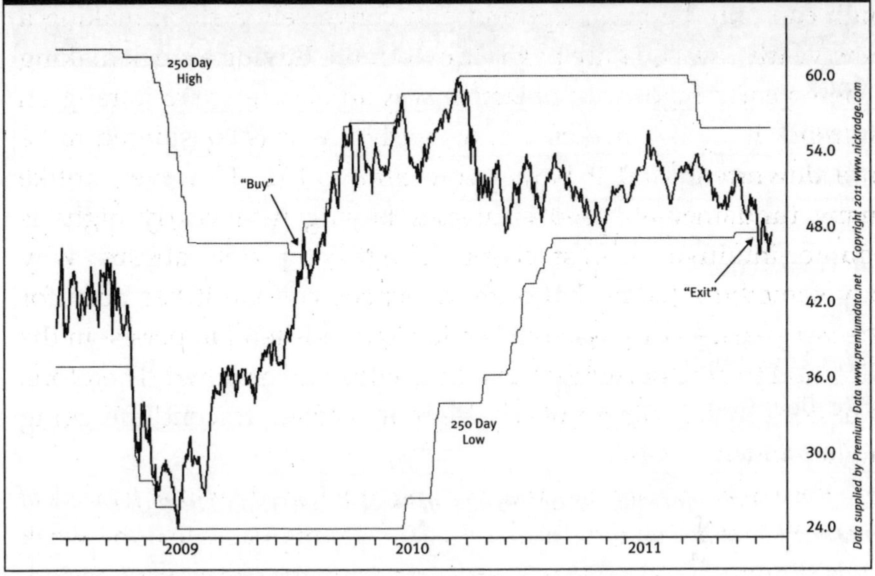

Figure 23: Commonwealth Bank, July 2008—August 2011.

The above example did not unfold in a sustained trend but next we see Bathurst Resources (BTU) penetrating the 250-day high level in late 2010 at $0.40 before trending all the way to $1.25. Note however the 250-day low, our exit level, is well below the current market price.

FIGURE 24

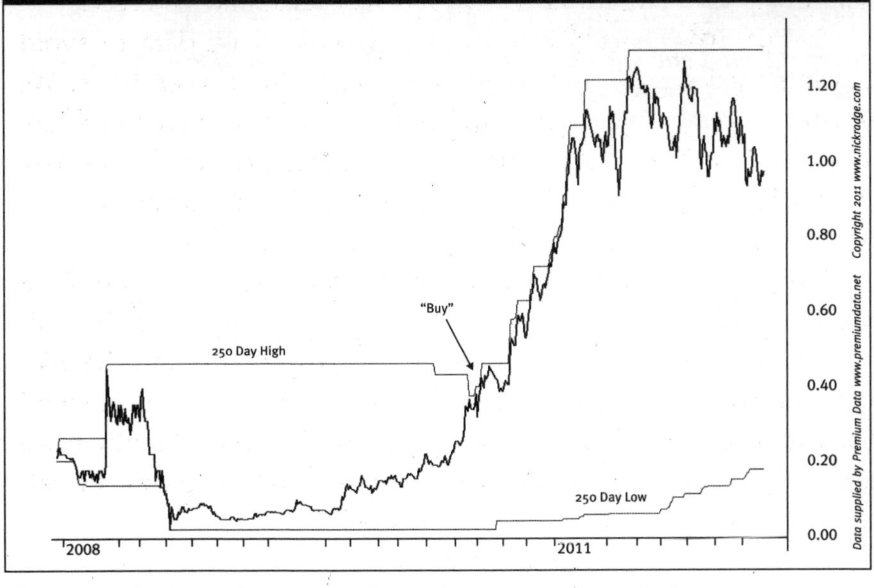

Figure 24: Bathurst Resources, December 2007—August 2011

Summary Statistics

	XAOA	Yearly High
CAGR	8.78%	18.21%
maxDD	-51.4%	-50.04%
MAR	0.17	0.36
Exposure	100%	92.6%
# Transactions	-	170
Win %	-	53.3%
Win/Loss Ratio	-	3.63
Std Dev. (pa)	18.88%	35.12%
Sharpe Ratio	0.204	0.395

Table 6: Single run simulation results of New Yearly High strategy verse Buy & Hold statistics.

	XAOA	Average	Range Min	Range Max
CAGR	8.78%	19.17%	13.50%	31.99%
maxDD	-51.4%	-53.30%	-73.86%	-33.90%
MAR	0.17	0.36	0.18	0.94
# Transactions		165	144	188
Win %		51.9%	43.8%	58..5%
Win/Loss Ratio		4.14	2.44	12.58

Table7: Monte Carlo simulation statistics of New Yearly High strategy based on 1000 iterations.

FIGURE 25

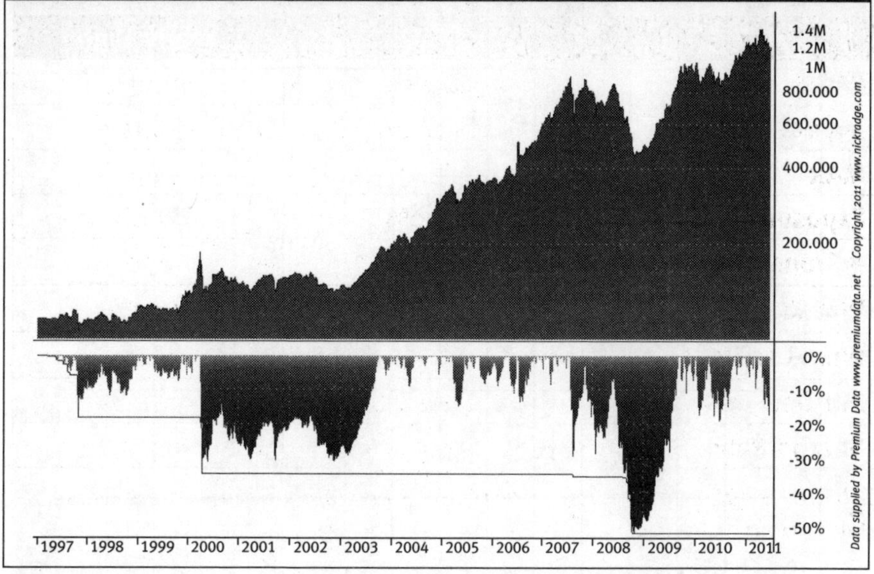

Figure 25: Equity growth of $100,000 from January 1997 through June 2011 (log scale).

	3-month	6-month	12-month	18-month	24-month	30-month
XAOA	68.6%	73.4%	79.8%	79.6%	79.4%	79.3%
Yearly Highs	55.7%	69.0%	81.7%	89.3%	89.5%	93.2%

Table 8: Rolling window analysis of New Yearly High strategy from 3-months to 30-months.

Year	Jan	Feb	Mar	Apr	May	Jun	Jul	Aug	Sep	Oct	Nov	Dec	Yr%
1997	n/a	n/a	-0.2%	0.1%	0.3%	3.0%	2.0%	-5.4%	9.0%	-11.8%	0.4%	3.1%	**-0.8%**
1998	0.7%	0.9%	1.6%	1.2%	-3.4%	1.0%	1.4%	-6.4%	3.1%	2.9%	3.8%	3.5%	**10.5%**
1999	3.8%	-2.8%	1.3%	-0.9%	-1.6%	-0.4%	-0.3%	0.6%	-0.0%	1.4%	9.1%	6.7%	**17.7%**
2000	-4.5%	11.0%	20.2%	-21.9%	2.5%	11.5%	-1.4%	9.0%	-6.3%	-3.9%	2.5%	-5.2%	**6.9%**
2001	2.2%	-3.0%	-5.7%	5.4%	4.0%	4.6%	1.1%	-2.1%	-6.0%	4.9%	0.3%	2.3%	**7.5%**
2002	1.4%	0.8%	-1.4%	-0.6%	4.7%	-6.6%	-5.9%	1.6%	-4.2%	-0.6%	-0.3%	1.4%	**-9.8%**
2003	0.5%	-2.2%	4.5%	2.9%	4.9%	5.8%	3.1%	5.4%	7.9%	4.9%	-2.9%	5.0%	**47.2%**
2004	1.9%	7.8%	1.3%	-6.0%	2.6%	6.1%	3.0%	0.7%	6.8%	7.6%	12.0%	1.3%	**53.9%**
2005	5.4%	3.2%	-1.4%	-7.7%	3.2%	8.6%	3.8%	1.8%	6.0%	-7.0%	1.4%	1.4%	**18.9%**
2006	1.4%	-3.7%	7.7%	5.9%	-6.1%	12.0%	7.3%	5.1%	4.1%	3.2%	7.0%	11.3%	**69.3%**
2007	5.7%	-2.7%	8.7%	3.3%	14.2%	4.6%	-5.6%	-4.8%	9.1%	10.1%	-10.5%	-0.3%	**32.9%**
2008	-9.6%	1.2%	-4.8%	14.5%	9.2%	-11.0%	-9.9%	-10.0%	-14.8%	-13.9%	-0.4%	6.8%	**-38.6%**
2009	-2.7%	6.6%	17.6%	3.3%	9.4%	3.7%	13.9%	10.6%	6.8%	-2.1%	10.4%	-1.8%	**104.2%**
2010	-15.5%	7.6%	10.2%	-3.1%	-7.8%	-6.9%	11.8%	-1.9%	11.7%	4.7%	3.7%	14.0%	**26.4%**
2011	-5.7%	2.9%	6.4%	3.0%	-2.8%	-7.5%	n/a	n/a	n/a	n/a	n/a	n/a	**-4.3%**
Avg	**-1.0%**	**1.9%**	**4.4%**	**-0.0%**	**2.2%**	**1.9%**	**1.7%**	**0.3%**	**2.4%**	**0.0%**	**2.6%**	**3.5%**	

Table 9: Monthly profit table of New Yearly High strategy.

FIGURE 26

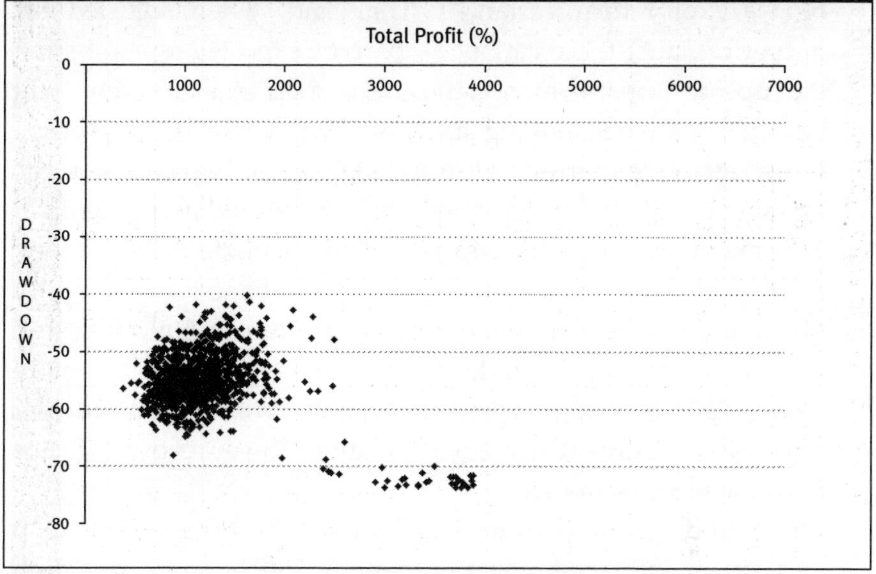

Figure 26: Distribution of total return plotted against maximum drawdown

Conclusion and Improvements

Taking into account simplicity, robustness, implementation and management, the New Yearly High strategy works reasonably well on a straight performance basis. The compounded return is over twice the Buy & Hold return enabling the MAR ratio to rise to 0.36, a figure still not considered overly high even if it is better than the broader market. The average holding period at 370 days suggests dividend income would be increased due to participating in two dividend payment cycles and tax liability decreased as the winning trade length, at 510 days, falls outside the 12-month threshold.

The monthly profit table shows that during the 14.5 years of testing the strategy has incurred a loss in three full years; 1997, 2002 and 2008. Probability of profit according to our Time Window Analysis also shows the strategy outperforms Buy & Hold on time intervals upward of 12-months and achieves a 93.2% probability of success at the 30 month interval.

However, there are three areas of concern:

1. **Volatility of returns**. The Standard Deviation of annual returns is high at just over 35% and roughly twice the broader market.

Investors trading smaller cap and more volatile stocks should be wary of return variances. That said, when adjusted for outperformance these variances are to be expected remembering that upside outperformance, the goal of most retail investors, will be penalized when looking at the standard deviation of returns.

2. **Long recovery period.** During 2002/2003 bear market the strategy remained 'underwater' for an extended period of time. This means that after the equity-high peak made in 2000 it took a number of years to regain that lost ground and for new equity highs to be made. The same occurs for a Buy & Hold investor. The broader market made a peak in February 2002 before sliding 22%. New highs were not seen until March 2004. Ideally an active investment strategy will have a lower recovery factor than the broader market.
3. **Depth of drawdown.** In 2008 global markets corrected in a deep and reasonably well sustained trend. The New Yearly High strategy was very slow to react to the changing environment and therefore suffered a similar decline in equity to that of the underlying market. In our opinion when equity declines exceed 30% most investors will opt out so a 50% drawdown is therefore not acceptable.

No strategy will be without some kind of capital decline during its lifetime. However, significant drawdowns occur in this strategy because the exit mechanism is quite wide, so to be more proactive in protecting capital when the market turns down we need to look at alternate exit mechanisms or portfolio management enhancements.

One way to lower volatility is simply selecting a lower volatility universe of stocks to invest in, specifically higher capitalized and institutionalized stocks found in the top 100. The trade-off for lower volatility will be a lower return but it's a worthy exercise to explore, especially for those in the latter stages of managing their own SMSF and not looking at higher growth rates.

The following table shows the returns of the New Yearly High strategy traded just on the ASX100[28].

---

28 ASX100 being the current constituent list as at June 30th 2011. Does not include delisted stock data.

	XAOA	Yearly High	Yearly High (ASX100)
CAGR	8.78%	18.21%	13.92%
maxDD	-51.4%	-50.04%	-36.03%
MAR	0.17	0.36	0.39
Exposure	100%	92.6%	82.3%
# Transactions	-	170	99
Win %	-	53.3%	55.5%
Win/Loss Ratio	-	3.63	3.69
Std Dev. (pa)	18.88%	35.12%	21.46%
Sharpe Ratio	0.204	0.395	0.416

Table 10: Single run simulation results of New Yearly High strategy traded on the test universe verse traded solely on the ASX100.

From the table we can see that the Standard Deviation of annual return drops considerably, almost to the same levels as the broader market. As expected the annual return also declines but MAR is lifted slightly to 0.39. Interestingly, exposure or 'time in the market' drops to 82.3%. If we were to take this lower exposure and equalize it to 100% exposure, the risk-adjusted return rises to 16.92%

The equity curve shows modest gains but of note is that a recovery to new-equity highs has not been achieved after the peak of 2007. One reason for this is lack of signal generation, specifically the number of stocks in the ASX100 making new-yearly highs after the GFC is limited so there are not enough drivers to take equity higher, whereas with the broader universe we did have those higher beta stocks that were able to make new yearly highs.

FIGURE 27

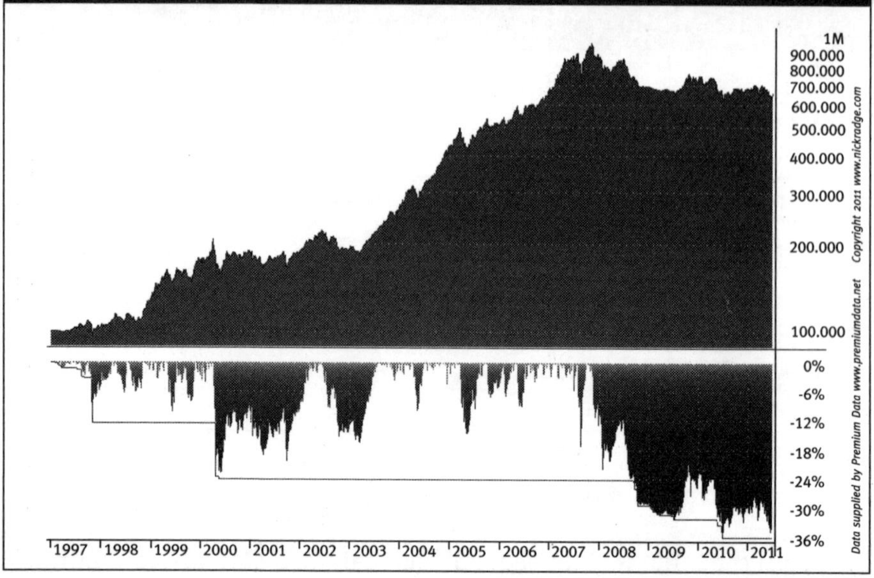

Figure 27: Growth of $100,000 trading the New Yearly High strategy solely on the ASX100 constituent list.

Another way to minimize capital declines without any significant shift in strategy is (a) defining when the broader market is in an uptrend and conversely when it's in a downtrend, and (b) taking appropriate position management action during those events. This mechanism is known as an Index Filter.

To create an Index Filter we place a 75-day moving average on the underlying index, in this case the All Ordinaries Index (XAO). 75 days is an arbitrary number – more conservative investors may wish to use a slightly longer filter thus delaying entries to the point that the trend has been confirmed by stronger price momentum. The following diagram shows the moving average during the lows of 2009. Once prices reverse above the moving average we can move from a cash stance to initiating new positions as the strategy signals are generated.

FIGURE 28

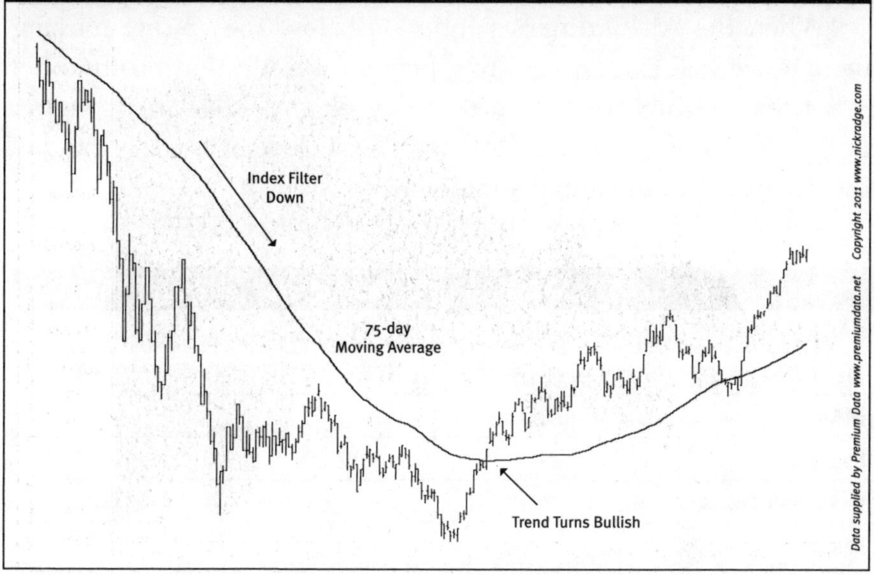

Figure 28: The inclusion of an Index Filter, such as a simple moving average, can offer a better risk adjusted return to a strategy. This chart shows the All Ordinaries Index with a 75-day simple moving average overlaid.

Entry with Filter:

If the All Ordinaries Index is above the 75-day moving average we acknowledge that the trend of the broader market is up and take any signals generated by the strategy. That is, when a stock closes above its 250-day high we enter on the next open.

Exit with Filter:

When the All Ordinaries Index is below the 75-day moving average we will exit any existing position should that position fall 10% from the high of the current day or any subsequent higher day—in other words we do not await for a close below the 250-day low according to the initial strategy rules.

Let's compare the raw strategy with the filtered (F):

	XAOA	Yearly High	Yearly High (F)
CAGR	8.78%	18.21%	17.66%
maxDD	-51.4%	-50.04%	-26.17%
MAR	0.17	0.36	0.67
Exposure	100%	92.6%	73.8%
# Transactions	-	170	459
Win %	-	53.3%	48.5%
Win/Loss Ratio	-	3.63	2.95
Std Dev. (pa)	18.88%	35.12%	22.09%
Sharpe Ratio	0.204	0.395	0.573

Table 11: Single run simulation results of New Yearly High strategy verse the same strategy with the Index Filter (F) added.

The addition of the Index Filter significantly improves the strategy's statistics across the board. The maximum drawdown has been dramatically reduced to 26.17% which is well within the realms of being acceptable for a growth investment.

	3-month	6-month	12-month	18-month	24-month	30-month
XAOA	68.6%	73.4%	79.8%	79.6%	79.4%	79.3%
Yearly Highs	55.7%	69.0%	81.7%	89.3%	89.5%	93.2%
Yearly Highs (F)	57.6%	63.4%	86.7%	95.0%	96.7%	95.9%

Table 12: The rolling window return profile shows the filter improving the odds of attaining profitability in less time.

The equity chart below offers a much more consistent rise as well as making new equity highs after the events of 2008. Apart from the 2002/2003 bear market, recovery periods have all been lessened.

FIGURE 29

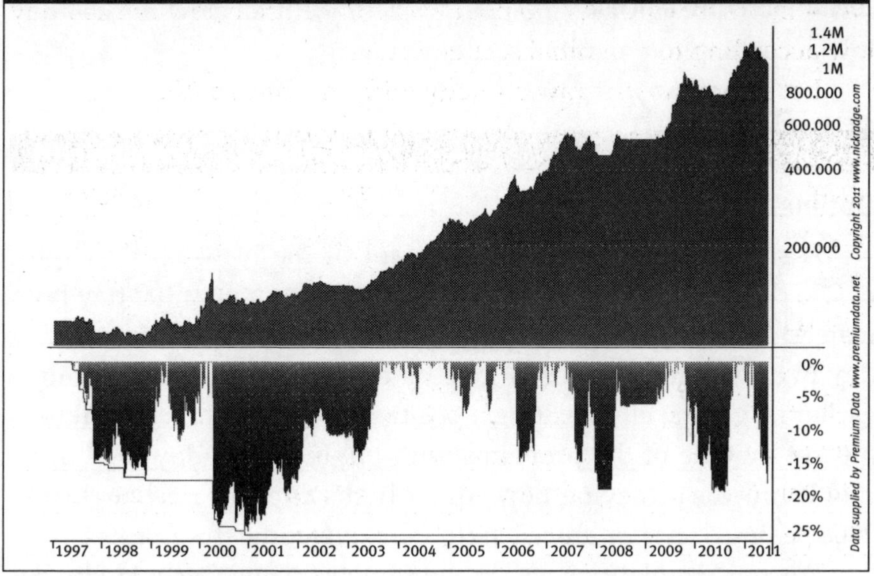

Figure 29: Growth of $100,000 using the New Yearly High strategy with the Index Filter added.

FIGURE 30

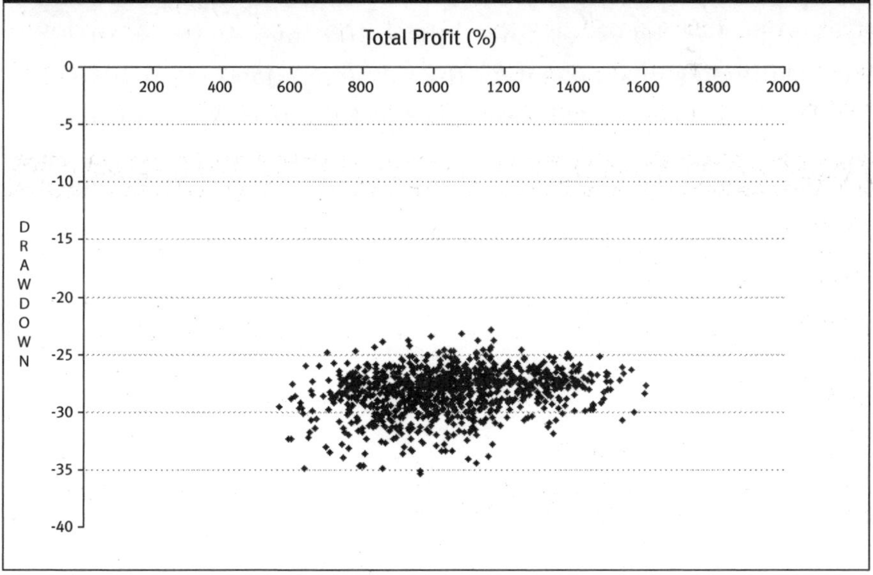

Figure 30: Scatter Plot showing total return verse maximum drawdown after the Index Filter has been added.

The only significant criticism is that the frequency of trading has risen: although whilst this is not overly critical, what has occurred is that the average winning trade length has declined to 174 days. This could increase the tax burden on the strategy in certain circumstances.

100-Day High

Outline

A slightly more aggressive variant of the New Yearly Highs, or 250 day highs, is buying a stock as it makes a new 100-day high instead. A key benefit of buying a 100-day high rather than a 250-day high is that the investor gets involved with a trend at a much earlier stage as well as exiting a position before too much weakness has set in. One of the problems with buying a 250-day high in its raw form was achieving new equity highs after the decline during 2008. Using a shorter entry length may overcome this issue.

For our simulations we do the same as New Yearly Highs but count back just 100 trading days. The strategy awaits a close above the highest high point of those 100 days then enters the next day on the open. The opposite is true for the exit: count back 100 trading days and select the lowest low of those 100 days. A close below that low point will signal an exit for the following day's open.

The following chart shows Forge Group (FGE) dropping to very low levels during the GFC before starting to recover in early 2009. The 100-day high trailed behind the falling share price before triggering an entry in May 2009 below $0.50.

FIGURE 31

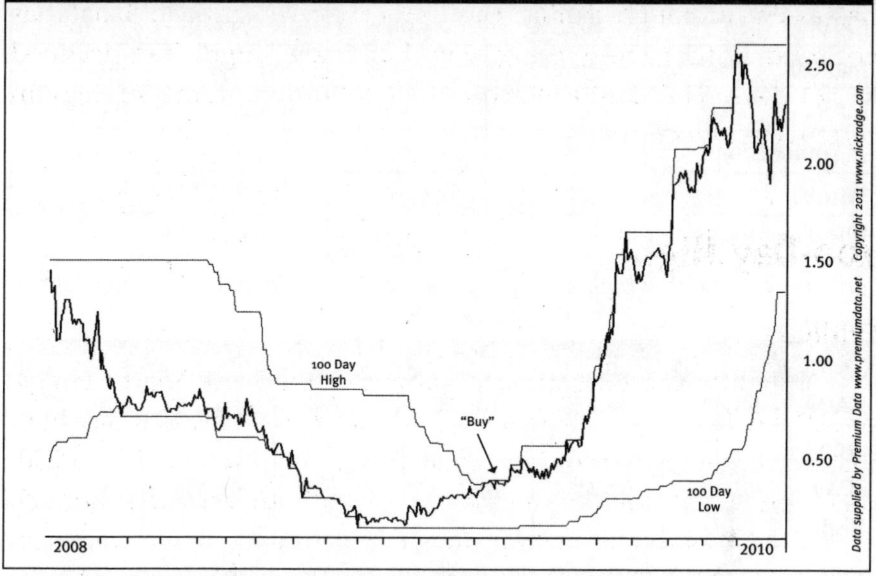

Figure 31: Forge Group, January 2008 to February 2009 showing a substantial trend occurring after a 100-Day High breakout.

Summary Statistics

	XAOA	100-Day High
CAGR	8.78%	23.74%
maxDD	-51.4%	-45.2%
MAR	0.17	0.52
Exposure	100%	93.1%
# Transactions	-	360
Win %	-	44.4%
Win/Loss Ratio	-	4.56
Std Dev. (pa)	18.88%	43.42%
Sharpe Ratio	0.204	0.432

Table 13: A single run simulation of the 100-Day High strategy verse our benchmark All Ordinaries Accumulation Index.

	XAOA	Average	Range Min	Range Max
CAGR	8.78%	23.95%	16.33%	33.36%
maxDD	-51.4%	-45.7%	-56.3%	-35.8%
MAR	0.17	0.52	0.29	0.93
# Transactions	-	351	325	379
Win %	-	44.91%	38.8%	51.2%
Win/Loss Ratio	-	4.39	3.06	6.74

Table 14: The 100-Day High strategy tested over 1000 Monte Carlo simulations.

	3-month	6-month	12-month	18-month	24-month	30-month
XAOA	68.6%	73.4%	79.8%	79.6%	79.4%	79.3%
100-Day Highs	58.3%	67.4%	76.4%	85.6%	94.1%	96.6%

Table 15: Time Window Analysis shows the 100-Day High strategy outperforms Buy & Hold after 18-months.

FIGURE 32

Figure 32: Growth of $100,000 using the 100-Day High strategy,

Year	Jan	Feb	Mar	Apr	May	Jun	Jul	Aug	Sep	Oct	Nov	Dec	Yr%
1997	n/a	-0.3%	-0.6%	0.1%	0.3%	3.5%	-1.0%	-3.7%	2.9%	-13.7%	-1.7%	3.9%	**-10.8%**
1998	0.9%	1.2%	0.2%	0.4%	-4.1%	-5.1%	3.3%	-5.9%	3.0%	4.7%	8.1%	14.3%	**21.4%**
1999	10.2%	-0.1%	10.0%	11.6%	-2.7%	-3.3%	2.3%	-1.9%	4.9%	5.5%	10.0%	9.7%	**70.4%**
2000	-5.2%	-2.2%	8.2%	-24.2%	-3.4%	8.1%	1.9%	1.1%	-2.1%	1.6%	7.1%	-2.0%	**-14.8%**
2001	1.4%	-1.7%	-1.9%	1.2%	5.7%	1.4%	-0.8%	1.9%	-7.1%	4.1%	4.3%	0.1%	**8.3%**
2002	1.5%	4.1%	7.9%	1.8%	4.3%	-5.4%	-6.9%	7.5%	-6.3%	0.9%	3.5%	1.1%	**13.3%**
2003	-0.5%	-1.8%	1.8%	5.9%	5.0%	3.3%	9.8%	9.2%	-0.1%	4.3%	-0.6%	5.7%	**49.9%**
2004	-2.6%	3.5%	1.5%	-5.7%	0.8%	6.1%	6.4%	2.5%	7.6%	7.0%	10.5%	0.4%	**43.7%**
2005	6.3%	0.9%	-1.0%	-13.2%	-1.8%	7.9%	5.1%	2.4%	6.9%	-11.3%	4.6%	1.9%	**6.5%**
2006	3.1%	1.6%	16.3%	4.8%	-5.3%	5.9%	0.7%	4.3%	5.0%	7.5%	8.4%	5.1%	**72.9%**
2007	7.0%	-3.5%	8.8%	2.9%	11.1%	5.6%	-8.4%	-4.3%	7.4%	7.8%	-9.2%	-3.5%	**20.5%**
2008	-11.4%	4.2%	-4.1%	9.2%	15.5%	-4.8%	-13.6%	-3.6%	2.4%	-19.4%	-4.3%	1.1%	**-29.3%**
2009	-4.5%	9.5%	11.5%	-2.5%	14.3%	-4.5%	22.1%	11.9%	26.0%	0.5%	14.1%	-1.0%	**142.3%**
2010	-12.8%	10.8%	8.5%	-1.6%	-6.5%	0.2%	5.9%	9.9%	9.3%	0.5%	7.4%	5.9%	**40.5%**
2011	2.1%	8.1%	3.8%	-2.7%	-4.0%	-7.7%	n/a	n/a	n/a	n/a	n/a	n/a	**-1.4%**
Avg	**-0.3%**	**2.3%**	**4.7%**	**-0.8%**	**1.9%**	**0.7%**	**1.9%**	**2.3%**	**4.3%**	**0.0%**	**4.4%**	**3.1%**	

Table 16: The breakdown of monthly returns shows reliable year-on-year results.

FIGURE 33

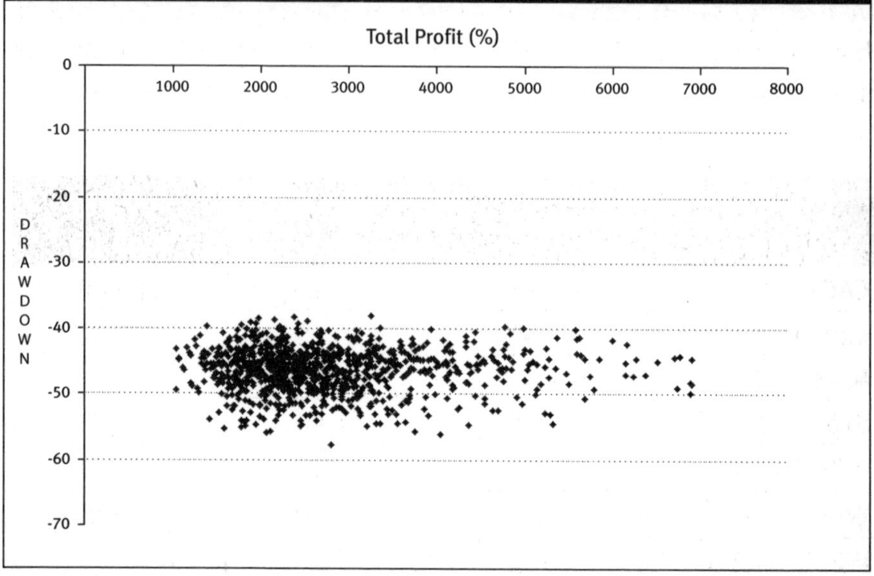

Figure 33: The Scatter Plot of total return verse maximum drawdown shows some outlier returns away from the main cluster.

Conclusion and Improvements

The one thing that stands out with this slightly more aggressive entry is that recovery from drawdown tends to be quicker, which in turn adds more profit to the bottom line. The ability to recover places this one at a higher ranking than the New Yearly High strategy.

The annualized return near 23% is certainly a worthy return for such a simple concept, plus the Time Window Analysis shows a reasonably high chance of achieving profitability from 18 months onward. The rolling returns divergence beyond 18 months between the XAOA and the 100-Day High strategy is due entirely to the ability of the strategy to pick stocks exhibiting strong upside momentum whilst steering clear of those unable to move higher.

Even with the 2009 equity recovery, the decline in equity during 2008 was probably still enough to send a large percentage of traders running for the exit door, even if it was still better than Buy & Hold. The inclusion of an Index Filter made for a much better risk-adjusted return with the New Yearly High strategy, so the obvious course of action is to see what impact, if any, the inclusion of an Index Filter will have here.

The following table shows the same 75-day Index Filter overlaid on the All Ordinaries Index (XAO). When the Filter turns negative we exit any positions that fall 10% from any respective high rather than awaiting the 100-day low point to trigger an exit. The data is almost identical to the improvements seen using the filter on the New Yearly High system.

	XAOA	100-Day High	100-Day High (F)
CAGR	8.78%	23.74%	15.32%
maxDD	-51.4%	-45.2%	-24.1%
MAR	0.17	0.52	0.63
Exposure	100%	93.1%	74.5%
# Transactions	-	360	545
Win %	-	44.4%	45.5%
Win/Loss Ratio	-	4.56	2.96
Std Dev. (pa)	18.88%	43.42%	23.06%
Sharpe Ratio	0.204	0.432	0.448

Table 17: The inclusion of the Index Filter greatly reduces the downside risks of the strategy.

What does improve dramatically is the drawdown during the downturn in 2008. The Underwater Equity Curve below shows a very minimal equity decline in 2008; indeed this single run simulation suggests it resulted in a +10.4% return during the calendar year—the strategy remained steadfastly in cash for 5 of the 12 months. This is a good example of how to improve the risk-adjusted return using strong defensive techniques during difficult times. Most fund managers saw their assets decline by at least 35% and many nearer 50% during 2008 simply because they were not mandated to take defensive action, such as going to cash.

FIGURE 34

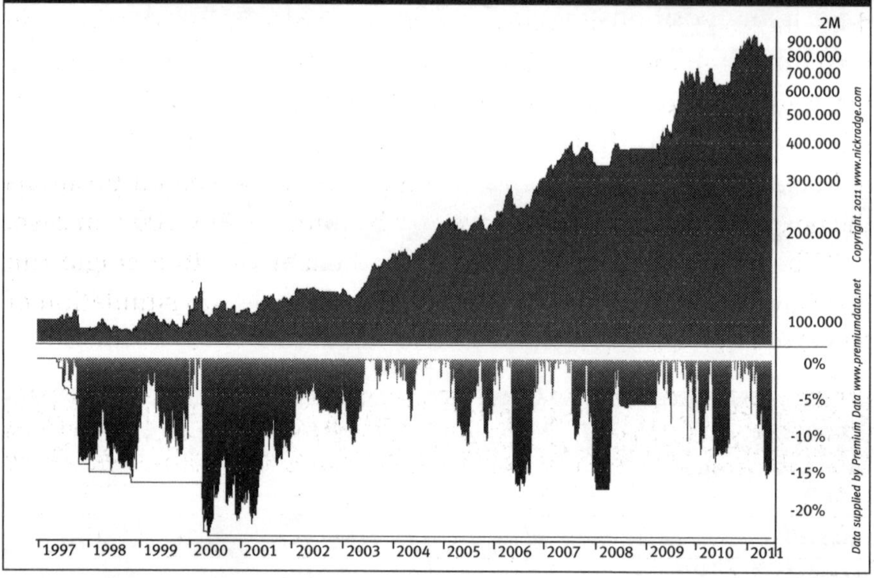

Figure 34: Growth of $100,000 using the 100-Day High strategy combined with the Index Filter.

Also worthy of note is the volatility of returns that have improved significantly, dropping from 43.42% to 23.06% and the market exposure falling from 93.1% to 74.5%. If we compare like for like at 100% exposure the risk-adjusted return lifts to 20.5%.

	3-month	6-month	12-month	18-month	24-month	30-month
XAOA	68.6%	73.4%	79.8%	79.6%	79.4%	79.3%
100-Day Highs	58.3%	67.4%	76.4%	85.6%	94.1%	96.6%
100-Day Highs (F)	58.7%	64.1%	83..0%	91.3%	96.7%	97.8%

Table 18: The inclusion of the Index Filter does not make a great deal of difference to the time window analysis.

We can see that using the filter and amending the trailing stop does increase the risk-adjusted return. Can it be improved even further? When the Index Filter turns the system off, instead of using the trailing stop, what if we reverted straight to cash instead? In other words, if our Index Filter turned negative, that is the market fell below the 75-day moving average, we would sell all positions the next day at the opening price and be immediately 100% in cash.

The following table compares our benchmark to a single run 100-Day High Filtered (F) and now adds a single run simulation of 100-Day High Cash (C).

	XAOA	100-Day High (F)	100-Day High (C)
CAGR	8.78%	15.32%	17.06%
maxDD	-51.4%	-24.1%	-22.9%
MAR	0.17	0.63	0.74
Exposure	100%	74.5%	56.2%
# Transactions	-	545	1020
Win %	-	45.5%	44.1%
Win/Loss Ratio	-	2.96	2.66
Std Dev. (pa)	18.88%	23.06%	14.1%
Sharpe Ratio	0.204	0.448	0.855

Table 19: Moving immediately to cash continues to increase the risk adjusted return of the 100-Day High strategy, although trade frequency also increases substantially.

Reverting to cash immediately generates a much-improved MAR ratio with substantially lower equity volatility. The standard deviation of annual returns drops to 14.1%, well below a Buy & Hold portfolio yet with twice the profit potential. The trade-off, and there is always a trade-off, is that the frequency of trades has rapidly increased to a level that may be unsuitable for a SMSF structure, although you should get guidance from your accountant on this. 1000 trades in a 14.5 year period is approximately 70 trades per annum.

FIGURE 35

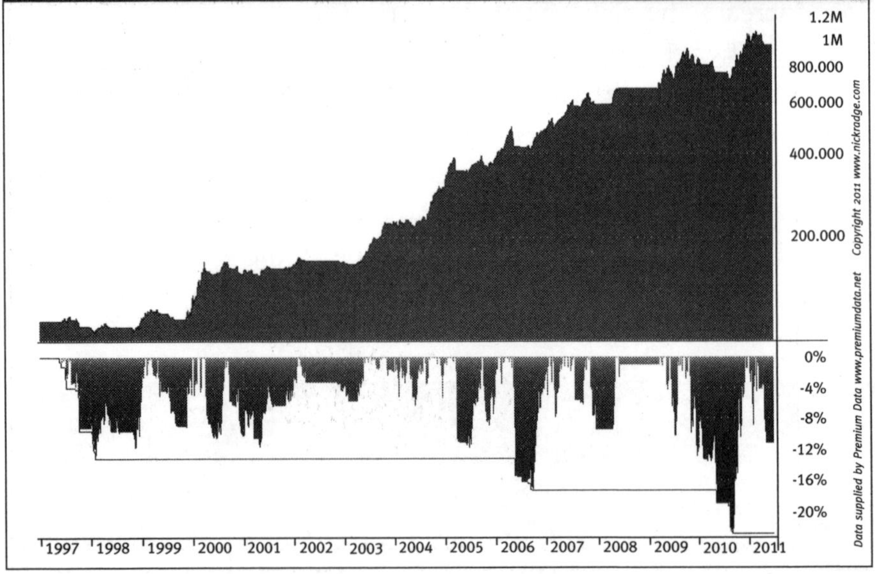

Figure 35: Growth of $100,000 using the 100-Day High strategy yet reverting to cash when the Index Filter is activated.

Lastly we analyse the possible distribution of returns using Monte Carlo simulations:

	XAOA	Average	Range Min	Range Max
CAGR	8.78%	15.89%	11.93%	19.81%
maxDD	-51.4%	-24.2%	-29.4%	-18.9%
MAR	0.17	0.66	0.41	1.05
# Transactions	-	1018	993	1044
Win %	-	43.8%	41.2%	46.5%
Win/Loss Ratio	-	2.66	2.32	3.00

Table 20: 1000 Monte Carlo iterations of the 100-Day High strategy combined with the cash option.

FIGURE 36

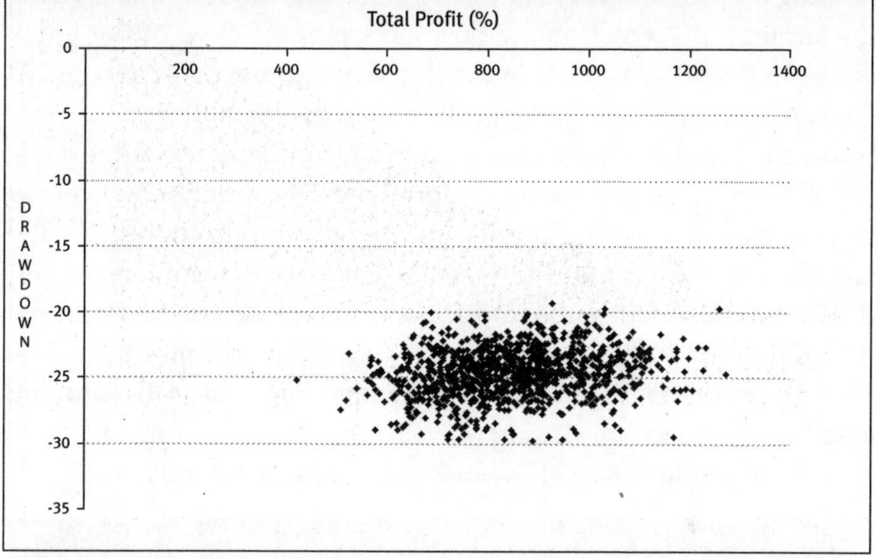

Figure 36: The addition of the filter and cash exit ensure a much tighter cluster of possible outcomes adding to the robustness of the strategy.

The simulation average is slightly below the single run data however these numbers are extremely encouraging on a risk-adjusted reward basis.

TrendPilot

Outline

TrendPilot is the name given to a new Exchange Traded Note (ETN) listed on the New York Stock Exchange Arca (NYSE Arca) issued by The Royal Bank of Scotland[29]. The NYSE Arca is a fully-automated trading platform that lists ETNs. ETNs are designed to provide investors with access to the returns of various market benchmarks, in this case a momentum approach. TrendPilot utilizes a systematic momentum strategy to provide exposure to the S&P 500 (SPY) index in positive trending markets and revert to 3-month cash yields in negative trending markets.

---

29 http://usmarkets.rbs.com/

Sounds impressive, but the concept behind TrendPilot is (a) nothing new, and (b) very simplistic, albeit robust. In layman's terms the strategy will enter a new position when the close of the index is above the 200-day simple moving average for five consecutive days. An exit occurs in the opposite situation, when the index closes below the 200-day simple moving average for five consecutive days.

A simple moving average is formed by computing the average price of a security over a specific number of periods, in this case the last 200 days. To calculate add the last 200 days of closing prices and divide by 200. As its name implies, a moving average is an average that moves: old data is dropped as new data becomes available. This causes the average to move along the time scale. Most moving averages are based on closing prices.

The following chart shows a TrendPilot entry setup.

FIGURE 37

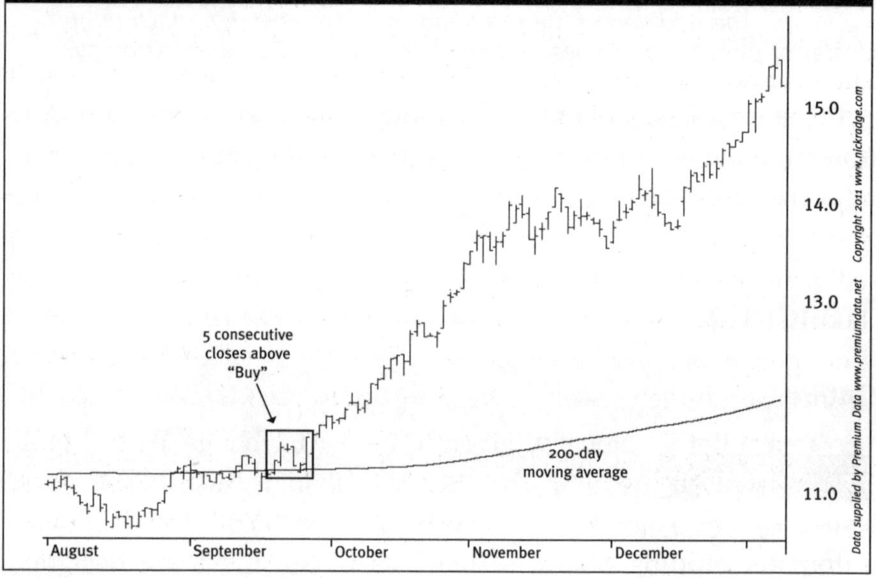

Figure 37: An entry setup occurs with five consecutive closes above the 200-day moving average.

The five consecutive closes above or below the average is designed to alleviate 'whipsaw'. Whipsaw occurs when prices move up, reverse and move down, reverse and move up and so on. As no sustained trend is forthcoming, any simplistic strategy, such as using a 200-day moving average on its own, will be forced to enter and exit repeatedly over a brief period of time. Each time there is a false entry the strategy will be dealt a small loss. This in itself is not an issue, but during a sustained period of sideways price action many false entries in a row may result in many small and frustrating losses. Essentially it becomes 'death by a thousand cuts'. Including the 'five consecutive closes' rule adds an element of confirmation to a move above or below the moving average.

As TrendPilot is designed to trade the underlying index only and not the individual constituents, we'll explore how the same technique would fare in Australia using our own underlying indices. TrendPilot also derives some benefit by investing in 3-month cash yields when funds are not invested in the system. However, that data cannot be extrapolated into the same test so it will be left out, with the understanding that some minor upside gains would be seen from interest accrued.

The next challenge is how to get a decent proxy for capital growth and dividends. The obvious broad-market gauge is the All Ordinaries Accumulation Index (XAOA) but it can't actually be traded—it's only an index. The next issue is that our test data period, January 1997 through June 30th 2011, will generate limited signals and therefore cannot be statistically relied upon.

Nick's Top Tips
How much capital is enough? More is always better due to commission drag. As account capital increases the drag of commissions and associated costs tend to fall.

With these impediments in mind here are the results for that period assuming we could actually trade the All Ordinaries Accumulation Index:

Summary Statistics

	XAOA	TrendPilot (XAOA)
CAGR	8.78%	9.75%
maxDD	-51.4%	-19.4%
MAR	0.17	0.50
Exposure	100%	69.9%
# Transactions	-	9
Win %	-	55.5%
Win/Loss Ratio	-	14.7
Std Dev. (pa)	18.88%	15.15%
Sharpe Ratio	0.204	0.314

Table 21: A single run simulation of TrendPilot traded on the All Ordinaries Accumulation Index.

FIGURE 38

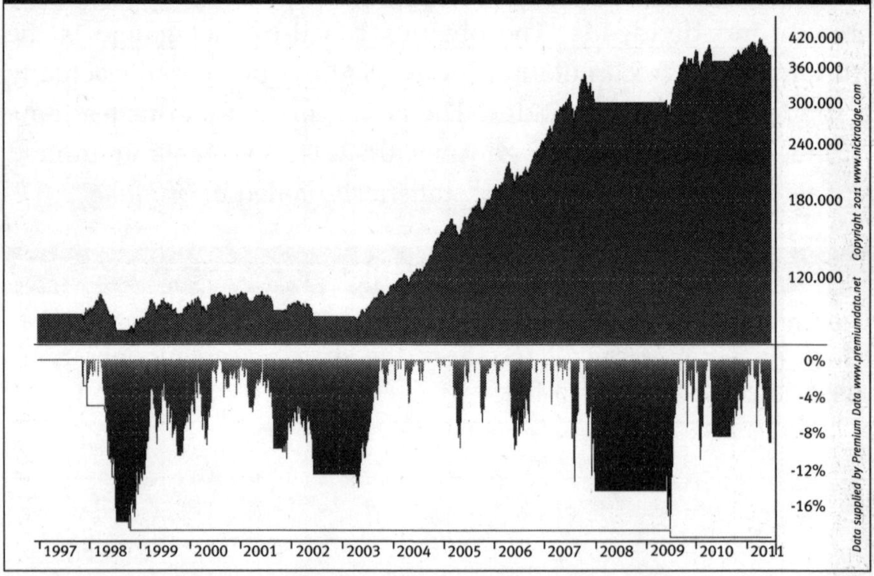

Figure 38: Growth of a $100,000 investment using TrendPilot on the All Ordinaries Accumulation Index.

Year	Jan	Feb	Mar	Apr	May	Jun	Jul	Aug	Sep	Oct	Nov	Dec	Yr%
1997	n/a	n/a	n/a	n/a	n/a	n/a	n/a	n/a	n/a	n/a	n/a	1.2%	**1.2%**
1998	2.1%	0.7%	2.6%	1.8%	-3.9%	-4.5%	-3.6%	-4.3%	n/a	n/a	1.2%	2.8%	**-5.6%**
1999	2.3%	-0.0%	3.6%	5.6%	-5.2%	3.8%	-0.1%	-0.7%	-1.3%	-2.8%	-0.4%	4.4%	**8.8%**
2000	-0.3%	3.7%	0.1%	-3.4%	-0.6%	6.9%	-1.4%	2.3%	-1.2%	-0.8%	0.8%	-0.2%	**5.8%**
2001	2.7%	-0.7%	-4.5%	0.3%	1.9%	2.0%	-1.7%	-2.6%	-4.4%	n/a	-0.4%	3.6%	**-4.2%**
2002	0.1%	-0.3%	0.0%	-0.8%	1.0%	-6.1%	n/a	n/a	n/a	n/a	n/a	n/a	**-6.1%**
2003	n/a	n/a	n/a	-0.4%	1.6%	0.8%	3.9%	3.3%	-0.5%	3.9%	-1.9%	5.4%	**17.2%**
2004	-0.8%	4.5%	2.5%	-2.8%	2.0%	3.0%	0.7%	1.6%	4.1%	4.8%	5.4%	4.0%	**32.6%**
2005	2.3%	2.4%	-1.2%	-3.9%	2.6%	3.9%	3.5%	4.0%	4.1%	-5.0%	3.1%	4.7%	**21.9%**
2006	5.1%	-1.7%	5.6%	5.9%	-5.4%	0.8%	-0.5%	3.3%	0.8%	7.4%	2.2%	5.6%	**32.4%**
2007	1.2%	1.6%	5.1%	5.3%	4.8%	1.3%	-5.7%	3.4%	12.1%	6.3%	-6.2%	-2.2%	**28.8%**
2008	-6.3%	n/a	n/a	n/a	n/a	n/a	n/a	n/a	n/a	n/a	n/a	n/a	**-6.3%**
2009	n/a	n/a	n/a	n/a	n/a	-2.7%	10.8%	6.7%	5.6%	-3.0%	5.6%	3.6%	**29.0%**
2010	-8.2%	4.8%	6.5%	-2.5%	-3.5%	n/a	n/a	n/a	0.5%	3.2%	-1.6%	4.2%	**2.4%**
2011	0.1%	2.3%	1.5%	-0.8%	-2.3%	-3.7%	n/a	n/a	n/a	n/a	n/a	n/a	**-3.0%**
Avg	**0.0%**	**1.1%**	**1.5%**	**0.3%**	**-0.5%**	**0.4%**	**0.4%**	**1.2%**	**1.4%**	**1.0%**	**0.6%**	**2.6%**	

Table 22: The monthly breakdown of returns using the TrendPilot strategy on the All Ordinaries Accumulation Index.

The largest point of difference is the significant reduction of the maximum drawdown. Losing 19.4% is more agreeable than losing 51% in anyone's language and even better the CAGR is more or less unchanged. However, nine transactions makes this simulation a moot point as it has no statistical substance.

Let us now turn back the test window for all available data back to 1980 to gain a better insight into longer term results for the index.

	XAOA	TrendPilot (1997–2011)	TrendPilot (1980–2011)
CAGR	8.78%	9.75%	8.67%
maxDD	-51.4%	-19.4%	-48.7%
MAR	0.17	0.50	0.18
Exposure	100%	69.9%	70.8%
# Transactions	-	9	26
Win %	-	45.5%	46.2%
Win/Loss Ratio	-	8.68	6.10
Std Dev. (pa)	18.88%	15.15%	20.7%
Sharpe Ratio	0.204	0.314	0.177

Table 23: Extending our test period back 30 years to 1980 shows consistent returns although highlights the impact of the 1987 crash.

Even taking the simulation back to 1980, the sample of 26 trades is still not enough to warrant dependence on the outcome, although looking at history does show one underlying flaw with this type of strategy. The significant difference here stands with the events of October 1987 when the broader market dropped some 25% on an opening gap—there was no scope for defensive action, and less so for a strategy like TrendPilot to adapt. As a result we see that the maximum equity decline slips considerably because of those events in 1987. We'll discuss the flaw within the strategy below.

Another instrument to consider is an index tracking exchange traded fund (ETF) such as the SPDR S&P/ASX200 ETF (STW) that is designed to closely match, before fees and expenses, the returns of the S&P/ASX200 Index (XJO). Unfortunately we run into an obstacle for testing because available data is limited to 2001 so yet again our trade sample is minimal and not statistically viable.

Summary Statistics

	XAOA	TrendPilot (STW)
CAGR	8.78%	7.70%
maxDD	-51.4%	-16.7%
MAR	0.17	0.46
Exposure	100%	63.1%
# Transactions	-	7
Win %	-	57.1%
Win/Loss Ratio	-	6.57
Std Dev. (pa)	18.88%	10.46%
Sharpe Ratio	0.204	0.258

Table 24: A single run simulation of the TrendPilot strategy trading the SPDR S&P/ASX200 ETF (STW).

Conclusion and Improvements

We've taken a look at TrendPilot applied to the underlying index and the required goal, albeit with minimal statistical significance, has been met: being invested when the market rises and reverting to cash during sustained declines. 2008 shows a very good working example of this. The strategy signaled an exit on 24th December 2007 above $60.00 in the ASX200 ETF before prices declined to $30.00 over the coming year.

FIGURE 39

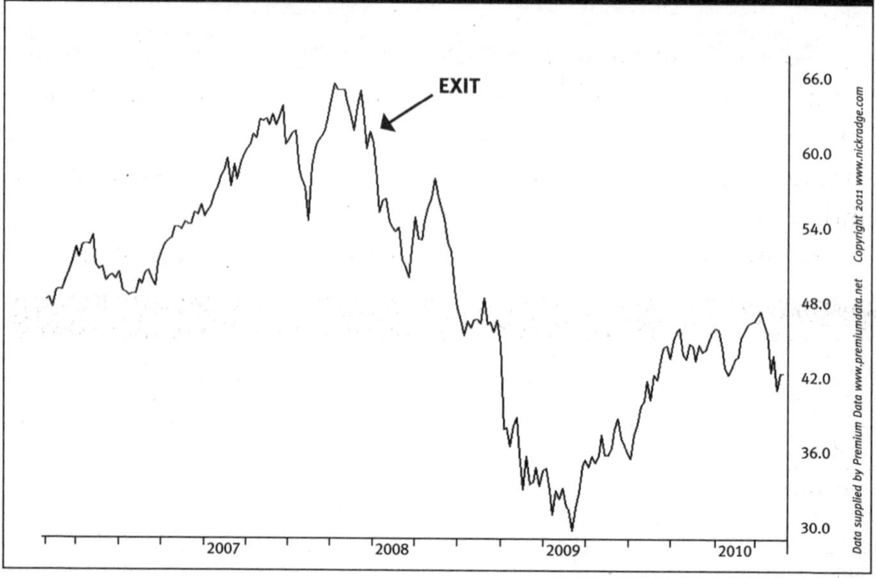

Figure 39: The SPDR/ASX200 ETF (STW), February 2007—April 2010

The risk-adjusted return increases simply because we enhanced the ability to remove downside risks rather than benefit from better upside gains.

Taking a closer look at the lead up to October 20th 1987, the market had slipped 10%, which, in the scheme of the bull market that preceded these events, was seen as a buying opportunity rather than a red flag. On the day prior to the collapse the All Ordinaries Accumulation Index (XAOA) was trading at 5702 with the 200-day moving average standing at 5072. On October 20th 1987 the XAOA opened at 4277.9, well below the 200-day moving average. Remember, TrendPilot requires five consecutive closes below the 200-day average to trigger an exit. By that stage the market had fallen another 10.3% to 3917, or 38.3% from the prior high point.

These five consecutive closes represent a pattern and this pattern must present itself to facilitate an entry and, more importantly, an exit. In the example above we saw five consecutive closes in an extremely volatile situation which, when combined, created an outsized decline in equity. With this in mind though, at other times a sustained down move could occur without the required pattern being seen. If we had a series of four consecutive closes below and one above, then the pattern criteria would not be met and no exit would be signalled. It is possible that an incomplete pattern could recur as the market falls resulting in a delayed exit.

Note it is impossible to beat the index's return on upward trends whilst invested in the index itself. Therefore, to enhance upside returns we need to be involved in higher beta instruments, specifically individual stocks that move at a faster rate than the underlying index.

Below is a standard simulation using a 20 stock portfolio:

	XAOA	TrendPilot
CAGR	8.78%	13.25%
maxDD	-51.4%	-53.6%
MAR	0.17	0.25
Exposure	100%	93.5%
# Transactions	-	689
Win %	-	27.1%
Win/Loss Ratio	-	5.36
Std Dev. (pa)	18.88%	25.64%
Sharpe Ratio	0.204	0.322

Table 25: A single run simulation of the TrendPilot strategy using our test universe.

At first glance the results appear to be slightly better than the benchmark with an annualized return just over 13%, although the maximum drawdown stands at -53.6%. What does stand out, and will be difficult to deal with for most investors, is the low winning percentage of trades at 27.1%. Whilst this certainly cements our introductory qualification that the winning percentage is not a critical factor to profitability, it is low enough to cause angst to the average investor, perhaps even for a seasoned investor.

As is always important we need to understand the broader possible outcomes using Monte Carlo simulations.

	XAOA	Average	Range Min	Range Max
CAGR	8.78%	15.40%	6.10%	25.52%
maxDD	-51.4%	-52.0%	-65.9%	-44.3%
MAR	0.17	0.30	0.09	0.58
# Transactions	-	657	595	730
Win %	-	28.8%	24.5%	34.1%
Win/Loss Ratio	-	5.66	3.66	8.69

Table 26: 1000 iterations using Monte Carlo simulations of the TrendPilot strategy on our standard text universe.

FIGURE 40

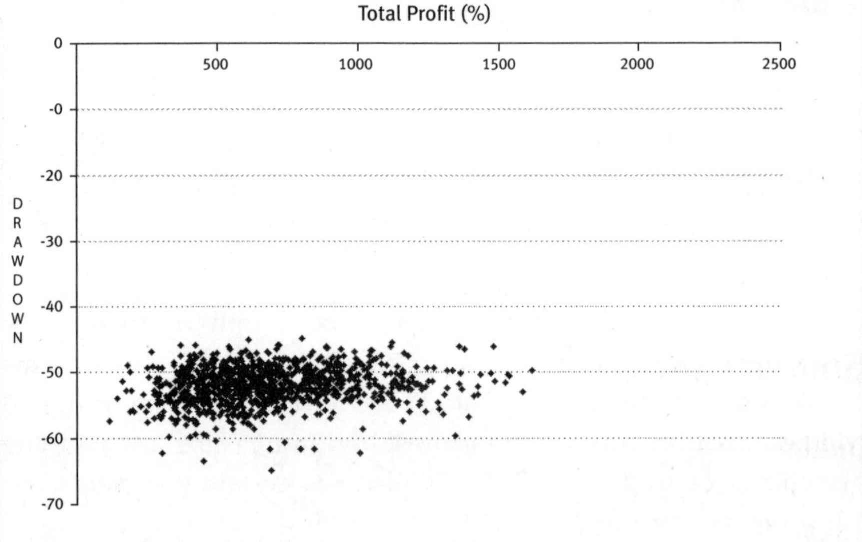

Figure 40: A reasonably tight cluster of data points yet risk adjust return still not enough to warrant using the strategy.

The same conclusions can be made after running a 1000-run simulation. The strategy keeps investors out of the worst of downturns whilst maintaining a similar return to the benchmark. However, the very low winning percentage of trades remains intact also and, as such, may be difficult for an investor to deal with psychologically. The reason for the low winning rate is more than likely due to whipsaw as individual stocks operate on a higher noise level than indices. In this case the whipsaw generates many small losing trades yet proffers substantial winning trades when market conditions are right. The following diagram shows where TrendPilot sits on the Expectancy Curve and, whilst profitable, ideally we'd like it sitting in the centre of the page.

FIGURE 41

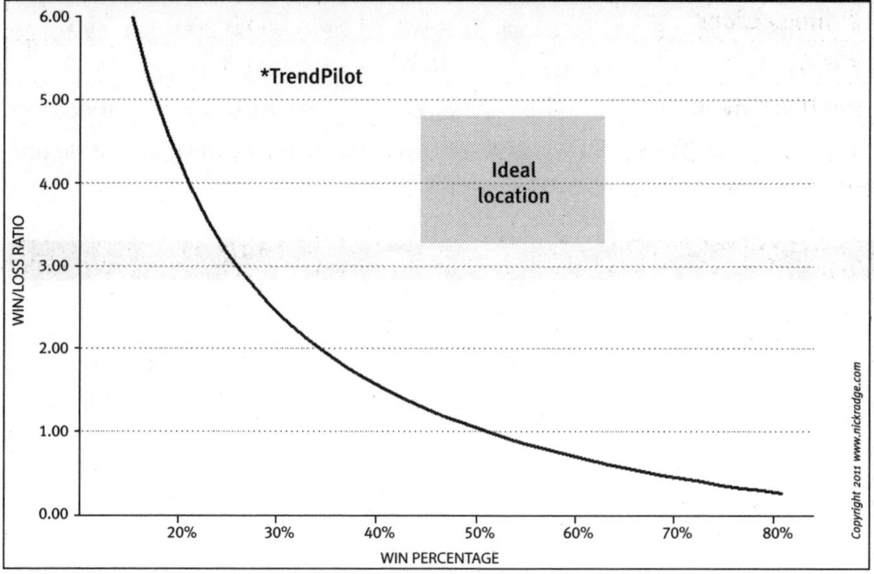

Figure 41: The location of TrendPilot on our Expectancy Curve

Golden Cross

Outline

The Golden Cross is quoted by many financial journalists, especially in the United States, as an important bullish signal predominantly when it occurs on major indices such as the Dow Jones or S&P 500. A Golden Cross is a variation of the moving average theme used by the TrendPilot strategy, however in this case a buy signal occurs when a 50-day moving average crosses up and through a 200-day moving average.

The philosophy behind this strategy is that the two moving averages are sensitive to different length trends and cycles in price movements tend to support momentum. The 50-day moving average is more sensitive to price changes and, as such, when it crosses the longer moving average, which is less sensitive, it is signalling that a new trend is potentially taking shape. As the 50-day average crosses up and through the 200-day average, the assumption is that enough upward momentum is occurring to indicate a new trend higher. Conversely, when the 50-day average crosses down below the 200-day average, presupposed downside momentum is enough that a new trend lower has started.

This 50-day average cross down and below the 200-day average is our exit signal and colourfully known as a Death Cross.

The following chart shows a Golden Cross buy signal generated in Biota Holdings (BTA) just before price exploded and started trending higher.

FIGURE 42

Figure 42: A Golden Cross buy signal occurs when the 50-day moving average crosses above the 200-day moving average.

The Death Cross, being the reverse of the Golden Cross and the exit signal, is shown here in Billabong International (BBG) before a sustained downtrend took hold.

FIGURE 43

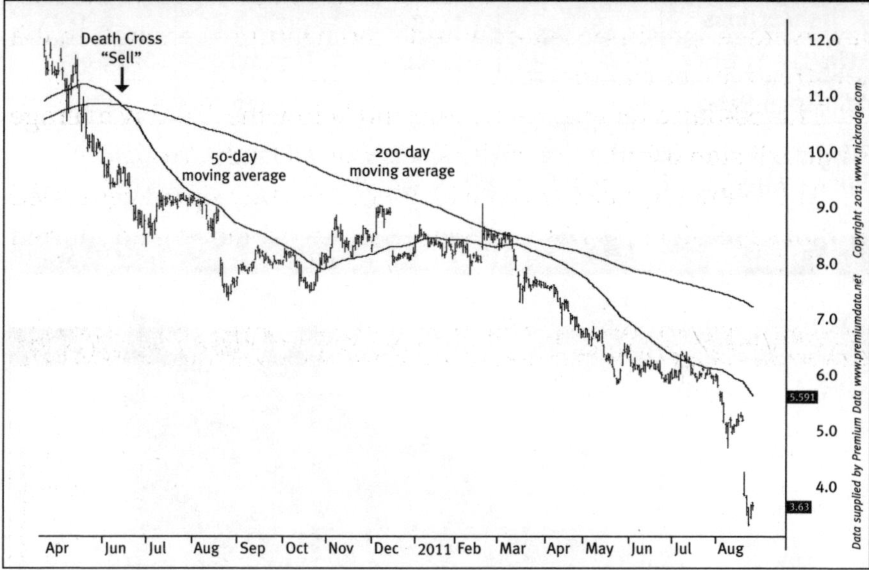

Figure 43: The Death Cross, or reverse signal to the Golden Cross, occurs when the 50-day moving average crosses below the 200-day moving average.

Summary Statistics

	XAOA	Golden Cross
CAGR	8.78%	11.63%
maxDD	-51.4%	-53.7%
MAR	0.17	0.22
Exposure	100%	91.6%
# Transactions	-	414
Win %	-	40.6%
Win/Loss Ratio	-	3.04
Std Dev. (pa)	18.88%	34.9%
Sharpe Ratio	0.204	0.191

Table 27: A single run simulation of the Golden Cross strategy shows only a very minor improvement to Buy & Hold.

	XAOA	Average	Range Min	Range Max
CAGR	8.78%	10.63%	4.45%	17.04%
maxDD	-51.4%	-51.9%	-62.4%	-44.1%
MAR	0.17	0.20	0.07	0.39
# Transactions	-	397	368	429
Win %	-	40.1%	35.2%	45.9%
Win/Loss Ratio	-	3.15	2.19	4.39

Table 28: A 1000-run Monte Carlo simulation confirms that the Golden Cross strategy adds minimal benefit to Buy & Hold.

FIGURE 44

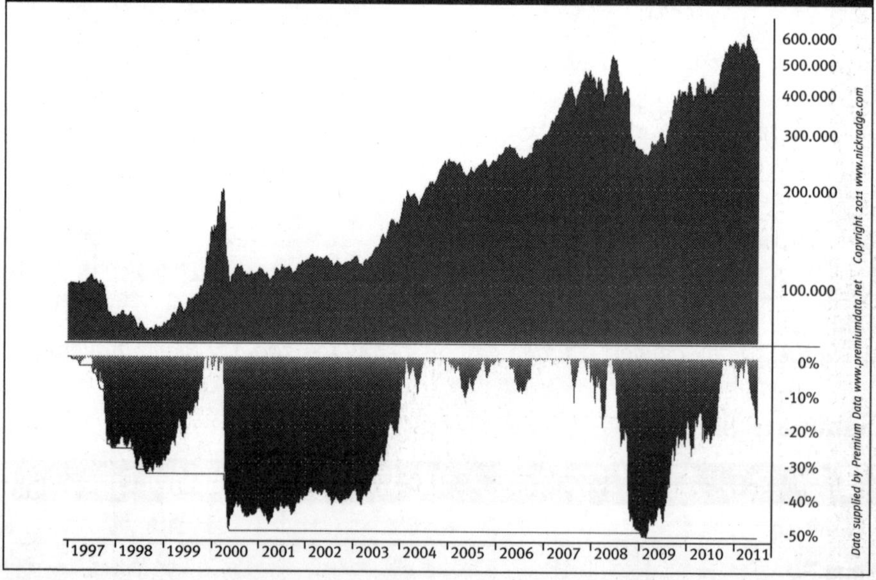

Figure 44: Growth of $100,000 using the Golden Cross strategy.

	3-month	6-month	12-month	18-month	24-month	30-month
XAOA	68.6%	73.4%	79.8%	79.6%	79.4%	79.3%
Golden Cross	48.3%	62.2%	74.5%	80.0%	82.4%	82.4%

Table 29: The Time Window Analysis suggests probability of profit is not much higher than Buy & Hold.

Year	Jan	Feb	Mar	Apr	May	Jun	Jul	Aug	Sep	Oct	Nov	Dec	Yr%
1997	0.7%	0.0%	-1.5%	1.9%	3.4%	1.8%	-3.1%	-0.5%	-3.3%	-17.7%	-2.5%	-0.6%	**-20.8%**
1998	1.1%	-0.7%	0.2%	1.5%	-6.2%	-0.4%	-2.9%	-1.6%	1.9%	2.1%	-2.3%	4.3%	**-3.8%**
1999	1.5%	3.2%	-0.1%	10.8%	-7.8%	5.8%	5.3%	2.8%	3.0%	10.2%	13.0%	17.2%	**84.0%**
2000	8.8%	10.9%	1.5%	-34.5%	-6.4%	7.6%	-0.4%	-2.5%	-1.7%	1.6%	-1.3%	4.2%	**-19.4%**
2001	-1.6%	-1.7%	-3.8%	3.2%	2.1%	1.3%	0.9%	-0.7%	-1.6%	4.8%	1.1%	2.0%	**5.7%**
2002	2.8%	-1.0%	-1.3%	1.2%	1.5%	-3.5%	-3.0%	2.1%	-1.7%	1.8%	0.2%	3.0%	**1.9%**
2003	-2.6%	-3.4%	4.9%	1.5%	4.6%	3.1%	5.1%	1.0%	8.1%	4.5%	-0.2%	6.4%	**37.5%**
2004	8.8%	3.9%	2.2%	-5.9%	2.9%	4.9%	7.1%	-3.0%	5.6%	8.1%	1.8%	2.3%	**45.0%**
2005	0.1%	-1.8%	-1.5%	-6.3%	2.4%	0.9%	1.5%	3.7%	0.5%	-0.9%	3.0%	2.4%	**3.7%**
2006	1.3%	5.8%	2.0%	-3.3%	-2.7%	-2.4%	-1.1%	4.0%	7.0%	2.7%	-0.1%	3.1%	**16.9%**
2007	5.7%	2.3%	9.2%	5.3%	9.3%	3.4%	-5.9%	1.4%	9.3%	8.0%	0.9%	-4.8%	**52.0%**
2008	-6.5%	0.1%	-5.9%	16.0%	11.7%	-9.8%	-5.8%	-10.2%	-6.8%	-20.9%	-6.8%	-0.2%	**-40.4%**
2009	-4.1%	2.6%	6.3%	-1.0%	9.3%	-9.4%	13.4%	16.0%	0.6%	8.0%	3.8%	6.6%	**62.5%**
2010	-15.0%	8.5%	8.6%	-11.5%	5.2%	-3.2%	7.0%	9.1%	10.7%	8.2%	2.7%	0.1%	**29.9%**
2011	-2.3%	4.4%	4.0%	-7.7%	-3.4%	-7.1%	n/a	n/a	n/a	n/a	n/a	n/a	**-12.2%**
Avg	**-0.1%**	**2.2%**	**1.6%**	**-1.9%**	**1.7%**	**-0.5%**	**1.3%**	**1.6%**	**2.3%**	**1.5%**	**0.9%**	**3.3%**	

Table 30: Monthly return data using the Golden Cross strategy.

Conclusion and Improvements

The results in the raw form are, at best, underwhelming, which is an interesting conclusion considering the triggers are widely written about. The strategy may perform better on indices but on a portfolio of stocks it definitely gets thumbs down. The increase in risk-adjusted return is very minimal, and when adding the cost of actually implementing and watching the portfolio there really is no benefit from Buy & Hold, at least not for a portfolio of stocks. Volatility of returns is extremely high and the equity curve is not encouraging, although it did recover from the depths of the 52% decline in 2008 reasonably quickly. This suggests the strategy is quick to jump on new upward trends yet quite slow to respond to changes in trend and therefore exit positions.

Perhaps the most obvious place to look for improvement is by adding an Index Filter, which has successfully improved the risk-adjusted returns of other strategies tested so far. To reiterate, the Index Filter is a 75-day moving average added to the underlying market, in this case the All Ordinaries Index (XAO). With the filter added, if the closing price of the XAO is above the moving average, take positions when a Golden Cross appears on an individual stock.

Another rule will be added for this exercise: when the closing price of the XAO is below the moving average, exit all positions the following day, regardless of the Golden Cross exit signal. As the slower moving average takes time to cross the longer moving average, the resultant lag increases the severity of the drawdown. By exiting immediately the goal is to quickly defend capital.

	XAOA	Golden Cross	Golden Cross (C)
CAGR	8.78%	11.63%	8.78%
maxDD	-51.4%	-53.7%	-19.8%
MAR	0.17	0.22	0.44
Exposure	100%	91.6%	40.4%
# Transactions	-	414	582
Win %	-	40.6%	42.1%
Win/Loss Ratio	-	3.04	2.75
Std Dev. (pa)	18.88%	34.9%	8.30%
Sharpe Ratio	0.204	0.191	0.455

Table 31: The use of an Index Filter and early exit enhances the risk adjusted return of the Golden Cross strategy.

The immediate exit option dramatically reduces the maximum drawdown and the annual volatility of returns. Essentially the changes result in a return similar to Buy & Hold yet volatility and downside pain have been greatly reduced. The MAR ratio increases to 0.44. Trade frequency does go up slightly, which is to be expected for cutting and running.

The big change is that whilst annualized return drops the actual exposure to the market, that is time invested in the market, is substantially lower at just 40.4%. Comparing like-for-like, that is, comparing returns purely on a time-weighted basis, then an 8.78% return using 40.4% exposure equates to a 21.72% return at 100% exposure. Obviously this is a theoretical comparison because when funds are not in the market they would be earning interest on cash held, therefore the 8.78% return would be supplemented by an interest component of around 3%. Not a bad return and being in cash for 60% of the time removes much angst for nervous investors.

The new equity curve rises at a steady rate:

FIGURE 45

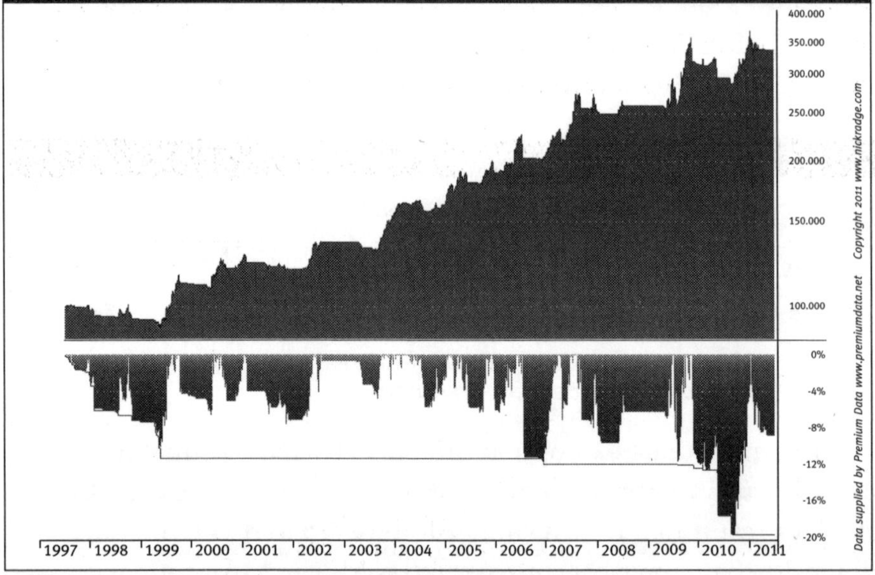

Figure 45: Growth of $100,000 using the Golden Cross strategy combined with an Index Filter and an early exit.

A Monte Carlo simulation will assess the broader distribution of returns as it was here that the raw strategy failed to live up to expectations:

	XAOA	Average	Range Min	Range Max
CAGR	8.78%	8.15%	4.58%	11.14%
maxDD	-51.4%	-17.6%	-21.4%	-13.7%
MAR	0.17	0.46	0.21	0.81
# Transactions	-	534	508	558
Win %	-	43.2%	39.5%	47.1%
Win/Loss Ratio	-	2.66	2.18	3.14%

Table 32: 1000-run Monte Carlo simulation confirming decreased drawdown using the Index Filter and early exit.

The Monte Carlo results are aligned nicely to the single-run simulations suggesting a degree of robustness for future returns. More importantly the Scatter Plot below shows a very high density of data points in a tight band between -15% and -20%, confirming this strategy offers a lower risk exposure to the market.

FIGURE 46

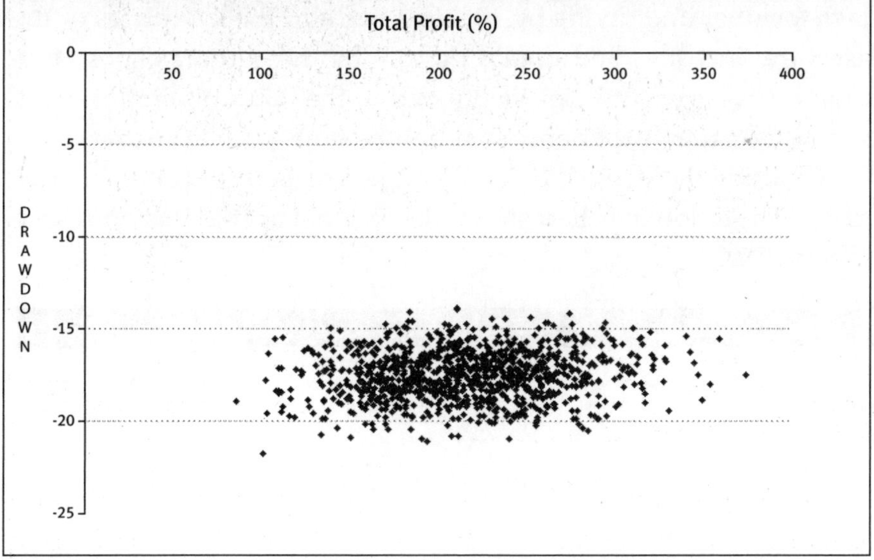

Figure 46: The Scatter Plot shows a consistent maximum drawdown (y-axis).

Moving Average Channel (MAC)

Outline

Each of the previous strategies has incorporated moving averages as they are an easy way to identify and ride trends. The Moving Average Channel or MAC is a unique way to view moving averages. The MAC is the creation of Jake Bernstein[30] and is discussed in his book *Stock Market Strategies that Work*[31] co-authored with Elliott Bernstein. The MAC is presented in the book as a discretionary setup with various guidelines offered depending on the user's situation although it is difficult to take away a specific

30 www.jakebernstein.com
31 McGraw Hill, 2002

strategy to replicate. The MAC is an interesting concept and worthy of pursuing further, so some of the guidelines from the book will be put to the test here.

The MAC is created using two moving averages. The first is a 10-day moving average of the daily highs (as opposed to close prices that have been used in the previous strategies). To calculate the 10-day moving average, add the high prices of last 10 trading days together and divide by 10. Next, we add the low prices of the last 8 trading days and divide by 8. Why the authors choose two separate averages was not mentioned in the text, although it could be based on their experience that tighter stops perform better.

Charting these two moving averages creates a 'channel' in price action. The following chart shows the channel overlaid on Fortescue Metals (FMG).

FIGURE 47

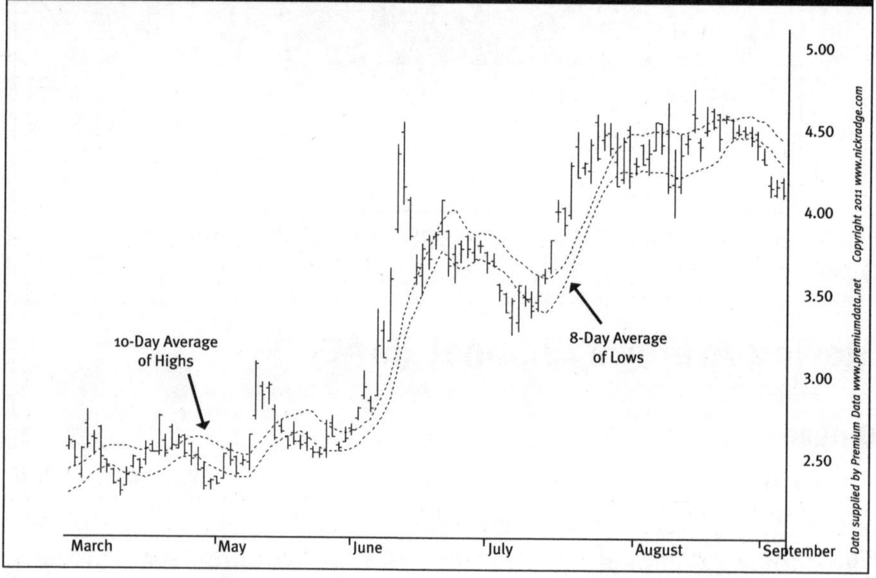

Figure 47: Jake Bernstein's MAC indicator offers a unique application of moving averages.

One specific guideline from the book will be investigated here:

"A 'very strong rally' develops once there have been five or more successive price bars completely above the top of the MAC. A 'large decline' develops when there have been five of more successive bars below the bottom of the MAC."[32]

In layman's terms an entire daily price bar must fall fully above or below the MAC—the low or the high. A partial bar will be excluded from the setup sequence and the requirement for five consecutive days will need to start again.

Below is an example entry and exit in Bannerman Resources (BMN):

FIGURE 48

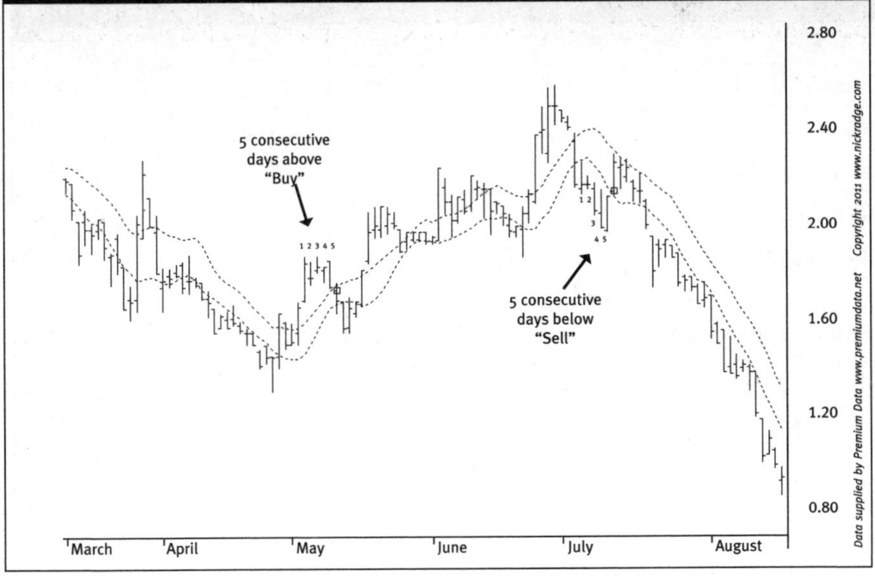

Figure 48: Entry and exit signals generated by the MAC indicator.

---

32 Bernstein, J & Bernstein E, 2002, *Stock Market Strategies that Work*, McGraw Hill, New York, page 107

Summary Statistics

	XAOA	MAC
CAGR	8.78%	26.76%
maxDD	-51.4%	-49.2%
MAR	0.17	0.54
Exposure	100%	95.8%
# Transactions	-	784
Win %	-	43.1%
Win/Loss Ratio	-	3.50
Std Dev. (pa)	18.88%	36.12%
Sharpe Ratio	0.204	0.602

Table 33: A single run simulation using the MAC strategy on our test universe.

	XAOA	Average	Range Min	Range Max
CAGR	8.78%	24.55%	16.54%	33.68%
maxDD	-51.4%	-51.2%	-64.5%	-37.6%
MAR	0.17	0.48	0.26	0.90
# Transactions	-	774	710	823
Win %	-	43.15%	39.6%	47.4%
Win/Loss Ratio	-	3.14	2.19	4.52

Table 34: Monte Carlo simulations run over 1000 iterations offer a risk adjusted return almost 3 times greater than Buy & Hold.

FIGURE 49

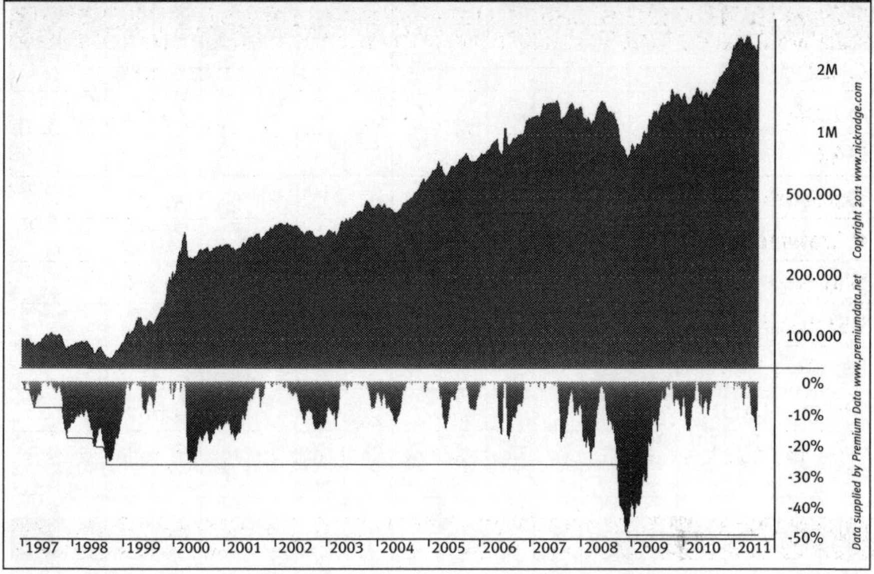

Figure 49: Growth of $100,000 using the MAC strategy has been consistent over time.

	3-month	6-month	12-month	18-month	24-month	30-month
XAOA	68.6%	73.4%	79.8%	79.6%	79.4%	79.3%
MAC	59.4%	68.6%	77.6%	81.2%	86.8%	92.1%

Table 35: As has been the case with strategies to date, the MAC increases its probability of profit after 18-months when compared to Buy & Hold.

Year	Jan	Feb	Mar	Apr	May	Jun	Jul	Aug	Sep	Oct	Nov	Dec	Yr%
1997	0.0%	-3.3%	-5.1%	4.2%	4.8%	5.3%	1.2%	-1.5%	0.7%	-11.3%	-2.9%	2.3%	**-6.6%**
1998	1.2%	0.5%	0.5%	-0.6%	-8.3%	1.3%	0.1%	-5.8%	-3.6%	4.3%	4.1%	10.7%	**3.1%**
1999	10.9%	0.0%	4.4%	12.6%	-6.8%	1.1%	2.7%	1.5%	9.5%	8.2%	28.2%	2.3%	**99.4%**
2000	25.5%	8.4%	10.6%	-13.3%	-0.8%	8.3%	0.2%	4.3%	-3.9%	3.7%	1.5%	0.8%	**49.2%**
2001	1.6%	-5.0%	-0.3%	0.4%	5.1%	7.3%	1.3%	2.8%	-3.0%	5.7%	3.0%	5.2%	**26.2%**
2002	1.6%	-2.3%	0.0%	-0.5%	-0.1%	-5.8%	-3.7%	4.1%	-4.8%	-1.7%	-0.1%	3.2%	**-10.1%**
2003	3.3%	-5.2%	6.8%	8.9%	1.8%	2.0%	5.8%	3.5%	5.5%	2.2%	-3.1%	3.8%	**40.3%**
2004	-4.3%	0.5%	-0.3%	-4.6%	1.8%	5.8%	6.4%	3.2%	5.8%	6.4%	9.7%	0.4%	**34.1%**
2005	9.8%	2.1%	0.8%	-9.2%	6.3%	5.4%	2.7%	6.0%	1.6%	-4.9%	-0.3%	6.2%	**28.1%**
2006	1.5%	4.6%	8.0%	4.3%	-11.5%	29.8%	-17.2%	4.5%	2.8%	4.9%	7.4%	11.0%	**52.8%**
2007	1.2%	2.0%	8.5%	5.6%	0.7%	-1.1%	-4.2%	-9.8%	7.4%	9.7%	-6.2%	2.0%	**14.7%**
2008	-13.0%	-2.4%	0.3%	10.1%	13.3%	-7.2%	-4.3%	-6.9%	-13.6%	-16.4%	-13.4%	15.7%	**-36.5%**
2009	-1.4%	3.7%	17.1%	1.1%	16.9%	1.9%	7.7%	2.3%	1.8%	8.3%	3.3%	0.1%	**80.8%**
2010	-11.1%	3.2%	9.2%	-4.3%	5.0%	-6.4%	13.9%	4.5%	9.1%	9.8%	10.0%	13.3%	**67.2%**
2011	12.3%	-0.3%	0.1%	-6.4%	-4.2%	17.7%	n/a	n/a	n/a	n/a	n/a	n/a	**18.2%**
Avg	**2.6%**	**0.4%**	**4.0%**	**0.5%**	**1.6%**	**4.4%**	**0.9%**	**0.9%**	**1.1%**	**2.1%**	**2.9%**	**5.5%**	

Table 36: When the markets get moving the MAC strategy tends to operate strongly as seen in this breakdown of monthly returns.

FIGURE 50

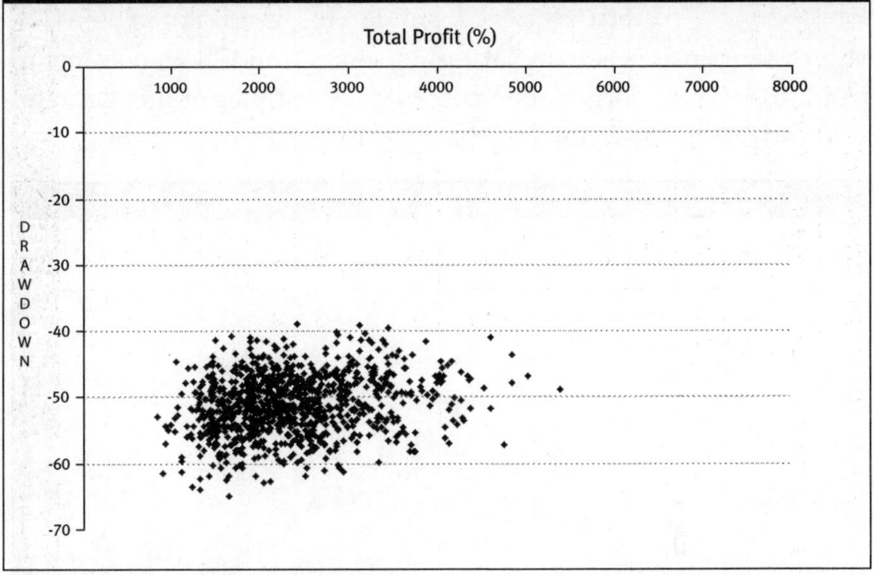

Figure 50: The MAC strategy offers quite a tight cluster within minimal outliers or tails. Whilst interpretation is subjective it is a good sign of robustness.

Conclusion and Improvements

In its raw form the MAC offers some very impressive results. A key to profitability is trade frequency as any edge gets exploited more often. This strategy has a trade frequency of around 54 trades per year, a little on the upper end of the scale, with the average hold time on the lower end of the scale at 14 weeks. Whilst the standard deviation of annual returns is a little high, the commensurate reward is worth the extra volatility. The MAR ratio is above 0.50 and the Sharpe Ratio is one of the highest so far that we've seen. All in all this strategy looks impressive even in its raw form.

If a fault had to be identified, it would be that the exit mechanism is based on a pattern sequence, similar to TrendPilot. The MAC pattern sequence is somewhat tighter than TrendPilot so seems to avoid giving back larger open profits but examples of this flaw can be found as per the following chart:

FIGURE 51

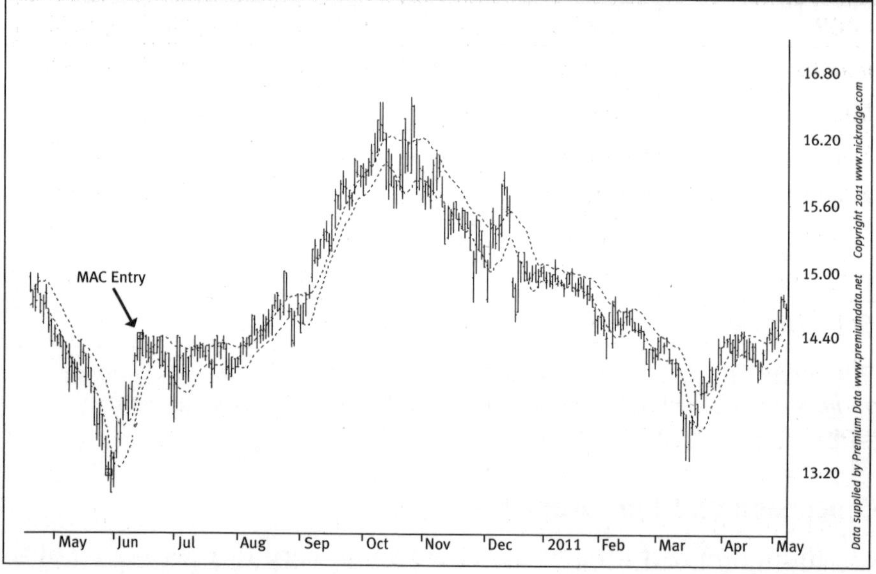

Figure 51: AGL Energy, April 2010—May 2011. An entry signal was generated in June 2010 but no exit signal pattern formed as prices fell away.

Nick's Top Tips

A secular bear market is an extended period, usually in excess of 5 years, where share price growth is zero or negative. However, during these times there are significant bullish phases where large gains can be made. During the secular bear market after the 1929 crash there were four significant bull phases that each had an average return exceeding 100%.

To overcome the risk of a pattern sequence failing to exit a losing position, a 'fail safe' exit mechanism can easily be adopted: exit any positions should the stock drop *n*-% from any high point. The following table highlights the impact on results when adding a fixed percentage exit point from 25% through to 10%:

	Raw	25%	20%	15%	10%
CAGR	26.76%	27.67%	19.05%	15.47%	5.02%
maxDD	-49.2%	-49.9%	-50.3%	-46.3%	-53.8%
MAR	0.54	0.55	0.38	0.33	0.09
Exposure	95.8%	94.6%	94.7%	93.4%	90.9%
# Transactions	784	1006	1159	1491	2349
Win %	43.1%	41.1%	40.6%	40.2%	38.5%
W/L Ratio	3.50	2.89	2.68	2.25	1.78
Std Dev. (pa)	36.12%	30.36%	26.04%	26.97%	17.26%
Sharpe Ratio	0.602	0.747	0.541	0.388	0.116

Table 37: The additional of protective stops tends to 'strangle' the performance of the MAC strategy.

The addition of a protective stop dramatically dilutes results and does nothing to help the drawdown of the system. In fact adding a protective stop that is too tight completely destroys the strategy. If the user is uncomfortable about not using some sort of protective mechanism then a larger stop, set at 25% or higher, is prudent and should allow the strategy to operate without deterioration.

TechTrader

Outline

TechTrader is an open source momentum strategy which has been freely available on various internet trading forums since 2003. It has amassed many thousands of posts from a variety of users looking for a strategy that is robust, easily managed and, more importantly, able to be freely discussed, dissected and ridiculed in public. It was designed by John Rowland. John is not professionally involved in the markets; indeed he owns a business that specialises in soil retention and has constructed over 4000 retaining walls in South Australia. His goal was to show that someone completely outside the financial markets industry could design a strategy that was profitable long term.

The rules for TechTrader are more comprehensive than the systems previously discussed. They have been divided into objective and subjective, the latter of which cannot be programmed into a computer. Consequently only the objective rules will be tested to provide comparative performance consistency to the other systems in this text. Should a user wish to pursue this strategy then the subjective rules should be investigated further. The rules are summarised as:

Objective:

1. The stock should be trading above its 40-day simple moving average.
2. It should be trading below $10.00
3. The closing price on the trigger day should be greater than the opening price.
4. The 21-day average turnover should be greater than $500,000.
5. The trigger day must be the highest value over the last 70 trading days.
6. The trigger day must also cross the highest high value for the last 10 trading days.
7. The initial protective stop should be placed 10% below the entry price.
8. The trailing stop is a 180-day exponential moving average of the lows.

Subjective:

1. The stock must be in an obvious uptrend or obviously breaking out of a down trend.
2. The stock cannot be trapped in a trading range.

Summary Statistics

	XAOA	TechTrader
CAGR	8.78%	21.33%
maxDD	-51.4%	-38.5%
MAR	0.17	0.55
Exposure	100%	93.0%
# Transactions	-	809
Win %	-	31.2%
Win/Loss Ratio	-	5.22
Std Dev. (pa)	18.88%	30.77%
Sharpe Ratio	0.204	0.543

Table 38: From a single-run simulation TechTrader is a strong performer against Buy & Hold.

	XAOA	Average	Range Min	Range Max
CAGR	8.78%	21.29%	14.53%	30.82%
maxDD	-51.4%	-39.3%	-49.9%	-32.7%
MAR	0.17	0.54	0.29	0.94
# Transactions		757	686	823
Win %		31.2%	27.8%	34.8%
Win/Loss Ratio		5.38	3.96	7.58

Table 39: Using Monte Carlo simulation across 1000 iterations the TechTrader strategy shows stability.

FIGURE 52

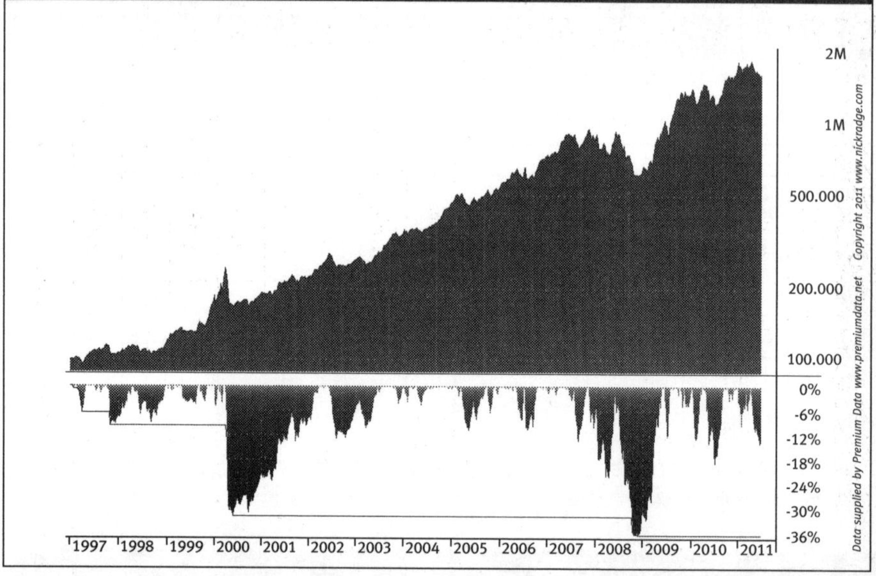

Figure 52: Growth of $100,000 from January 1997 through June 2011.

	3-month	6-month	12-month	18-month	24-month	30-month
XAOA	68.6%	73.4%	79.8%	79.6%	79.4%	79.3%
Tech-Trader	48.0%	58.1%	78.1%	86.2%	92.8%	97.8%

Table 40: TechTrader almost attains a 100% probability of profit at 30-months, well above other strategies we've reviewed so far.

Year	Jan	Feb	Mar	Apr	May	Jun	Jul	Aug	Sep	Oct	Nov	Dec	Yr%
1997	0.8%	-0.3%	-5.6%	6.1%	4.7%	3.9%	0.8%	-0.0%	3.8%	-9.4%	0.7%	1.3%	**5.9%**
1998	1.9%	0.6%	2.8%	1.7%	-2.5%	-1.4%	-2.6%	-1.4%	3.0%	1.8%	0.1%	10.2%	**14.3%**
1999	5.8%	0.1%	2.7%	-2.1%	1.5%	0.4%	-0.6%	6.5%	2.1%	-0.2%	14.2%	5.3%	**40.7%**
2000	12.7%	4.4%	5.4%	-18.8%	-3.0%	4.9%	0.8%	1.5%	-2.2%	0.3%	4.3%	5.0%	**12.8%**
2001	-1.2%	2.4%	-1.0%	5.0%	3.4%	1.5%	3.2%	3.2%	-4.0%	3.2%	-0.6%	1.5%	**17.5%**
2002	2.6%	3.9%	4.1%	4.1%	8.1%	-7.2%	-5.9%	1.6%	-0.3%	1.5%	2.7%	3.3%	**19.0%**
2003	0.1%	-3.5%	-1.0%	2.0%	5.3%	3.6%	7.0%	4.1%	5.9%	1.6%	-1.9%	6.3%	**33.0%**
2004	-3.7%	4.6%	0.5%	-2.3%	1.1%	2.0%	2.6%	2.1%	3.3%	10.7%	1.8%	4.4%	**29.9%**
2005	8.8%	-1.6%	-2.2%	-5.4%	4.0%	-0.0%	2.2%	2.4%	2.3%	-0.5%	6.2%	2.6%	**19.6%**
2006	3.1%	3.5%	6.6%	1.6%	-2.7%	6.4%	-10.9%	4.8%	4.5%	9.2%	1.4%	2.8%	**32.7%**
2007	3.5%	-0.9%	10.3%	6.4%	4.1%	-3.4%	-4.3%	-3.0%	4.7%	10.5%	-5.4%	0.9%	**24.6%**
2008	-12.9%	1.8%	-6.2%	7.5%	11.2%	-6.8%	-3.6%	-10.5%	-7.5%	-8.9%	0.1%	8.5%	**-26.8%**
2009	-2.1%	5.5%	23.6%	2.7%	13.8%	-6.6%	15.2%	13.1%	4.2%	3.3%	3.4%	5.9%	**113.8%**
2010	-13.5%	4.5%	11.9%	-6.2%	-2.4%	-10.5%	10.7%	10.5%	7.7%	3.4%	1.2%	7.0%	**22.3%**
2011	0.9%	4.9%	-0.8%	-7.4%	-1.4%	-2.0%	n/a	n/a	n/a	n/a	n/a	n/a	**-6.1%**
Avg	**0.4%**	**2.0%**	**3.4%**	**-0.3%**	**3.0%**	**-1.0%**	**1.0%**	**2.5%**	**2.0%**	**1.9%**	**2.0%**	**4.7%**	

Table 41: Since 1997 the TechTrader strategy has only experienced one completed negative year—2008.

FIGURE 53

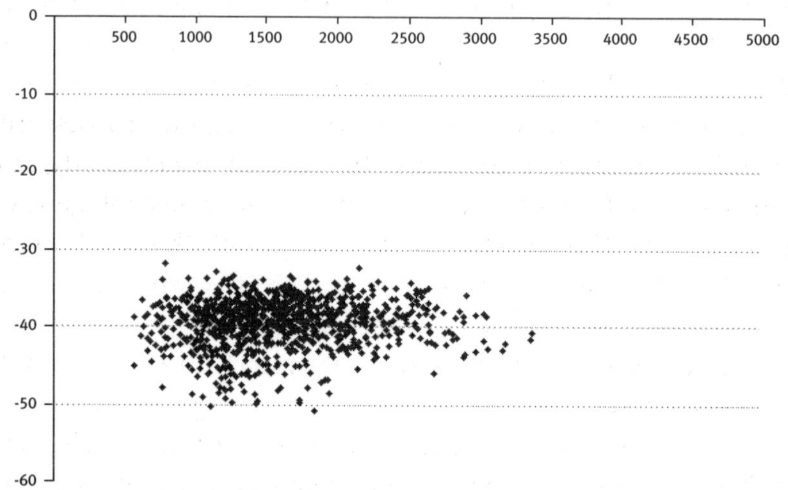

Figure 53: A reasonably tight Scatter Plot suggests TechTrader is quite a robust strategy.

Conclusion and Improvements

For a homegrown strategy developed by an amateur trader, TechTrader is without doubt a solid performer and it is obvious why it has become popular across trading and investing forums. It provides a strong annualized return of over 20% yet limits maximum drawdown to below 40%, both of which outperform the benchmark and other strategies discussed so far. The MAR ratio is above 0.50 which is very acceptable and the standard deviation of returns is 30% which for a strong growth performer is also very accommodating. The Time Window Analysis exceeds 90% at the 24-month stage and just misses the 100% probability at 30-months. One would naturally assume 100% would be seen within another 6-month window, well ahead of Buy & Hold.

If there are criticisms to be made they would be that TechTrader has more degrees of freedom than other strategies reviewed so far. A degree of freedom is a variable that may be changed or adjusted by the user. The more degrees of freedom, the closer a strategy moves toward optimisation as well as increasing the chances of something breaking down in future. Obviously we've tested the strategy across a very broad universe and market conditions and it still came up with excellent results so robustness in this case is difficult to argue against. Also we only tested the strategy using the defined objective inputs yet there were two subjective inputs that could not be coded into the computer. We are unable to determine what difference these will make to the bottom line profitability, although we can assume they could be interpreted differently by different users. Lastly, and more importantly for most investors, the winning percentage is on the lower side at 31% which may be a deterrent; the result being the investor may discard the system out of frustration or fail to implement the strategy correctly over the longer term.

On the basis that the strategy already has numerous inputs and degrees of freedom I would not attempt to better it by adding further rules. It could be beneficial to remove some of the rules and strip it back a little to see how it then performs. Potentially, with fewer rules, one could then tack on other parameters to achieve a better outcome, but on the whole I can see why it has been a popular strategy in its current form.

20% Flipper

Outline

The 20% Flipper is probably the purest form of momentum investing and very easy to understand. As stated previously, there is nothing new in the world of investing and this concept is derived from the book *Winning on Wall Street* by Martin Zweig[33]. Zweig discusses the 4% Rule—a market timing system developed by Ned Davis. The buy and sell signals are based upon a single week's movement, specifically 4% up or down, of the Value Line Composite Geometric Index[34]. If the Index moves up 4% in any given week it is a signal to buy. Should it move down by 4% it is a signal to sell. In *Adaptive Analysis for Australian Stocks*[35] I discussed the same theory

33 Warner Books, 1994
34 An equally weighted price index of all stocks covered by The Value Line Investment Survey. Source: www.valueline.com
35 Nick Radge, Wrightbooks, 2006

in a more discretionary context[36] using 'segments' or 'zones' so here we take the same type of movement, specifically a percentage move off a low or high to trigger a signal.

Logically, a stock that is going to double in price, that is, increase in value by 100%, must first increase in value by 20%. The 20% Flipper is a strategy that buys a stock that has risen 20% off a low point with the expectation that it will continue to rise by an unknown yet larger amount—a stock in motion tends to stay in motion. Conversely if a stock is going to fall by a substantial amount of its value it must first fall 20%. Therefore, if we hold an existing position and the stock falls 20% from any high point we exit on the next day's open.

A 20% rise from any low is a buy. A 20% fall from any high is an exit.

The following diagram shows a stock that has made a low at $1.00. We cannot know if this low will be the absolute low but we do know that a 20% rise from this low equals $1.20. A close above $1.20 at some stage in the future generates a buy signal. If the stock drops below $1.00, recalculate the 20% rise from the new low point, wherever that may be.

FIGURE 54

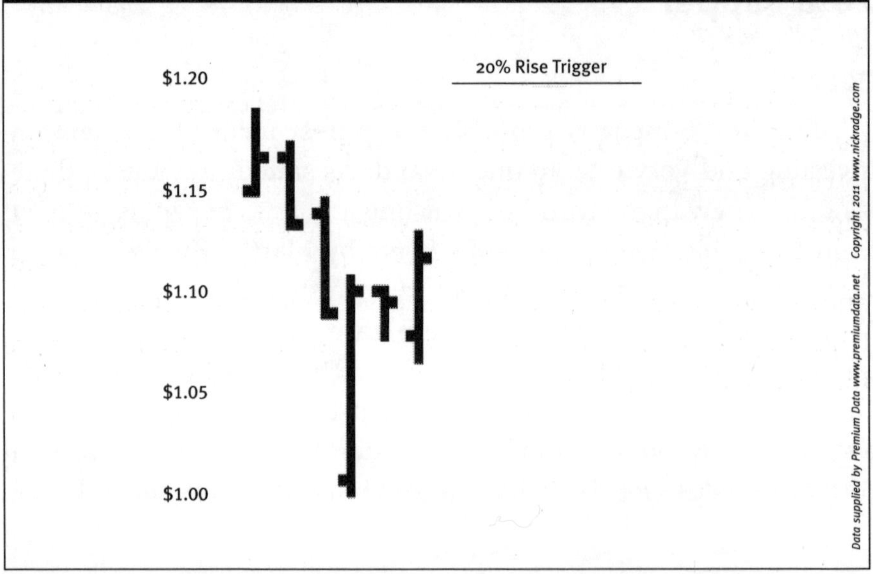

Figure 54: A stock that makes a low of $1.00 will need to rise beyond $1.20 to trigger a buy signal.

36 Nick Radge, 2006, *Adaptive Analysis for Australian Stocks*, Wrightbooks, Milton, page 99

Next we have a close above the $1.20 trigger level so the strategy will generate a buy signal for the following day's open and at the same time place a protective stop-loss order 20% below this day's highest point.

FIGURE 55

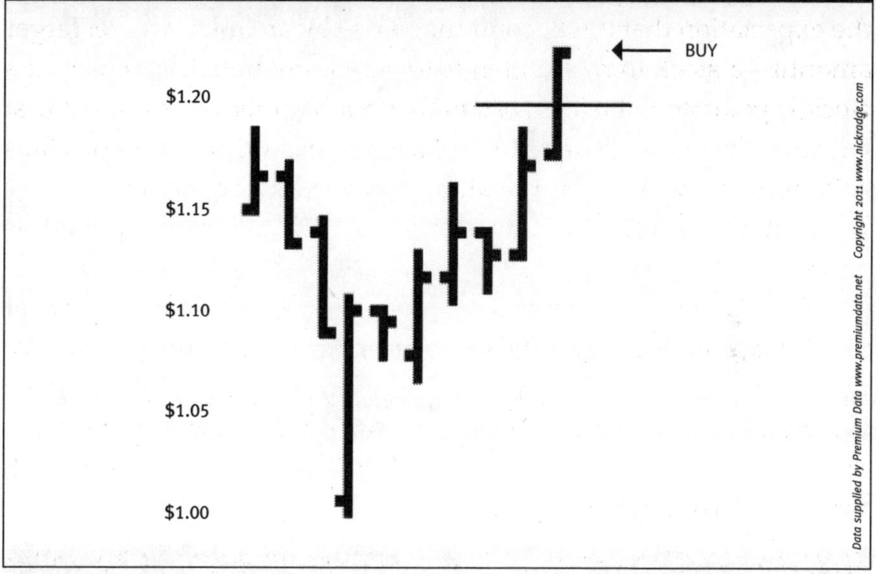

Figure 55: A close above the 20% trigger level confirms a buy signal for the following day.

The following Commonwealth Bank (CBA) chart demonstrates the 20% Flipper strategy. The stock rose 20% off the March 2009 lows triggering a buy signal at $28.83. Prices continued to move higher finally reaching a peak of $60.00. The black line following prices higher represents a 20% reversal from each successive peak and, as can be seen in July 2010, as prices fell to $48.00 an exit was triggered. In its basic form this example risks a 20% decline in price for a substantial upside gain.

FIGURE 56

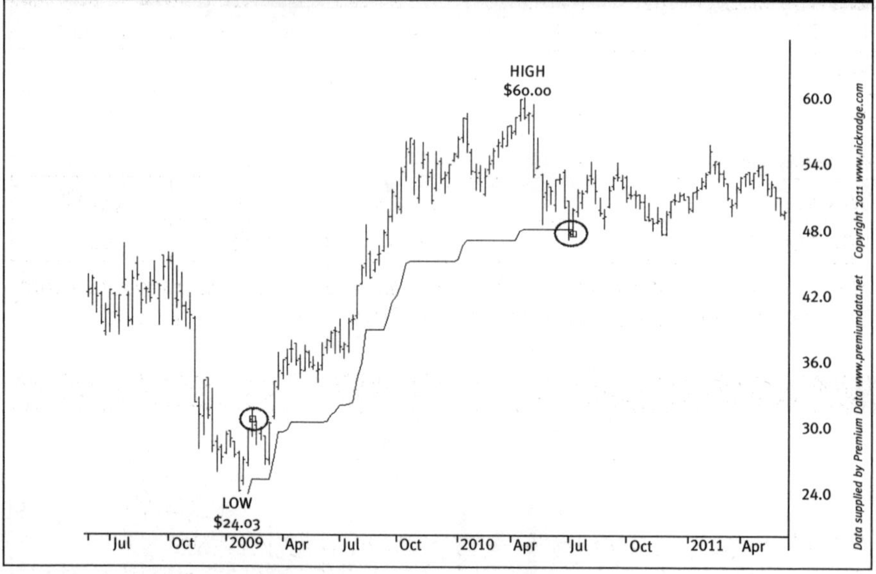

Figure 56: Commonwealth Bank rises quickly off the $24.03 low in early 2009 before continuing to trend higher to $60.00 before stalling.

Summary Statistics

	XAOA	20% Flipper
CAGR	8.78%	30.81%
maxDD	-51.4%	-35.3%
MAR	0.17	0.87
Exposure	100%	96.5%
# Transactions	-	952
Win %	-	40.8%
Win/Loss Ratio	-	3.19
Std Dev. (pa)	18.88%	28.74%
Sharpe Ratio	0.204	0.898

Table 42: The 20% Flipper strategy exhibits an extremely strong risk adjusted return profile.

	XAOA	Average	Range Min	Range Max
CAGR	8.78%	27.86%	18.20%	37.04%
maxDD	-51.4%	-38.2%	-53.9%	-27.3%
MAR	0.17	0.73	0.34	1.36
# Transactions	-	933	839	1020
Win %	-	40.9%	36.9%	44.9%
Win/Loss Ratio	-	3.31	2.46	4.44

Table 43: Whilst slightly lower performance than a single run, this 1000-run Monte Carlo simulation still concludes that the 20% Flipper strategy is very powerful.

FIGURE 57

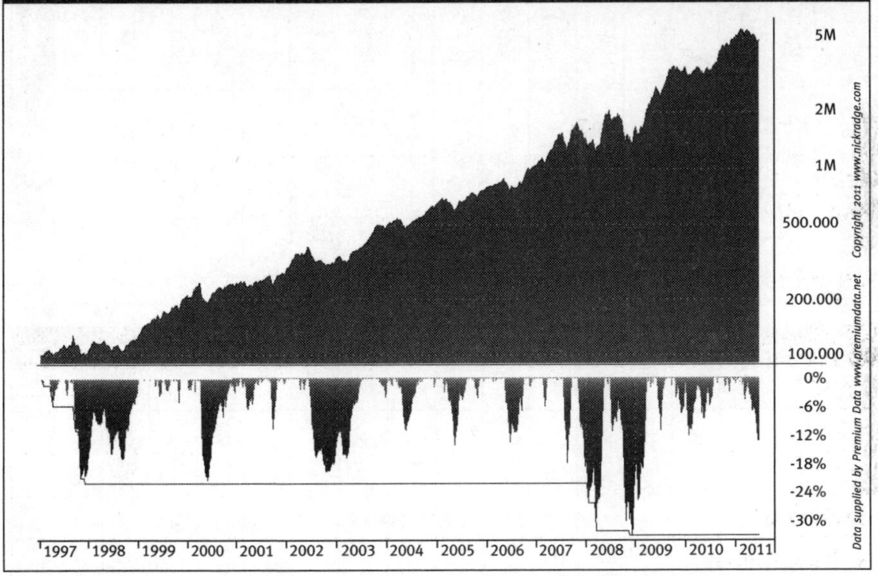

Figure 57: Growth of $100,000 using the 20% Flipper strategy.

	3-month	6-month	12-month	18-month	24-month	30-month
XAOA	68.6%	73.4%	79.8%	79.6%	79.4%	79.3%
20% Flipper	54.2%	65.7%	84.2%	91.8%	100%	100%

Table 44: The probability of profit hits 100% at the 24-month time window. No other strategy to date has been able to achieve this goal.

Year	Jan	Feb	Mar	Apr	May	Jun	Jul	Aug	Sep	Oct	Nov	Dec	Yr%
1997	2.7%	3.3%	-5.9%	4.0%	5.0%	3.6%	-0.4%	13.0%	-10.6%	-10.6%	-1.0%	6.5%	**7.1%**
1998	10.0%	-2.5%	-0.6%	1.2%	-6.5%	2.6%	-1.3%	-3.6%	7.1%	5.0%	0.2%	8.6%	**20.5%**
1999	10.4%	1.1%	3.3%	3.0%	2.2%	5.2%	1.2%	3.9%	6.8%	-4.5%	13.7%	0.3%	**56.3%**
2000	3.3%	9.9%	-3.4%	-10.4%	-3.0%	9.9%	4.8%	4.4%	1.0%	1.8%	1.4%	0.4%	**20.0%**
2001	2.7%	-0.5%	-4.1%	-1.2%	4.0%	1.8%	4.6%	1.9%	-5.6%	7.4%	2.1%	4.7%	**18.5%**
2002	6.9%	7.3%	4.0%	1.2%	9.7%	-11.1%	-6.1%	1.1%	-3.1%	-1.3%	1.7%	5.5%	**14.8%**
2003	-1.2%	-2.0%	3.0%	9.7%	1.9%	3.8%	5.1%	8.1%	10.5%	3.4%	-0.1%	-0.4%	**49.5%**
2004	2.3%	4.8%	1.5%	-8.1%	0.6%	2.7%	6.2%	0.1%	4.2%	6.9%	4.6%	4.1%	**33.1%**
2005	4.4%	-0.7%	-3.1%	-9.6%	5.7%	6.1%	3.3%	4.2%	1.2%	-0.4%	5.6%	3.9%	**21.2%**
2006	1.9%	2.1%	1.7%	3.8%	-3.4%	-4.6%	-1.8%	5.9%	6.5%	12.4%	-0.6%	4.9%	**31.4%**
2007	4.9%	-1.4%	7.8%	8.7%	12.0%	6.3%	-7.2%	-1.4%	16.4%	10.5%	-9.6%	-9.3%	**39.2%**
2008	-7.1%	-2.8%	0.5%	15.6%	28.8%	-4.6%	-0.2%	1.2%	-4.4%	-16.0%	-9.3%	17.9%	**11.6%**
2009	-7.2%	11.2%	23.5%	6.3%	19.0%	-3.3%	6.9%	14.2%	6.9%	2.3%	-0.4%	4.7%	**116.8%**
2010	-12.3%	5.3%	5.4%	-5.8%	1.7%	0.7%	8.6%	6.5%	13.5%	8.2%	-1.9%	7.6%	**40.6%**
2011	6.9%	5.1%	-2.1%	-5.1%	-0.5%	-4.3%	n/a	n/a	n/a	n/a	n/a	n/a	**-0.6%**
Avg	**1.9%**	**2.7%**	**2.1%**	**0.9%**	**5.2%**	**1.0%**	**1.7%**	**4.2%**	**3.6%**	**1.8%**	**0.5%**	**4.2%**	

Table 45: The monthly performance shows that the 20% Flipper is yet to have a losing year.

FIGURE 58

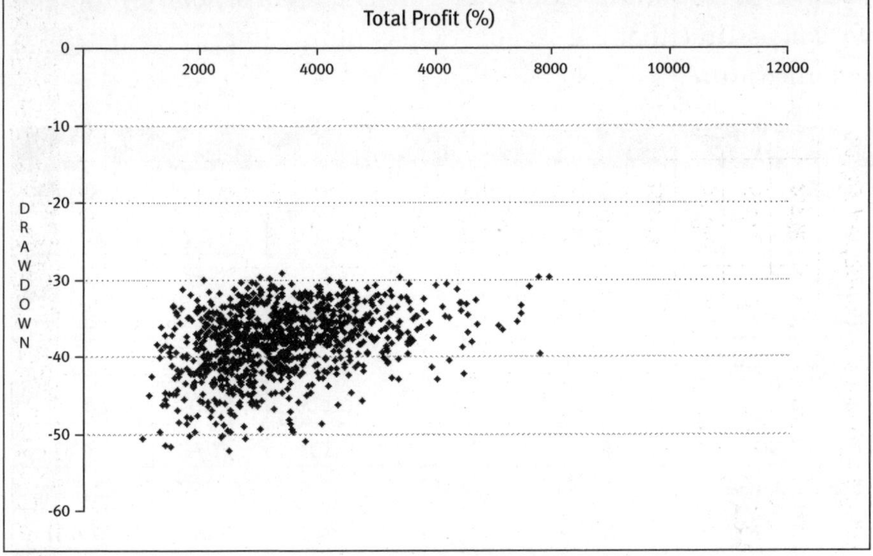

Figure 58: An important visual representation of robustness is ensuring that the distribution of possible outcomes is reasonably tight, which subjectively it is here.

Conclusion and Improvements

The 20% Flipper displays very impressive results on most fronts. The equity curve is not only smooth but drawdowns are well contained to reasonable levels and, more importantly, recovery time from major declines is quick. This is also shown within the Time Window Analysis where the strategy has a 100% probability of making a profit inside any 24-month period. No other strategy discussed thus far has achieved 100% profitability within a 24-month window or even a 30-month window for that matter.

The two drawbacks appear to be the usual suspects that have been seen elsewhere, specifically the higher trading frequency and the lower winning percentage. The higher trade frequency is certainly a positive contributing factor to the increased profitability, although the lower win rate at 40% could present psychological issues for some investors.

In a simplified test of robustness the following table compares various input parameters around the default 20% trigger level. Whilst the 20% level seems to be a sweet spot, all other settings exhibit strong profitability and therefore robustness, though volatility and drawdown do increase as the input value increases. Because surrounding parameter values are consistently profitable we can assume that the strategy will continue to provide reliability into the future.

	16%	18%	20%	22%	24%
CAGR	24.51%	26.97%	30.81%	26.22%	28.77%
maxDD	-39.8%	-39.4%	-35.3%	-43.4%	-46.2%
MAR	0.61	0.68	0.87	0.60	0.63
Exposure	96.2%	96.4%	96.5%	96.2%	96.2%
# Transactions	1388	1163	952	776	757
Win %	40.0%	39.4%	40.8%	42.0%	41.2%
W/L Ratio	2.71	3.10	3.19	3.72	3.83
Std Dev. (pa)	32.08%	36.83%	28.74%	47.94%	44.77%
Sharpe Ratio	0.608	0.596	0.898	0.443	0.531

Table 46: The basic concept of the 20% Flipper works across a variety of input values intimating its robustness.

Investors concerned by the equity decline levels may consider the use of an Index Filter. As in previous examples the 75-day simple moving average of the underlying index will be used. When the market falls below this average the 20% Flipper strategy will:

1. Tighten stops to 10% rather than 20%
2. Not initiate any new positions

	XAOA	20% Flipper	20% Flipper (F)
CAGR	8.78%	30.81%	20.49%
maxDD	-51.4%	-35.3%	-23.6%
MAR	0.17	0.87	0.87
Exposure	100%	96.5%	75.6%
# Transactions	-	952	901
Win %	-	40.8%	44.6%
Win/Loss Ratio	-	3.19	2.86
Std Dev. (pa)	18.88%	28.74%	35.48%
Sharpe Ratio	0.204	0.898	0.437

Table 47: Adding a trend Index Filter with a slightly tighter stop loss decreases market exposure to 75.6%.

As expected when filtering a strategy, the risk reward attributes do pick up. The CAGR drops to 20.49% yet the maximum equity decline also drops to a more comfortable 23.6% scoring a MAR similar to the raw strategy. Note that exposure to the market drops to 75.6% which equates to a risk-adjusted return of 27.09%.

The following equity curve shows minimal capital erosion during 2008 as the strategy was very quick to revert to cash.

FIGURE 59

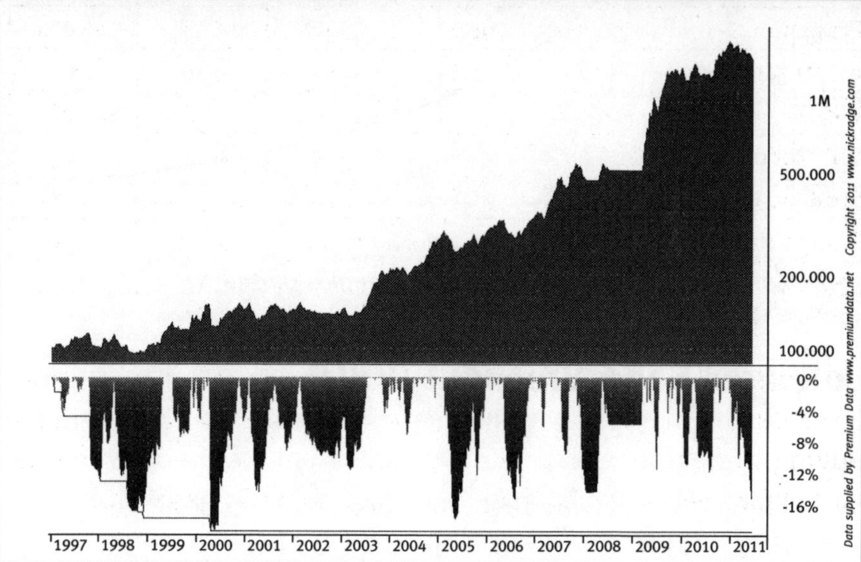

Figure 59: Growth of $100,000 using the 20% Flipper with the added Index Filter rules.

Nick's Top Tips

Many who try to predict markets are living in hope and riding the highs and lows of being right and wrong. Expectations create an attachment to an outcome and if that outcome is not realised then disappointment will prevail. **Have no expectations. Experience no disappointment.**

FIGURE 60

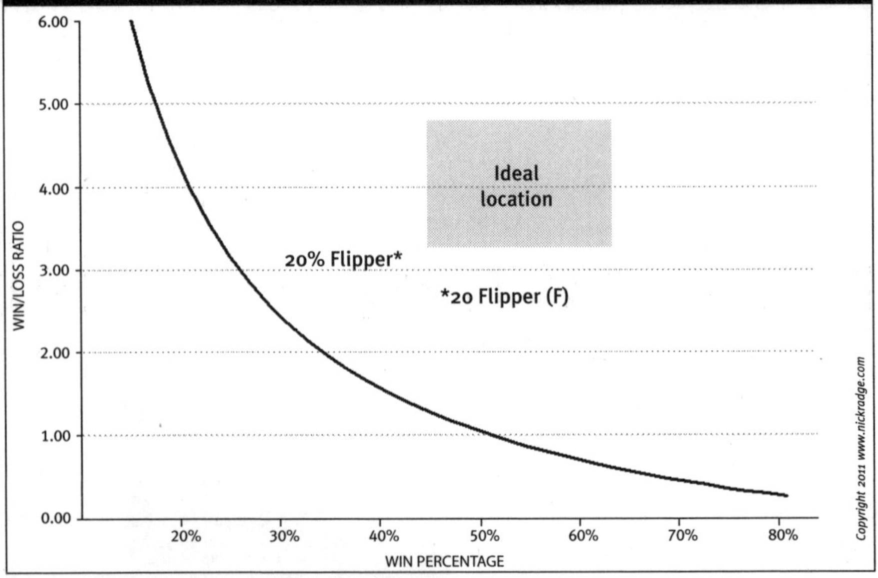

Figure 60: Location of the 20% Flipper strategies on the Expectancy Curve.

Bollinger Band Breakout (BBO)

Outline

Bollinger Bands were first introduced by John Bollinger[37] in the early 1980s and have since become popularised and written about extensively. Today almost every trading software package and broker platform offers Bollinger Bands as a default technical tool.

Bollinger Bands consist of three price levels, the first being a simple moving average plotted over a predefined period. An upper and lower band is then calculated based on a specified number of standard deviations above and below that central average. The bands therefore offer a reflection of volatility of the instrument at any given time. During periods of congestion the bands tend to contract as volatility declines whereas during periods of high volatility the bands expand.

The following chart shows Atlas Iron Ltd (AGO) with a 100-day moving average as the central level and the upper and lower bands set to 2-standard deviations.

---

37 www.bollingerbands.com

FIGURE 61

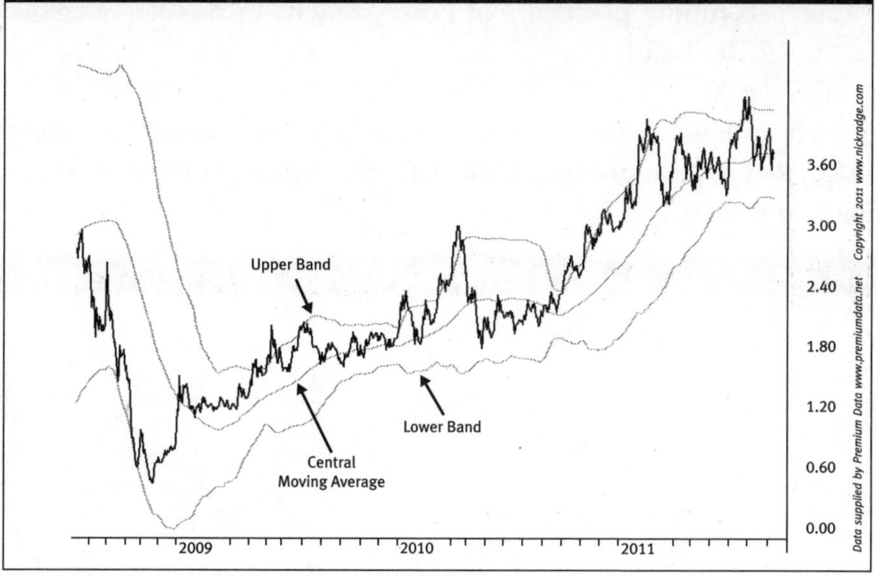

Figure 61: The addition of Bollinger Bands accounts for volatility of the instrument.

Bollinger Bands can be used in a variety of ways but as a momentum strategy tool the most common use is entering a new position when price closes above the upper band and exiting positions when price closes below the central moving average. However, the main concern with using simple moving averages is that stock markets tend to have more noise and therefore, more often than not, a simple moving average will prematurely close positions out.

Most texts and broker platforms use default settings of a 20-day simple moving average central line coupled with upper and lower bands set at 2-standard deviations. These settings are too tight for longer term momentum investing and need to be loosened to allow for longer hold times and to overcome general stock market noise. For the purpose of this book some slight enhancements to the default settings will be made:

1. Firstly the upper entry band will be set at 3-standard deviations, yet the lower band will be set at 1-standard deviation.
2. The 20-day moving average period will be set to 100 days, effectively a 20-week variant.

3. Lastly, rather than exit positions at the central moving average as is common practice, exit positions when price closes below the lower band.

The following chart shows a significant trend in Regis Resources (RRL) that was caught and ridden using the Bollinger Band breakout method with the above criteria.

FIGURE 62

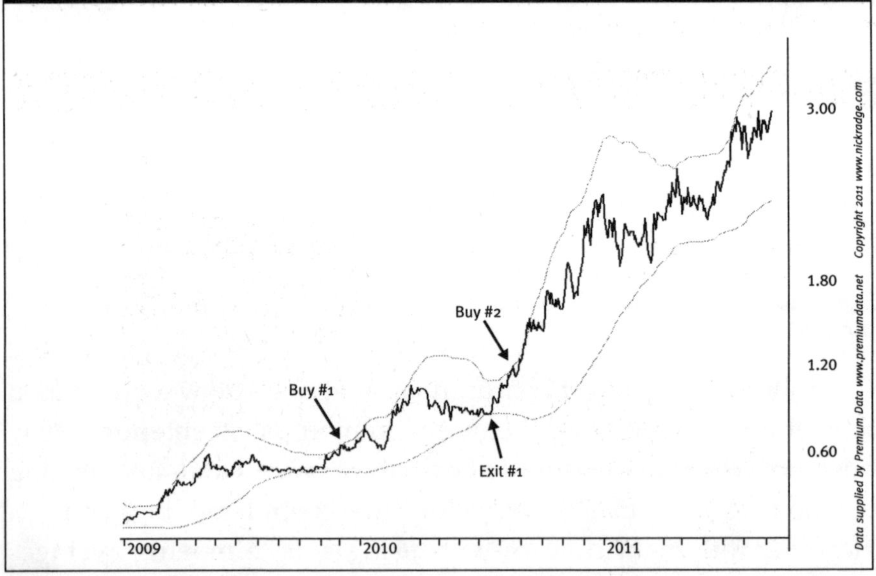

Figure 62: This chart shows a slight variant of traditional Bollinger Bands, specifically using two separate standard deviation inputs.

Summary Statistics

	XAOA	BBO
CAGR	8.78%	33.59%
maxDD	-51.4%	-43.7%
MAR	0.17	0.77
Exposure	100%	89.6%
# Transactions		470
Win %		48.32%
Win/Loss Ratio		4.00
Std Dev. (pa)	18.88%	47.83%
Sharpe Ratio	0.204	0.636

Table 48: A single run simulation using the BBO strategy shows very promising returns.

	XAOA	Average	Range Min	Range Max
CAGR	8.78%	29.88%	17.78%	39.25%
maxDD	-51.4%	-41.0%	-57.1%	-28.8%
MAR	0.17	0.73	0.31	1.36
# Transactions		463	429	499
Win %		47.3%	41.9%	53.0%
Win/Loss Ratio		3.71	2.64	5.65

Table 49: Over 1000 Monte Carlo simulations, the single-run return profile is confirmed. A very strong performer.

FIGURE 63

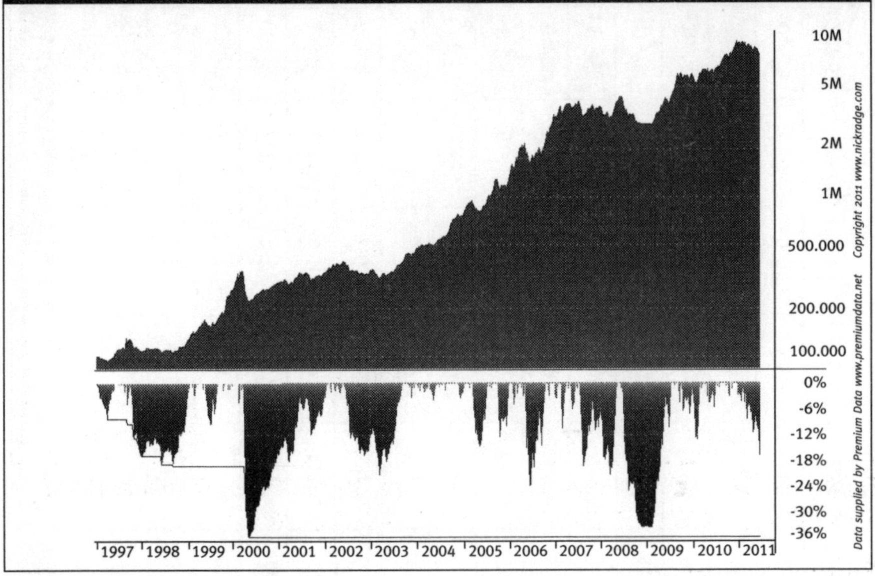

Figure 63: Growth of $100,000 from January 1997 to June 2011 using the BBO strategy.

	3-month	6-month	12-month	18-month	24-month	30-month
XAOA	68.6%	73.4%	79.8%	79.6%	79.4%	79.3%
BBO	57.7%	67.4%	80.6%	85.0%	95.4%	99.3%

Table 50: The BBO strategy was not quite able to make the 100% probability of profit by 30-months but even so it outperforms Buy & Hold by a considerable margin.

Year	Jan	Feb	Mar	Apr	May	Jun	Jul	Aug	Sep	Oct	Nov	Dec	Yr%
1997	-2.9%	-1.5%	-4.2%	4.8%	9.1%	5.9%	1.0%	15.3%	-0.1%	-11.8%	-2.1%	-3.8%	**7.2%**
1998	0.6%	1.6%	0.8%	-0.2%	-2.2%	0.6%	-0.6%	-2.1%	2.6%	5.6%	-0.4%	11.1%	**18.1%**
1999	8.8%	0.5%	4.3%	9.1%	4.1%	-4.9%	3.2%	4.6%	9.0%	3.0%	23.5%	10.3%	**103.0%**
2000	17.5%	2.1%	0.9%	-23.2%	-4.2%	7.3%	3.4%	5.0%	0.2%	3.2%	2.8%	3.8%	**12.3%**
2001	2.6%	2.3%	-5.1%	0.9%	7.1%	5.3%	0.1%	-1.0%	-4.9%	0.8%	2.7%	4.9%	**16.0%**
2002	4.1%	-0.1%	6.4%	1.0%	4.7%	-5.2%	-7.7%	-1.3%	-2.0%	0.3%	-0.3%	2.7%	**1.7%**
2003	-1.8%	-6.3%	2.5%	-0.8%	3.7%	2.6%	8.7%	3.9%	6.9%	7.0%	1.2%	8.3%	**41.1%**
2004	1.3%	1.7%	2.7%	-1.0%	2.2%	3.1%	6.8%	4.3%	16.4%	7.9%	5.2%	-1.5%	**60.0%**
2005	15.2%	5.6%	-4.2%	-7.6%	1.2%	6.4%	13.8%	8.2%	11.6%	-2.9%	0.2%	8.2%	**67.9%**
2006	25.1%	9.8%	16.2%	-1.5%	-5.7%	-4.1%	2.5%	8.9%	-2.5%	20.8%	14.5%	14.1%	**144.3%**
2007	5.1%	-0.0%	15.2%	1.7%	-5.1%	2.9%	-4.0%	-7.6%	4.6%	9.1%	-5.1%	2.7%	**18.6%**
2008	-11.3%	-0.2%	-3.0%	12.8%	20.1%	-11.2%	-7.9%	-6.4%	-2.9%	-9.4%	-1.2%	0.1%	**-22.6%**
2009	-0.4%	5.2%	11.3%	5.9%	12.5%	-1.7%	13.9%	16.4%	5.9%	1.2%	4.9%	1.9%	**107.2%**
2010	-12.9%	7.2%	8.4%	-1.4%	4.5%	-3.9%	10.9%	9.1%	6.1%	3.3%	5.1%	8.8%	**52.0%**
2011	3.6%	-0.3%	-2.3%	-8.4%	3.4%	-7.0%	n/a	n/a	n/a	n/a	n/a	n/a	**-11.1%**
Avg	**3.6%**	**1.8%**	**3.2%**	**-0.5%**	**3.7%**	**-0.3%**	**3.1%**	**4.1%**	**3.6%**	**2.7%**	**3.6%**	**5.1%**	

Table 51: The BBO strategy has only had a single losing year—2008 but has also shown itself to produce triple digit return years when markets are trending well.

FIGURE 64

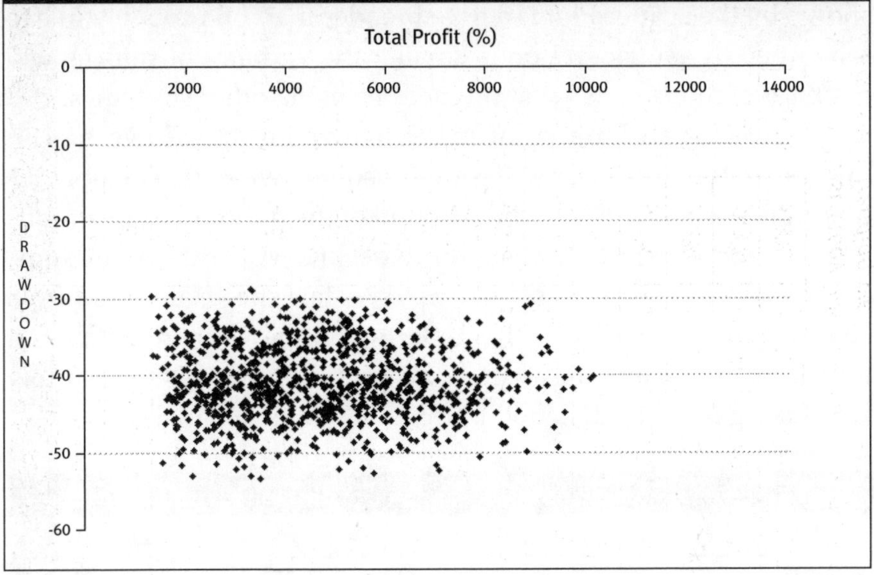

Figure 64: The dispersion of returns verse drawdown is a little broad which may bring into question the possible variance of outcomes.

Conclusion and Improvements

The CAGR is by far the highest of all strategies tested so far in this book, although it does come with higher volatility of returns. It's important that an investor be aware of, and respects, the higher volatility rather than simply chase the strategy with the highest return.

Two other positive attributes stand out against other strategies: the win rate is high at 47% and the strategy operates at a lower trade frequency of 32 trades per year. In the world of momentum strategies a winning percentage of 47% is very high especially when the average win is some 3.7 times the average losing trade. These are extremely strong numbers.

Growth of $100,000 exhibits a very strong and smooth upward trend although the two distinct drawdowns are quite sharp. That said, a very strong trait is that recovery time is extremely fast.

A unique element of Bollinger Bands is that they take into account the volatility of a stock and not just momentum. This ensures a stock is not only moving higher, but doing so at an accelerating rate. A by-product is the quantity of signals generated by this type of strategy will be a lot less than those generated by a simplistic strategy such as the 100-Day High. The distribution of returns shown by the Scatter Plot is a little broader than I'd probably like to see but as signal generation is smaller the variance of returns will not be as significant as what it would be using other strategies.

A possible sticking point is the maximum drawdown at 41% may be on the uncomfortable side for some investors. The obvious question is whether or not the addition of the Index Filter technique will make a difference to that equity decline. We will use the same parameter settings as has been used so far, specifically adding a 75-day moving average to the underlying index. When the market trades below this moving average we'll instruct the system to simply stop taking new signals. Stop placement will not change.

	XAOA	BBO	BBO (F)
CAGR	8.78%	33.59%	29.86%
maxDD	-51.4%	-43.7%	-32.6%
MAR	0.17	0.77	0.92
Exposure	100%	89.6%	79.8%
# Transactions	-	470	397
Win %	-	48.32%	50.1%
Win/Loss Ratio	-	4.00	4.37
Std Dev. (pa)	18.88%	47.83%	39.85%
Sharpe Ratio	0.204	0.636	0.624

Table 52: A simple rule that stops new signals being generated when the trend of the broader market is down reduces the maximum drawdown by 25%

The inclusion of the filter shows the maximum drawdown drop from an uncomfortable 43.7% to a slightly more acceptable 32.6%. Simply put the Index Filter removes about 14.6% of the transactions – obviously those taken against the broader market trend. The MAR ratio moves higher from 0.77 to 0.92 and the volatility of returns drops to 39.8%. The Index Filter is certainly an added benefit.

FIGURE 65

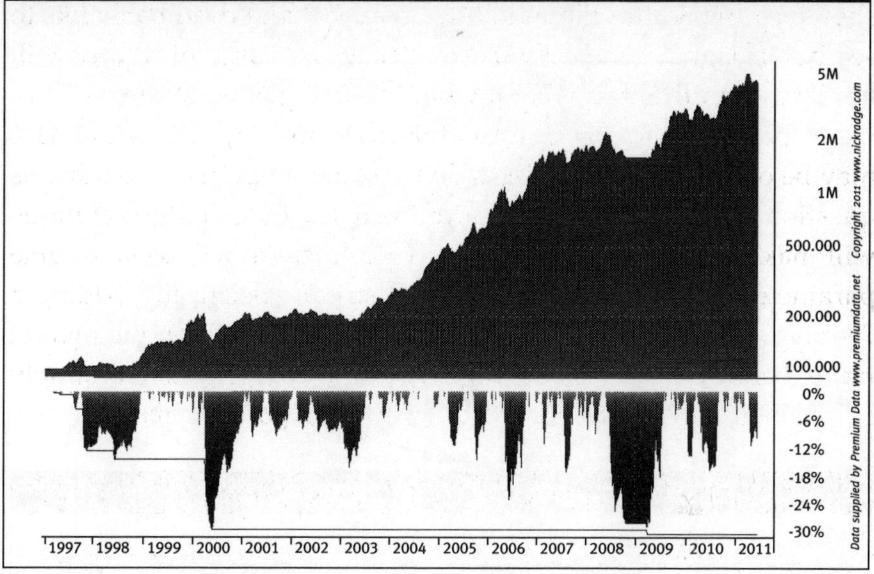

Figure 65: Growth of $100,000 using the BBO strategy and an Index Filter.

Strategy Conclusions

The following chart offers a graphical representation of all tested strategies plotted by CAGR and Maximum Drawdown. Whilst different investors will have different gauges for a strategy comparison, these two are critical. Usually an investor wants the highest return on their investment but they also need to be able to deal with the inevitable decline in capital that occurs with all strategies at some stage.

FIGURE 66

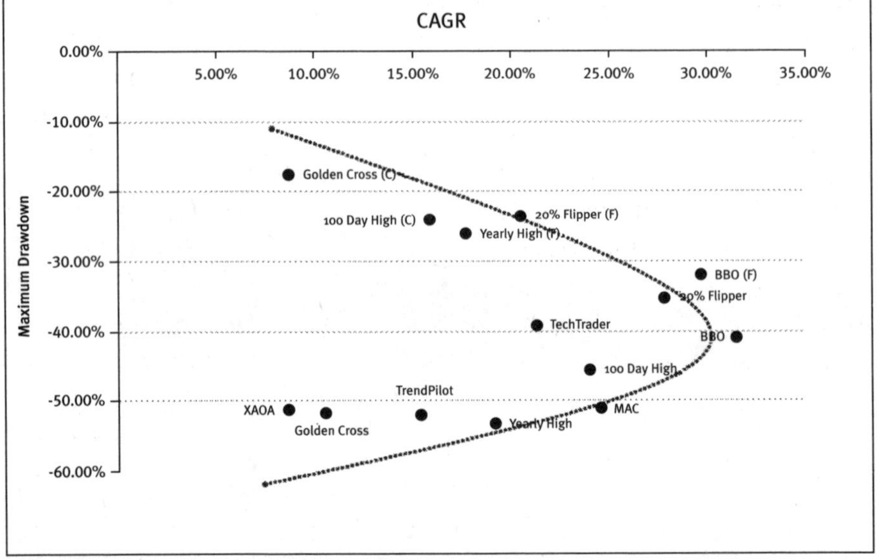

Figure 66: Comparison of all tested strategies using CAGR vs. Maximum Drawdown.

The average investor can withstand an equity decline around the 20% level. Once this is exceeded doubt starts to creep into the process and the investor tends to start looking for another strategy. On this basis the 20% Flipper using an Index Filter or the Yearly High with an Index Filter tend to be the strategies that offer better than market returns with a decent risk adjusted reward.

An investor that can stomach a little more downside, yet keen on higher growth rates, would be studying the Bollinger Band Breakout (BBO), with or without the filter, or the raw 20% Flipper.

The worst performer?

Buy & Hold as measured by the XAOA.

SECTION 3
Proof of Concept

Real Time Results

So far the philosophy behind momentum investing has been assessed: what and why it should work. We explored the intricacies of how returns can be generated – the mathematics of allowing profits to run their natural course yet stopping losing positions before they imparted too much damage on the portfolio. We ridiculed our cultural belief that success can only come from making correct decisions rather than managing the poor ones. Using this philosophy allowed us to remove the need for prediction, the most salient point being that markets, sectors and stocks that are going to trend will automatically be brought to our attention without input and foreknowledge. In other words, momentum investors don't pick stocks, stocks pick momentum investors.

Various strategies were tested including strategies commonly discussed in the media, on internet forums or in trade publications. Some of these were simple, others slightly more complex. Rather than looking at performance in terms of returns only, we used the two-dimensional frame of risk adjusted returns: is it worth chasing a 15% annual return, if it means enduring a 40% decline in your capital? In simulations momentum investing tended to increase risk adjusted returns across a variety of different strategies and, to some degree, becomes a foul-weather friend for investors. We saw how an Index Filter can be beneficial for keeping us out of sustained bearish environments yet also allow participation on bullish trends.

In this section the philosophy and theory discussed so far will be taken a step further by reviewing a small sample of real-time trades[38]. These results come from a momentum strategy that contains (a) all the aspects of momentum investing discussed in Section 1, and (b) most of the key attributes discussed in Section 2. The goal is to test and prove the concept of momentum investing in the real world, as best as possible.

Before we get started it's important to lay some groundwork. The momentum strategy that generated these recommendations has evolved over the years. I first developed it back in the late '90s to trade commodity futures. A strategy designed for trading commodity futures that can be applied to equities is a great example of why the philosophy of momentum investing is robust and should remain plausible over the long term. Commodity and stock markets are vastly different, not only driven by different fundamental factors but also used by vastly different participants, yet they both exhibit the same tendency to trend.

The time period for this real time sample, mid-2006 through mid-2011, encompasses one of the most chaotic periods seen in the markets for 20 years; the late stages of the big bull run from the 2003 lows, the significant decline through 2007 and 2008, the spectacular bounce off the 2009 lows and the very frustrating sideways congestion during 2010 and 2011.

---

38 Recommended to subscribers of the Growth Portfolio at www.thechartist.com.au (now also www.nickradge.com) between May 2006 and October 2011.

FIGURE 67

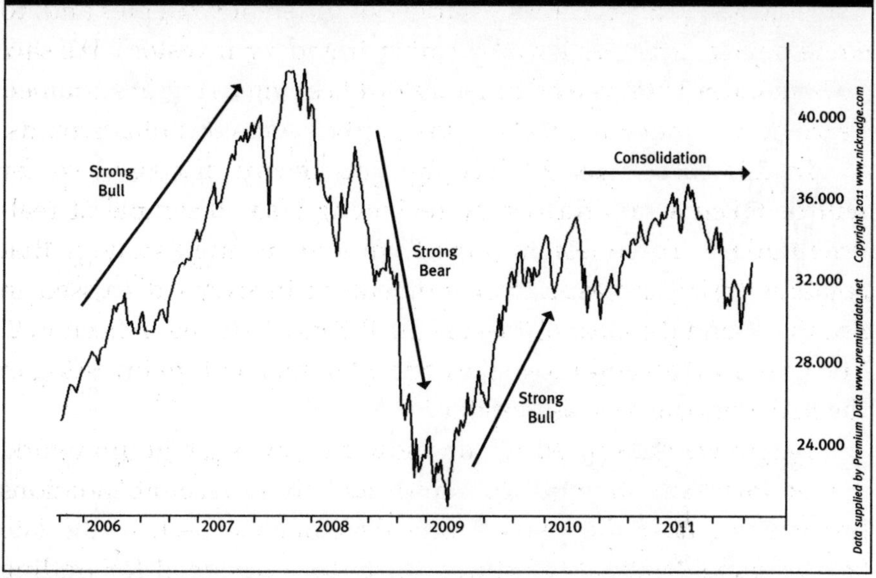

Figure 67: The All Ordinaries Accumulation Index between May 2006 and October 2011.

Markets can go through periods of non-trending, but ultimately trends will reappear and profits can be extracted for those that are patient enough and able to protect capital during the down times. The early 70s saw one of the most devastating bear markets since the depression. The following charts show some US stocks that felt the brunt of that nasty bear market yet were followed by exquisite trends that any system outlined in this book would have caught and ridden with ease. As is commonly said, the darkest hour is before the dawn.

FIGURE 68

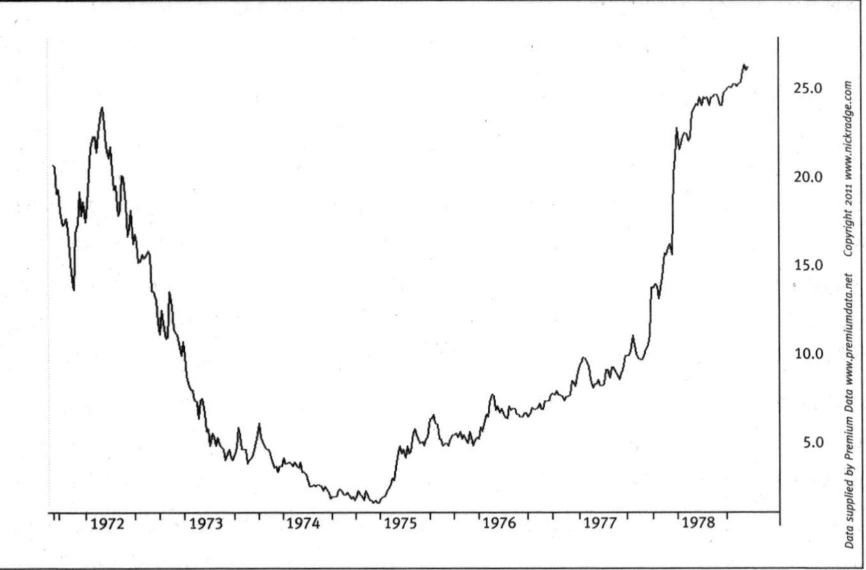

Figure 68: American Medicorp, 1972 to 1979.

FIGURE 69

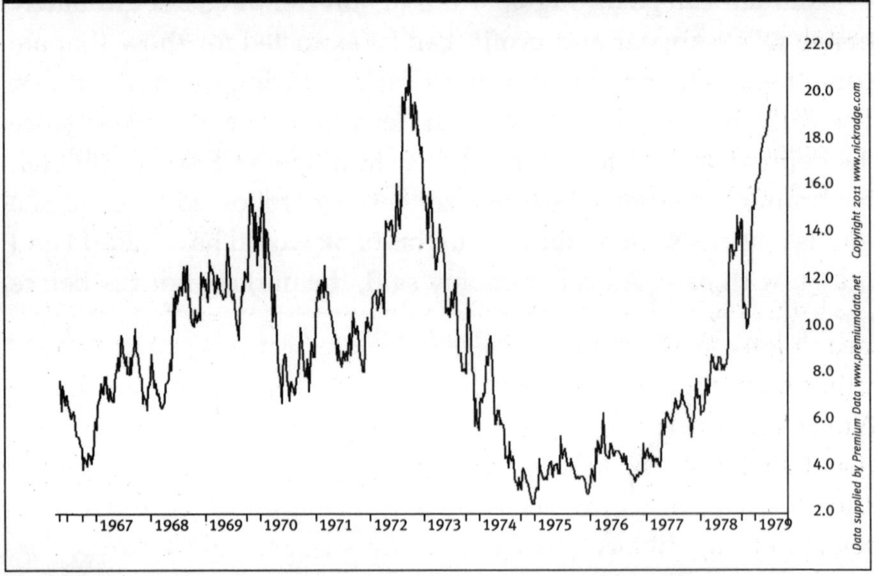

Figure 69: Executone Inc, 1967—1979

A key element of failure is discarding a long term strategy experiencing short term difficulties. Amateurs want a strategy that's always working, always profitable, and are very quick to jump from one strategy to another chasing performance. In professional money management circles the term 'style drift' refers to a manager changing strategy during a poor performance period. It's considered taboo by institutional investors. A manager with style drift is a red flag. Think of it another way. If owning an airline becomes a tough business, would it be acceptable for Qantas to move into iron ore or gold mining? Of course not. During the Tech Boom in the late '90s, did BHP Billiton join the frenzy of internet and communications technology? Absolutely not. If Warren Buffettt was unable to find value investing opportunities would he get into high frequency trading? No. Yet this is what amateurs do. The focus is usually based on a very small subset of the total possible outcomes, known as sample bias, so they never allow a strategy to do what it's designed to do over the longer term. On the other hand, professionals understand that patience is a hallmark of success. They understand the short term idiosyncrasies of the markets or of a strategy and will not be swayed by short term emotions.

> *"Whenever we get a period of poor performance, most investors conclude something must be fixed. They ask if the markets have changed. But trend following presupposes change."*
>
> **John W. Henry**

Data records for these trades do not include daily revaluations, meaning the performance presented is based on closed equity only rather than open equity—as has been done throughout this book. Whilst this does not impact on the return it will impact on the visual shape of the equity curve and the depth of the maximum drawdown. A drawdown is defined as the decline of equity from a peak to a trough which also includes any open profits that are given back, even if the trade is profitable.

Other considerations:

- Commission was 0.08% or minimum $6
- Includes dividends and capital adjustments
- Does not include compounding
- Does not include interest earned on cash.

	XAOA	Real Time
Total Return	5.27%	96.46%
AROR	0.94%	13.12%**
maxDD	-51.4%	-13.1%***
MAR	0.17	1.00
Exposure	100%	n/a
# Transactions	-	158
Win %	-	43.0%
Win/Loss Ratio	-	3.52

*Table 53: A snapshot comparison of performance between the real time strategy and the All Ordinaries Accumulation Index (XAOA) from May 8th 2006 through October 30th 2011.**

"The challenge is to not learn more, but rather to ignore more so that you can focus on the principles and the few techniques that are important."

Garr Reynolds

* Based on a signals generated and recommended via the Growth Portfolio at www.thechartist.com.au and now also available at www.nickradge.com

** Does not include compounding. All investments have been made based on the same start capital.

*** This drawdown is based on 'closed only' equity which inherently underestimates the true peak to trough drawdown. The real figure is approximately 20% – 22%.

The following Expectancy Curve shows the real time results plotted against the longer term simulated results.

FIGURE 70

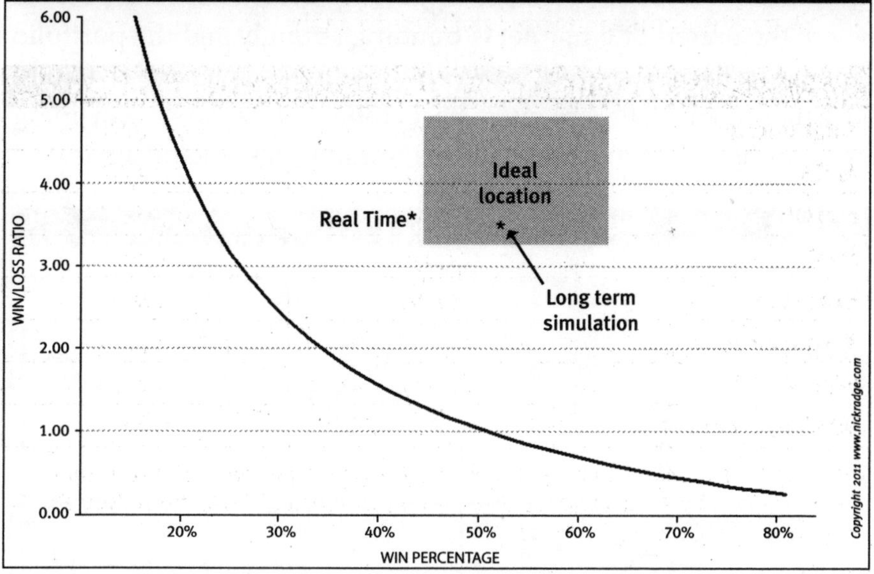

Figure 70: The Expectancy Curve showing both the real time and longer term simulation results.

The slight drop in the winning percentage of trades is more than likely caused by the difficult market conditions of 2008 and the congestion of 2010–2011. This is why we want to operate well above the Expectancy Curve because short term adverse market conditions will cause results to move around the mean. A large buffer ensures we retain a profitable outcome when these adverse conditions come along. Strategies that tend to hug the curve can fall below the Expectancy Curve during adverse conditions.

The strategy has generated 158 trades in its 6.5 years of operation with an expectancy of 12.1%. Expectancy measures the expected return of capital invested on each individual trade. These types of strategies tend to have higher expectancy levels but lower trade frequency. The 158 trades in 6.5 years are below the long term average, mainly because we spent half of 2008 sitting in cash. Over the longer term the yearly trade frequency is 30 transactions per year with an average hold time of approximately 8 months.

The following equity curve is based solely on closed equity and does not include swings in open equity. It shows three significant jumps: May 2006 to May 2007, March 2009 to September 2009 and again between September 2010 to January 2011. These are periods where the underlying market is trending strongly and the portfolio becomes fully invested. In between these times you can see equity retreat as open profits are given back, followed by the system going 100% to cash and the equity curve flat-lining as we stand aside.

FIGURE 71

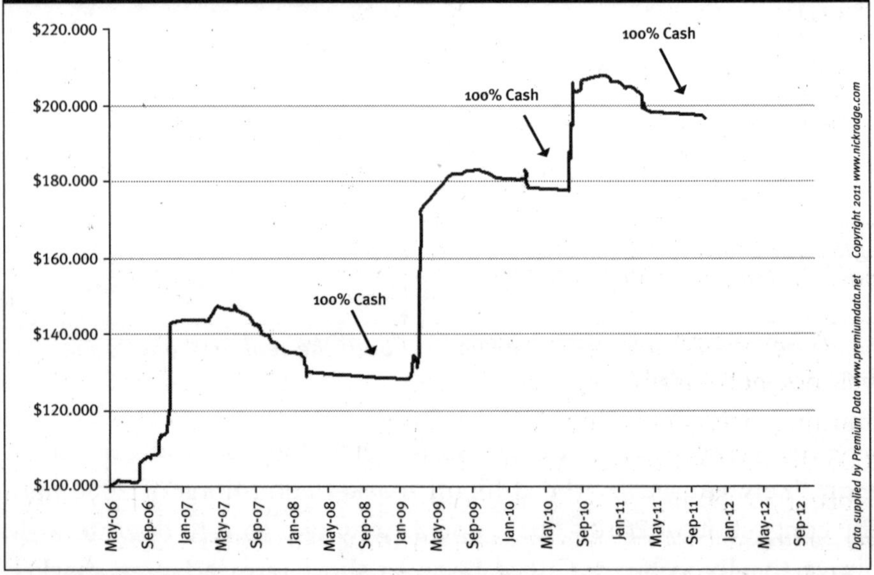

Figure 71: A non-time weighted closed trade equity curve from May 2006, when the strategy was introduced, to October 2011.

Next we have the value of $100,000 invested in the All Ordinaries Accumulation Index (XAOA) for the same period, although this chart exhibits the day-to-day fluctuations of the investment. The shape and outcome here is very different to the shape and outcome of an investment in the real time momentum strategy.

FIGURE 72

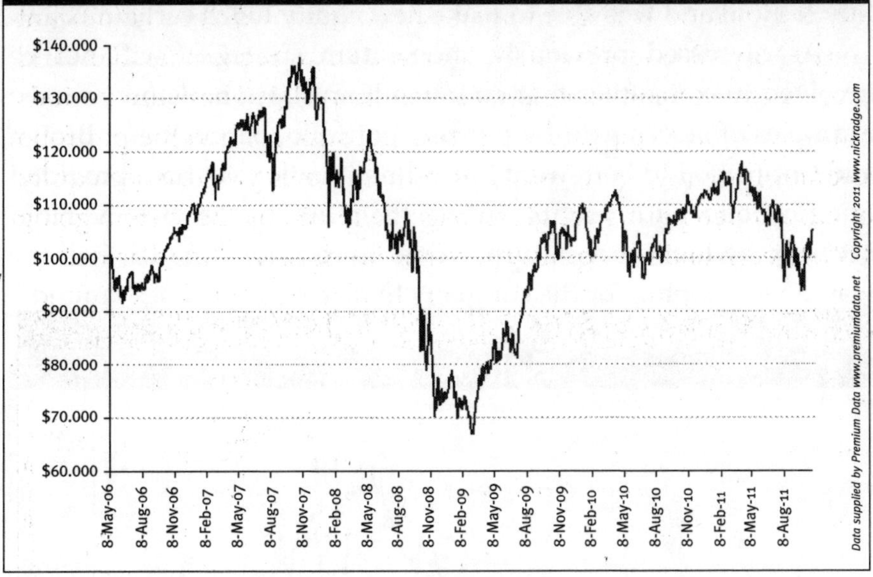

Figure 72: Growth of $100,000 invested in All Ordinaries Accumulation Index for the period May 2006 to October 2011.

A key element of the success of the strategy during this period was not necessarily capturing great trends and trades but rather standing aside between May 2008 and February 2009. In May 2008 the All Ordinaries Accumulation Index stood at 38,435 and in February 2009 it was 41% lower at 22,655. From its absolute peak the index lost 51.4%. We've seen strong evidence throughout this book that the addition of an Index Filter greatly enhances the risk adjusted returns on most strategies and this real time performance is a key insight into how and why this will occur.

Financially the benefits are obvious although another element is that the strategy has been able to make new equity highs above and beyond the 2007 high water mark. As at October 2011, some 4 years after the 2007 peak, the All Ordinaries Accumulation Index is still languishing 23.5% below its highs. Needless to say almost every Australian fund manager is also underwater and it's proving a long wait for their investors to recover losses.

The real time strategy is not immune to pain though, although quite clearly there are differing degrees of pain to contend with. On a closed trade basis equity fell by 13% and on an open mark-to-market basis the decline was circa 20%. Either way you wish to measure it, the drawdown had substantially less financial pain than Buy & Hold and was able to make new equity highs early in 2009.

As discussed previously, momentum strategies will not be involved in companies that go into administration. Below are two examples of stocks held by our real portfolio. Babcock and Brown and Copperco Ltd both went into administration yet both provided our portfolio with profits during their lifetime. A Buy & Hold investor, by their very nature, would have ridden the dive all the way down, hoping for the company to turn their fortunes around.

FIGURE 73

Figure 73: Babcock and Brown was bought on 9th May 2006 and sold on 30th July 2007 for a gain of 24%. The stock continued to slide into the abyss in the ensuing years.

FIGURE 74

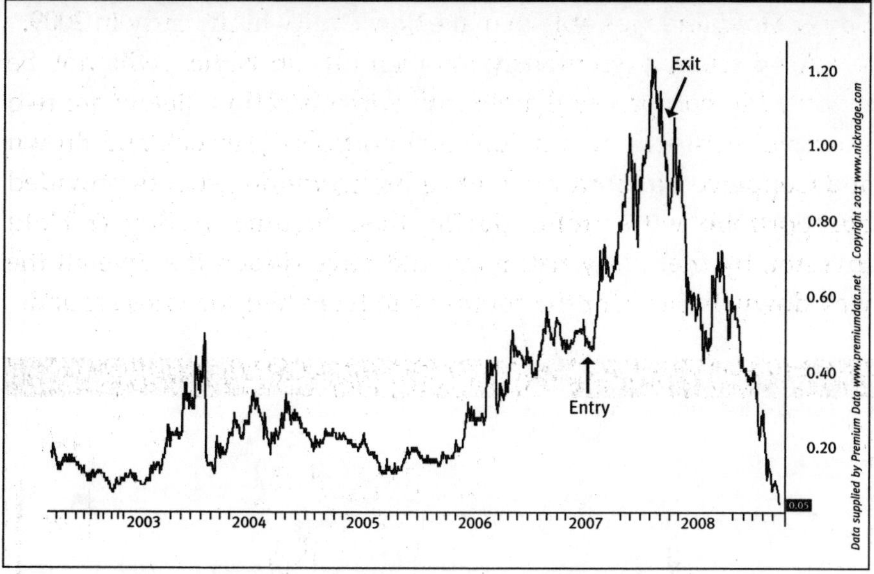

Figure 74: Copperco Ltd was bought on 11th April 2007 and sold on 20th November 2007. Like Babcock and Brown it was unable to recover from its dive.

Also of important consideration are those once high-flying stocks that, whilst still listed, have little hope of returning to their former glory. Here are two examples that the portfolio held.

FIGURE 75

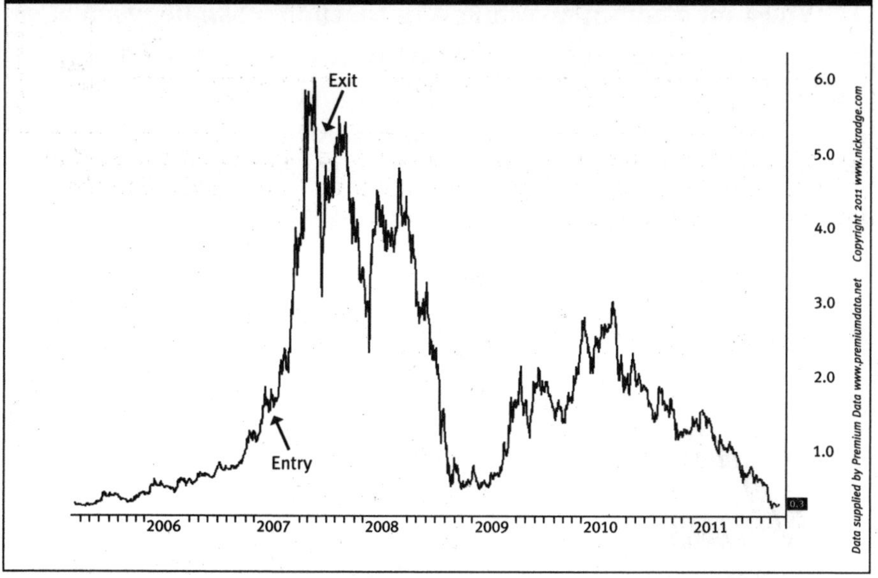

Figure 75: Murchison Metals was a stock that provided a windfall profit before falling back to earth. Will it ever attain those highs again?

FIGURE 76

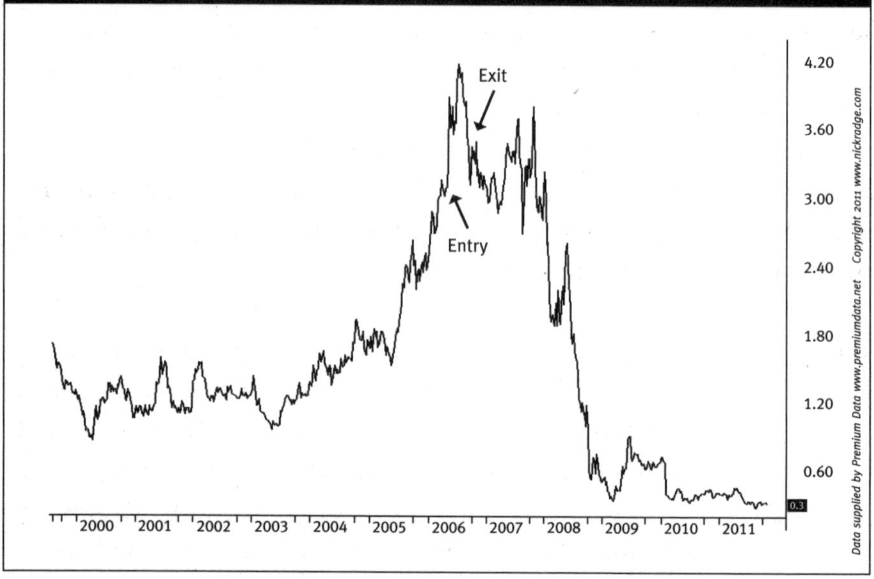

Figure 76: Whilst not a successful trade Roc Oil was exited as the bullish trend reversed. The new down trend saw prices collapse over the next year.

No strategy is perfect but momentum investing can, and does, work during times of market stress. If you can overcome the need for constant profit gratification and take a longer term view of creating positive expectancy, then you'll be well ahead of most investors.

Whilst momentum investing is not a common strategy amongst the herd, four highly-successful individuals kindly agreed to discuss their trading strategies for inclusion in this book. Two are individuals trading their own accounts, one is the director of a financial planning group and one a stockbroker. These interviews provide insights into their success as well as lessons they have learned along the way.

Interviews with the Experts

Interview with Gary Scott

From Academic Theory to Market Reality

Each investor's personal journey will be influenced by different factors: a chance encounter with a likeminded person, a book that switches on an internal light or even discussion and the sharing of ideas on an internet forum. These can all be life-changing events. In Gary's case it was a newspaper advertisement that sent him on a path away from strong beliefs formed at university and ultimately to new theories solidified by mathematical algorithms that he personally developed. His journey is full of lessons that many of us learn the hard way—as he did, but ultimately his passion and perseverance paid off, allowing him to achieve independence and success with his investment decisions.

Gary: I completed a Bachelor of Commerce at the University of Queensland thinking I wanted to be an accountant, but didn't really like that after the first year, so I selected as many electives in computer science as I could. After university I worked for Burroughs Computers and then the state government as a computer analyst and programmer.

Nick: During this time were you doing any investing or trading?

Gary: No, absolutely none.

Nick: No interest in the market at all?

Gary: As part of my degree I did a finance course which explained the efficient market hypothesis[39] arguing that you could not beat the market. That was my belief for the next 15 years. My father used to dabble in the stock market and I'd tell him you can't beat the market. That's what I'd learnt in university and I was convinced—based on what they'd presented to us—that this was the truth.

Nick: How successful was he in the market?

---

39 An often-disputed theory that it is impossible to beat the stock market because all available information is priced in making it impossible to buy below fair value or sell above.

Gary: He actually picked a couple of good mining speccies and made a fair bit of money.

Nick: That would have been in the '70s?

Gary: Yes.

Nick: They had the mineral boom with Poseidon and all the nickel stocks.

Gary: Yes, although he didn't get on Poseidon he did get a few good ones. In those days there was no capital gains tax either so it was a bit of a free for all.

Nick: What did your father say when you brought up the efficient market hypothesis with him?

Gary: He didn't believe in it. He thought that he could read the newspaper and pick out some stories. In some respects he had success which defied the theory I had, but I was firmly sticking to my academic view. After four years as a programmer my brother and I started a business from a very lowly base and that's all we focused on for at least the first 10 years. It was about 1999 that we decided to invest in the market, so I took my knowledge of the efficient market hypothesis and spread my capital between Australian and international managed funds. It was virtually the top of the market in 2000—couldn't have timed it any worse.

Nick: What made you pick these funds? Did you pick them yourself? Did you have a financial planner—where did you get your information on the funds?

Gary: Through the internet. I looked at the ones that had performed best over the last 10 years.

Nick: They were the ones you went with?

Gary: Yes—the ones that had performed best. Over the prior 10 years they were pretty good—a lot of them were making 20% a year.

Nick: Up until 2000?

Gary: Yes. It seemed pretty exciting to me that you could earn 20% just tipping money into these funds, so we proceeded to do that and used a bit of dollar cost averaging[40] as more capital came in. Unfortunately it was all downhill virtually from the first month. It just kept going down and then we had the tech crash.

Nick: How many of these managed funds would have been investing in tech stocks? By the sounds of it you had some good diversification there.

Gary: I did have some good diversification but I remember specifically buying into a Colonial First State technology fund that invested in technology mainly in the US. It just went down like a stone—dropped 50% in quick time. So even though I had diversity, everything was going down—the market was going down. That's when I started to think there had to be a better way of doing this—obviously it wasn't going like I'd planned.

Nick: How much of your equity do you think you had lost when that realisation hit you?

Gary: Overall it was probably only about 20% and I think what partially saved us was the dollar cost averaging. But the decline was consistent—it was just going down and down. I've since learned 20%

---

40 A strategy of investing equal dollar amounts regularly over a period of time which allows more shares to be purchased at lower prices and less shares at higher prices.

is about as much pain as I can tolerate with most investments, even my own systems. In 2001 I saw an advertisement for a US company that was offering a free seminar so my brother and I went along. They had a system that to me seemed pretty magical. They were putting up charts that were cherry picked.

Nick: The well-chosen examples? Seems nothing's changed today.

Gary: Yes. It just looked so easy—it was like 'wow'. I started to challenge my belief about the efficient market theory. These guys were making incredible profits and it was all pretty easy. They actually had two green arrows to buy and two red arrows to sell. I didn't understand it at the time, but after lots of reading and research I realised that one green arrow was a slow stochastic crossing up above the 20 line. The other green arrow was a MACD. Theory was that you bought if these arrows crossed within two or three days of each other. You sold when they crossed to the down side. The whole platform was very professional in appearance. They also had a fundamental overlay where you could screen the whole US market and pick out fundamentally good stocks and apply these indicators.

Nick: Was their software predominantly for the US markets or could it be used here in Australia?

Gary: No, it was all US-based. I remember quite clearly our first couple of trades because we were buying in a seriously down-trending market. They didn't really have any market filters and the trades lasted about two or three days before they tanked.

Nick: So you purchased this US software?

Gary: Yes.

Nick: Was it expensive?

Gary: Yes, it was. You had to buy a course with the software which was US$5,000.

Nick: Just for the course? Back then the Aussie dollar was certainly below 60c.

Gary: Yes, so probably A$10,000. On top of that was a monthly fee of around US$300 or US$400.

Nick: So that's A$6,000 to A$8,000 a year?

Gary: Yes.

Nick: And are they still in business these days?

Gary: No, they're not around anymore. I remember at the seminar there were 100 to 200 people and they gave a number of presentations whilst in Australia. The figures were staggering.

Nick: But it's no different now, is it? You get these companies that come out with software packages at exorbitant prices still around that $8,000 to $15,000 level.

Gary: Yes, there's plenty of that around.

Nick: With 10 years' experience behind you, what's your feeling about it now?

Gary: My feeling is that these firms need a consistent stream of new suckers. The fact is there are many people looking for a way to utilise their money.

Nick: I would argue that if it looks really good, people will pay any amount of money to get their hands on it.

Gary: I think that's the case—that's what we felt after going to the initial two-hour seminar. It just looked so good we signed up on the spot. We had to be involved. After losing money with the managed funds, we thought this was the way to go.

Nick: Let's just go back—you did your first few trades during what was a stiff bear market back then—'02/'03 was the last recession.

Gary: That's right. I cannot remember a winning trade. We did play around with it for a long time. We spent more time researching the whole strategy than actually trading it.

Nick: Was it a disclosed system?

Gary: No.

Nick: You paid US$5,000 for the course. What kind of things did they teach you in the course?

Gary: The one good thing that came out of the course was the exit strategy—the two red arrows. It was basically a stop and they stressed that when you saw the two red arrows you must get out. I've never really had a huge problem doing that because my tolerance to drawdowns is relatively low. The other positive aspect was they had a system that you could follow mechanically.

Nick: What made you step from managed funds, which are arguably fully fundamental, to something that's almost purely technical?

Gary: The thing that allowed me to make the transition was their software had a fundamental overlay. Even though they were entering and exiting on technicals, they had some fundamental filters. That appealed to me.

Nick: So the fundamentals made you feel comfortable?

Gary: Yes. It made me feel that I was trading in good stocks so things would be fine.

Nick: And the first year or two were pretty rough?

Gary: Yes. We abandoned that software before the next bull market started though. It was definitely the beginner's cycle and basically we didn't give it a chance to work. If we had hung in a little longer, we probably could have done okay because it was a tremendous run-up from 2003.

Nick: Was it doing a lot of transactions?

Gary: Yes, it was very short term. It wouldn't catch a trend of more than a month. You would then watch those trends continue on without us. That didn't suit me either.

Nick: How long did you use this software?

Gary: Less than two years. We got sick of it.

Nick: Sick of losing money.

Gary: Yes.

Nick: It was also a very expensive piece of software to keep running.

Gary: Yes. But it taught me to adhere to stops and it also made me realise there may be a better way than just buying managed funds and watching them plummet 50%.

Nick: Being a little bit more active.

Gary: Yes, being proactive. I thought there had to be a better way to do things so I started reading lots of books. I'd collect books and read everything and anything I could find.

Nick: Were they technical books or just anything to do with investing?

Gary: Anything to do with trading and investing. After the bear market in 2003 it really started to shake my belief in fundamentals because there were companies that were in seriously big down trends, getting cheaper and cheaper, and they just kept going down.

Nick: Even though the fundamentals were very good.

Gary: The fundamentals were fantastic. HIH Insurance was one of them. I realised that just using fundamentals was a pretty dangerous game in a bear market and that you could lose a lot of money. So I learnt that lesson from them.

The next thing I got involved in was an investment strategy promoted by an Australian educator. They offered complete systems that you could implement—all with good rules. We traded one of their systems for three or four years from late 2003 to 2007.

Nick: This system being a weekly momentum-type strategy?

Gary: Yes, although it relies on having long term stable trends. A stable trend is defined as having an upward trend on weekly charts for at least six months with low volatility. So it works fantastically well in a long bull market that goes straight up. It has a trailing stop and distinct areas where you place buy orders—an up-week after a pullback in price. The weakness of the strategy is that you really need a bull market for it to operate. For example, there's probably not one stock in the ASX300 that you'd actually buy using that system right now.

Nick: Would they only trade the ASX300 stocks?

Gary: I can't recall, but they also had a basic fundamental filter based on data from Lincoln Indicator's Stock Doctor. It's a weekly newsletter and effectively you follow the buy and sell signals.

Nick: So there was no software required to run your new strategy? Was there any back testing provided?

Gary: A little bit of back testing. In a sense they took two years of signals that had appeared in their newsletters, put them into a portfolio manager and followed it over the course of two years. You could see the results of the system.

Nick: What year was that?

Gary: About 2005.

Nick: So about 2 years into the new bull market...

Gary: Yes, it was a really good period.

Nick: Was there any back testing done during the '02/'03 period?

Gary: Not that I'm aware of. They also used an Index Filter to try and keep you out of those markets. It's based on a moving average cross-over of the XAO so in a big down trend it won't let you buy stocks. It's a reasonably good filter.

Nick: You've gone from efficient market hypothesis to the expensive US software to a momentum strategy. You seem to be trying to find something that suits you and you're just fine-tuning it a little bit more? What were the lessons you learnt from the momentum strategy? Obviously the Index Filter was very beneficial.

Gary: An Index Filter and to have a proven system you could follow. However all through that period that we were trading I still don't think I was a mature trader because it didn't take much to shake my confidence and get me out of the market. When things got a little bit rocky I tended to run for the hills and sell everything and think the world was going to end.

Nick: So you were overriding the system?

Gary: Yes.

Nick: Why do you think that was happening? Were you scared of losing more money? Were you unsure of the system?

Gary: It was a combination. A lot of the time I was scared of losing open profits. When you've got a substantial profit sitting there and the market is not behaving properly, it's hard psychologically to see it evaporate. In your mind you think it's your money. I also think it has to do with the fact that I didn't build the system.

Nick: So, we're now in 2005. What was your next step?

Gary: I became interested in building trading systems myself and back testing. I was never really comfortable following someone blindly. I could also see that the system relied on having really long term trends that you waited preferably a year before jumping on board.

Nick: You had to wait for a year before entering? Even though the trend was firmly in place?

Gary: You had to wait six months, but their preference was a year. There was a subjective filter being the MMA[41] which is a series of moving averages without the price overlaid on the chart. The preference was to have the longer term group of moving averages virtually straight and moving up at a 45 degree angle across your screen. It takes time for that to happen. I could see there was an opportunity to jump on all of those trends way earlier and capture the first year.

Nick: It would be quite a substantial lag?

Gary: A huge lag. That's why you really needed a sustained bull market to get a number of those trends.

Nick: So by their definition, was 2009 a bull market even though the market returned some 30%?

Gary: No. I think they sat out most of 2009 with this system.

Nick: The market only went up from March to October so that would have only just made the six month criteria. I guess the sudden reversal off the lows would have taken some time for those longer moving averages to get the pattern required.

---

41 Multiple Moving Averages

Gary: To turn around, yes. I then bought MetaStock and wrote a number of strategies that I found on the internet. If you Google there's plenty of code out there.

Nick: You did mention that you had, apart from your commerce degree, done some programming which obviously has helped with MetaStock.

Gary: Yes, it has certainly helped me to write a script in some of these languages. You could see a system then build on that and get an idea of how it worked.

Nick: Okay, so you're building systems in MetaStock. What kind of strategies were you looking at?

Gary: Longer term momentum strategies. I started out looking at daily bars, but I really couldn't find anything that suited me. I noticed that if you skewed your system to have a few big winners and lots of small losers, then it was pretty easy to make a reasonable return in a year.

Nick: What's your definition of long term?

Gary: 12 months. During that time the shares might go up 100%, 300% or 400%.

Nick: You mentioned that when you were initially testing these daily systems the strategies you were testing didn't suit. What do you mean by they didn't suit? What were you looking for? What were your criteria for a good system?

Gary: They didn't suit because of the number of trades and the shortness of the holding period. Holding shorter term is a bit draining—every day you're making decisions and buying and selling and jumping out of trends only to watch them go further, so that's when

I switched to weekly. MetaStock was a bit frustrating because you could only back test one symbol at a time. Eventually I bought CompuVision's TradeSim for portfolio testing, but eventually I came across AmiBroker and I used it from then on.

Nick: Are you self-taught with the AmiBroker programming?

Gary: Yes, I taught myself, although in the early stages I outsourced to a programmer because I had some ideas that were reasonably complicated to code.

Nick: Trade frequency seems to be an important element. Can you give us an idea of how many trades a year is too many?

Gary: More than 50 transactions a year. One of my systems runs in my Superfund so I don't want to churn too many trades.

Nick: So you trade a Superfund and do you have other accounts that you trade?

Gary: Yes, I also trade an account in my Family Trust. In 2007 the account we were trading was a company as part of our overall business, with my brother. We built that account up to about $3 million but we had a real estate development we were doing and needed the funds so toward the end of 2007 we realised all profits, exited the market and walked away.

Nick: So you overrode your strategy and took the money completely out of the market?

Gary: Yes, but it was for external reasons and it made us look like geniuses to everybody in hindsight.

Nick: The top was November 2007.

Gary: Yes, it was within about a month of the top.

Nick: Great timing. You said you built that account up to $3 million. Do you have any idea what you started with?

Gary: We started with less than a million.

Nick: What kind of annualised return were you making in that period of time?

Gary: In the good years we were making 40%.

Nick: This was with the systems that you personally developed back in 2005?

Gary: Yes, but also with the system prior to this.

Nick: Can you give us an idea what's behind the systems?

Gary: They're actually quite simple. The entry is not hugely important—I'm just looking for strength coupled with an increase in volatility and a move above a high point.

Nick: So a break-out system?

Gary: Yes, but the break-out has to have high momentum and that's the only indicator I use in the system. I've found it gives a higher winning percentage than taking, just say, a 26-week break-out with no other filters on it.

Nick: In this book we test a 52-week break-out and also a 100-day break-out, but we didn't use any overriding filter to go with it. Can you give us an idea what that might be?

Gary: I look at how far and how fast the prices move prior to the break-out similar to a rate of change.

Nick: Okay, so a rate of change indicator.

Gary: Yes. I've looked at volume, but I haven't been able to add anything of value to my system using that.

Nick: Do you use an Index Filter?

Gary: I do use an Index Filter. It's extremely simple—if the XAO closes above the 10-week moving average, which is equivalent to a 50-day moving average.

Nick: And you're using weekly charts which mean you only run your data once a week then place the orders for the following week?

Gary: Yes. I like to get set in the opening auction of the next Monday and be done in the first half hour, then that's it for the week.

Nick: That entry is very simple. Do you think simple works?

Gary: Yes.

Nick: What's the winning percentage of your strategy?

Gary: About 50%—it's basically a coin toss. However in the last year it's certainly been lower—down towards 25%. Very few trades have worked.

Nick: What about the exits?

Gary: The exit is a little more complicated and relies on two aspects. The first is a trailing stop and the second is a lack of momentum, meaning if the stock goes sideways long enough without getting a trailing stop signal I'll sell out and look for a better opportunity.

Nick: A stale exit?

Gary: Yes—a stale exit. The trailing stop is based on ATR—average true range. The average true range stop just trails behind the price and will move up a little quicker if the price moves up quickly.

Nick: You mentioned that in your early days giving back open profits was an issue. With any type of trailing stop you're going to have periods of time where you give back open profit. Are you dealing with it better now or do you think the strategy deals with it better?

Gary: The strategy definitely deals with it better, although I don't have the same issues with open profits.

Nick: So in percentage terms, just roughly, because an ATR doesn't operate on percentages—approximately what kind of percentage give-back would there be on a particular run-up in a stock?

Gary: It's still going to be about 20% on average, unless the index turns negative which will close it up a bit more. Sometimes it can be a lot more.

In periods like we've had in the last year or 18 months the system will trigger lots of buy signals then the market has turned around quickly, the stop will be quite tight and you'll get stopped out quickly. That's actually comforting to me—that's what I feel works best for me.

Nick: You've got a win rate of—well at the moment, low—but on longer term testing 45 to 50%. What's your win/loss ratio?

Gary: It's pretty high, probably about three-and-a-half to one.

Nick: For every dollar you lose on a losing trade, you're going to make three, three-and-a-half dollars on the winning trades?

Gary: Yes.

Nick: That's good positive expectancy.

Gary: Yes—and helps when you get periods like we've had in the last year or two. No system can work fine all of the time and we're in pretty unusual times at the moment. Currently I'm sitting on a drawdown in the last year of about 10%.

Nick: What's your tested historic maximum drawdown?

Gary: Historic maximum goes to about 20%.

Nick: 10% now is pretty good.

Gary: I'm happy with the 10% given the market has chopped back and forth all year which doesn't suit trend following. Higher drawdowns are usually off the top of a really good run-up.

Nick: In your long term testing, what's your annualised return look like?

Gary: On long term testing annualised return is about 40%.

Nick: Wow. So you've got a 40% annualised return with a maximum 20% drawdown. So you've got a MAR ratio of about two.

Gary: Yes. If you get a MAR of one you're doing pretty good. The caveat is that there's not quite enough liquidity for me to get 40% in the real world. If I actually test my system to have a higher level of liquidity the annual return will drop down to 30%. So if I had a smaller account size I'd be confident of getting up to those figures.

Nick: Does your testing have any liquidity filters in it at all?

Gary: I have a basic liquidity filter just to make sure I'm not trading garbage stocks. I only test on the XAO stocks. It looks better on the ASX300, but there's a Survivorship Bias now if you test today rather than if you go back 10 years—there's certainly going to be Survivorship Bias in there.

Nick: Have you tested using delisted data?

Gary: No, I haven't.

Nick: Right, but you're aware of Survivorship Bias?

Gary: Yes—absolutely. You'll see stocks come into the 300 that have a really good run-up prior to getting into the index. If you run your test system on that it'll pick up the stock and say I would have made 200%, when the stock wasn't even in the index to start with so I wouldn't have traded it in the first place.

Nick: So you concentrate just on the top 300? Or you'll take anything in the All Ordinaries so long as liquidity's there?

Gary: I will actually take part positions in smaller stocks if they show up in my scan and the chart looks good.

Nick: On average how many signals would your system generate each week? What I'm getting at here is sample bias. So for example, you said you take 15 to 20 positions, how many signals would you have to stand aside from?

Gary: In a normal market there's quite a lot. I'm not sure exactly how many.

Nick: How long would it take you to fill your 15 or 20 positions?

Gary: When the market satisfies the Index Filter normally it's just a few weeks.

Nick: So quite quickly.

Gary: Yes. You can get in very quickly.

Nick: Did you run Monte Carlo simulations?

Gary: Yes. Over a thousand runs and then dumped that into a spread sheet that a trader friend of mine gave me. I did substantial testing on probably 200 systems I built all using Monte Carlo simulations. It took me a year of fanatical testing, working every single day testing ideas.

Nick: And where did the passion for that come from?

Gary: It's just how I am—I get onto something and I can't leave it alone. I think success is more to do with being dogged at it. Just keeping at it and learning from your mistakes and moving on. I say a year; my wife will probably say it was two years. I'd come home at night and sit at the dining room table. I'd have my laptop so I could do the testing while everything else was going on around me. I'd get different ideas off the net and test them. I've actually got quite a number of good tradable systems, but it's a matter of just picking something and going with it.

Nick: You've taken a big jump from a two-hour seminar where you signed up on the spot to doing at least a year of testing and research. Do you think a new person coming into the markets now would be inclined to do a year's worth of testing? I can tell you that my first system I researched and tested two hours a day, seven days a week for 18 months before I placed my first trade.

Gary: I think most people would pull out before they even got to the system testing point. I don't know a great deal of traders, but reading internet forums there's a consistent string of people that try and fail. People don't stick with it—they just give up.

Nick: Why do you think that is?

Gary: It's probably a lack of confidence. Normally when you start it's always the worst time to do so. A lot of people get that initial sharp drawdown and then doubts creep in. They override the system and I know every time you override the system you almost always do the wrong thing. You think you can beat it, but it's usually the wrong thing to do. 80% of the time, if a stock looks like it's going to hit the stop you'll sell it early and then it'll absolutely take-off.

Nick: How often do you override your system now?

Gary: Now, I don't ever. I've learnt my lesson. I've had lots of lessons—lots and lots of lessons.

Nick: What other lessons have you learnt?

Gary: I have a bad habit of reading financial press. I really wish I didn't although I do find it interesting. You always get someone that's got an opinion: the markets going to tank, it's going to be the biggest recession ever or the market's going to rocket up. That just messes with your head. To me the charts, what's before you, that's what's actually happening.

Nick: You don't use any fundamentals now?

Gary: No. One hundred percent technical on these systems.

Nick: So even though you read the press, you don't deviate from your plan—you just follow the signals...

Gary: I just follow it through. That's hard when the system kicks into gear and says there's 10 buys and there's negative news around, but I know when it comes off a bottom you can make a lot of money really, really quickly. It's that first bit of a new trend that makes profits really move along. You can make a year's return in a couple of months if you're on the right side to start with.

Nick: Absolutely. There's probably a lot of people who are more inclined to sit on the side-lines until things become more definitive. Would you say they're missing, or could miss, a substantial amount of the year's gain just by that tendency to stand aside and wait a little longer?

Gary: Yes, absolutely. It happened to a lot of people at the start of 2003 and it happened to a lot of people again at the start of 2009.

Nick: What would your weekly routine be?

Gary: I update the data every day and if I've got time have a quick look at the charts. Sort of keeps me in tune with the feel of the market—not that it changes anything. On a weekend I run the system and look at all the signals. You want to check to make sure there is not a takeover, for example. If I've got a selection of shares then I'll look at the charts and decide which ones I like best. I do have a filter that I'll look at if I've got two signals that look similar and not enough capital. It's the value of a standard RSI[42] multiplied by the ADX[43] and the higher the value, the faster the stock is moving.

Nick: So you'd only use this if you had to select between two different signals?

Gary: Yes.

Nick: So if you're fully in cash and you get 10 buy signals, you're going to take all 10 buy signals?

Gary: Yes.

Nick: But say you've got 19 positions already and you get another three buy signals and you can only take one, that's when you'll use the filter.

Gary: Yes.

Nick: It's been pretty tough conditions over the last couple of years, but by the sound of it your system's dealt with it reasonably well. After 2007 did your strategy make new equity highs?

Gary: Yes, absolutely.

Nick: But you weren't involved in the market in 2008 due to other business interests.

---

42 Relative Strength Index
43 Average Directional Index

Gary: That's right, but even if I didn't exit the market, my system has definitely made new equity highs.

Nick: So you pulled out of the market in late 2007—when did you get back in again?

Gary: July 2009.

Nick: You missed the first few months off the March lows.

Gary: I missed the first few months and that was a really good time for the system however I didn't have any available funds; they were all tied up in the other project.

Nick: What now? Do you keep tinkering with your system or are you just going to let it do its job?

Gary: I go for periods of time where I really don't look at the system at all—I just run it and don't think about it. But to me building systems is a passion. So I'll always go in and look at some old systems and run those on the data, say, for three years since I built them to see how they work. But the actual system I'm using I don't intend to change. It's been nice to have the last three years of difficult market conditions to see how it's performed.

Nick: Any advice for someone new coming into the game? I would say don't pay US$5,000 for black box software when AmiBroker is $300?

Gary: That would definitely be my advice, yes. It's quite amazing that start-up costs are really low—besides your trading capital, and you do need a reasonable amount of capital to start up. Besides that you need quite a high amount of intellectual capital, and determination, although I don't think it's rocket science.

Nick: In terms of capital to start with, dollar-wise, how much would you recommend someone start with?

Gary: For my type of system, and given transaction costs, I doubt you could start with under $50,000.

Interview with Stephen Rowe

Taking It Month by Month

Juggling a large and successful business creates various hurdles, some of which are easily overcome and others which require a little more thinking through. With time a dwindling asset, Steve intuitively adjusted his investment strategy to a monthly time frame so operational input was decreased. It also inadvertently allowed him to better manage another obstacle: how to inject substantial new capital into the strategy as his business grew. Regardless of account size, Steve's solutions can go a long way in helping others manage their investment strategies.

Nick: Can you tell us a little bit about your background and how you got into the market and what made you get involved?

Steve: To invest some money that I had. I actually remember my first trade back in 1995 very well. I rang a broker my brother recommended and said I wanted to buy some shares and asked him what was good. He suggested Commonwealth Bank (CBA) and he went ahead and bought them. It was only after he bought them that he asked me for my name. That was my first trade and it was that simple.

Nick: Why did you want to get into the market? What was that precursor to actually getting involved?

Steve: I had some money and thought, "what am I going to do with this?" I'm not real keen on property as I was already reasonably invested in terms of owning commercial and residential properties, so I decided to put the money somewhere else. I think my brother was probably talking to me, saying you should try this.

Nick: He was involved in the market?

Steve: In a small way.

Nick: Macquarie Bank was listed in '95 and CBA was listed in '92, so the popularity of getting into the stock market was reasonably high. So you've rung a broker, and asked what's good? And he's told you.

Steve: Yes. I bought some CBA.

Nick: Do you still hold them?

Steve: No.

Nick: Can you remember what reasons he gave you to buy them?

Steve: He said it's a blue chip bank. I think it was all fundamentals. I started looking at prices and PE ratios and reading things along the lines of Warren Buffett.

Nick: How long did the relationship with your broker last?

Steve: He retired and they put me on to someone else who didn't work out so then I got into online broking.

Nick: When you say it didn't work, what happened? Were you losing money?

Steve: The relationship changed. He seemed pretty good, gave good advice but I just didn't feel comfortable with him. I'd done a bit of reading and thought it couldn't be too hard. I started writing down prices and ratios and reading annual reports and going through those motions.

Nick: So you started off with a fundamental tilt?

Steve: Yes.

Nick: When you went to an online broker where were you getting your information for the fundamentals from? The internet was still relatively new back then.

Steve: StockDoctor—I took a subscription with them for a year. It wasn't until 2002 when I really went to charting and system building so up until then it was all fundamentals—reading the reports and chatting with various people. We had the dot com boom and bust in there as well which was a bit of fun.

Nick: How did you go over the Tech crash?

Steve: I didn't lose a lot but I didn't make much. Based on the fundamentals you wouldn't touch most of the companies. I did dabble a little bit because my brother's girlfriend at the time was really keen on some stock that was shooting right up so I bought some of those.

Nick: Like a Davnet?

Steve: Yes, it was Davnet.

Nick: I think everybody was on Davnet.

Steve: I was doing some rudimentary charting back then. She rang me one day and said she had just bought some more whilst I had just sold mine. That was pretty close to the top and so she rode it all the way down. I was lucky on that one but I probably lost money overall.

Nick: From memory Davnet went from 22c to $5 or $6 and all the way back down again.

Steve: Something ridiculous. I remember selling at around that $5 or $6 mark although I didn't hold them at 20c. I bought them at $4 when everybody was talking about them.

Nick: You mentioned you were drawing some lines on a chart. Is that why you got out of Davnet?

Steve: Possibly, but the thing was the fundamentals were crap. They weren't working so what else was there? I didn't know what I was doing but if it was going up you jumped on. I think that was the approach everyone used and I was suckered into the same type of strategy.

Nick: You mentioned that you made a shift into technical analysis and system building in 2002.

Steve: Yes. One of the big things I did was buy MetaStock. I bought it in 2001 and dabbled with it. The problem was it wasn't a portfolio tester—you could only put one chart up and test it. I found Roy Larsen, an interesting character who wrote software for MetaStock called Trade Equity. It allowed you to test portfolios and test the whole market. I thought this was amazing and I stuck with that for quite some time until I stumbled upon AmiBroker. I also bought TradeSim and used the software initially with Metastock, but then also used it with AmiBroker. I can also Monte Carlo test in AmiBroker but it is a lot slower than TradeSim.

Nick: Let's just take a step back. What was the trigger? What made you even think about going to some kind of software package and testing a strategy?

Steve: Fundamentals don't mean anything, like the dot com boom-bust—it just doesn't work. If you bought Davnet at 20c or at $5, you don't care if it's a great company or a pile of garbage, as long as it goes up and in the right direction. Drawing lines on charts was too subjective. You could draw a line here or you could draw a line there or you can change the timeframe. It didn't mean anything to me.

Nick: Do you come from an engineering or mathematical background? That's a fairly big step going from discretionary and subjective to something that's completely objective.

Steve: I've always dabbled with computers. I bought my first computer in '81 and started learning basic programming code at uni[versity] back in the late '70s so I actually liked coding. I enjoyed it and found it a lot of fun. So I had no fear of writing code and learning it. It was a fair jump getting into AmiBroker because I learned it from scratch. I've done a lot of statistics at uni[versity] and have a science degree so that's helpful. I've always had a little bit of a bent for maths, although I'm no great mathematician. I love the idea of testing things.

Nick: It was quite possibly a subconscious jump, if you like, especially with that kind of a background?

Steve: Yes. I went for a job interview once and, even though I wasn't really good at maths at school, I was given all these IQ tests. The director of the company who hired me said I had a really good aptitude for it.

Nick: How did you find Metastock? A lot of people still use it today.

Steve: It was okay. I don't know where it went in the end. When I discovered AmiBroker it was just that much more powerful because you could do portfolio testing. I was using MetaStock initially, and using Roy's software, and then TradeSim, to find systems that worked, although they were fairly simple systems back then.

Nick: When you say "fairly simple", what kind of systems? Where were you getting the ideas from?

Steve: There was a little group of about three or four of us on this website sharing ideas. There was another group in the US and there was also your forum (www.thechartist.com.au/forum), which was very useful. I'm sure you've got blogs or posts from way back in the early 2000s where you could see people feeling their way with this sort of stuff.

Nick: Yes. I went back and had a look. You made an appearance in 2002 and there were a number of users back then all on the same kind of learning curve. So some of the ideas you were testing and some you were trading?

Steve: After the dot com boom I slowed down a bit. I was thinking "I've got to find something that I know works. I've got to have a system." I'm not a discretionary trader—I can't do it. Some people say they can do it. I can't.

Nick: So you intuitively knew what kind of a trader you were, what your personality can and can't do and you stuck with that. When we talk systems here, we're talking about specifically momentum or trend following strategies?

Steve: Yes.

Nick: What made you go towards those kinds of strategies rather than shorter term?

Steve: I work for a start so it's not like I could sit and day trade. I also read the William O'Neil book on CAN SLIM™[44] and there was one aspect that stood out—strength. I said, "Well, what's strength?" I started exploring the idea of strong stocks, specifically stocks that are moving more than the rest of the market. In the book he was ranking them; the ones at the top are moving the fastest and the ones you should be buying, not the ones at the bottom. Rather than trying to rank the stock in any sort of order, I thought I'd just use a simple momentum indicator to say which ones are moving. Then I added a cut-off and said if they moved more than x% over a certain period of time then they're worth testing. That's the sort of process I went through. The other book that I thought was really good was Dr. Van Tharp, *Trade Your Way to Financial Freedom*. I got a lot out of that. It was all the basics such as the positive expectancy and the position sizing. It wasn't trying to show you a system, it was more saying "This is what you've got to look for when you develop a trading system". I found that very good.

Nick: Then what?

Steve: I had a bit of a false start. I had a daily system in 2002 which was developed using MetaStock and it just didn't suit me. It might have worked, but it didn't suit me.

---

44 *How to Make Money in Stocks*, Third Edition, McGraw-Hill, 2002

Nick: It didn't suit you because you had a full time job and you had to check it every day or you just didn't feel comfortable with it?

Steve: Yes, I had to check it every day. That's probably part of it but it wasn't a good system either.

Nick: Was this the point at which you moved from a daily system to weekly?

Steve: It was a suggestion from one of the guys in the group who said to make it weekly.

Nick: So the original daily system that you were looking at was adapted to a weekly timeframe?

Steve: Yes. I found that weekly worked. I stuck with weekly systems up until 2009 before I flipped over to monthly. I don't know if many people trade on a monthly timeframe.

Nick: You're the only person I know that trades on a monthly timeframe.

Steve: I don't know if I should tell people but I think it's a great way to trade. It's a very comfortable way to trade.

Nick: When you say you trade on a monthly timeframe, you only run the strategy once a month?

Steve: Yes.

Nick: When I came here today you said you hadn't downloaded your data for quite some time. Is that because you've only got to do it once a month?

Steve: That's right.

Nick: If we go back to 2002—you've got MetaStock although it can't do the portfolio testing. You're still trading daily back then, but...

Steve: Roy's code allowed me to portfolio test, although it was fairly crude, but it was a heck of a lot better than just testing individual stocks.

Nick: And was that an eye-opening...

Steve: Oh yeah, that was a revelation.

Nick: Can you remember what you were looking for in a system back then? What made sense to you?

Steve: I really struggle with short-term. I really had trouble finding any sort of short-term system that worked for me. Swing trading and trying to hold it for three or four days—none of the systems that I tested using those timeframes with the data I had seemed to work for me. I found that the longer the timeframe, the better the system. I mean, the markets generally trend upwards. We've had a few wobbles but if you go back far enough there's a positive trend upwards.

Nick: So you've always naturally gone for the bigger swings?

Steve: Yes.

Nick: Can you remember what type of stocks you were looking to trade? Was it the top stocks or just any old stock?

Steve: I've pretty much stuck to the All Ordinaries index.

Nick: The top 500?

Steve: Yes.

Nick: Do you still trade the top 500 today?

Steve: Yes.

Nick: So you'll trade a BHP just as readily as you'll trade something smaller?

Steve: It would be very unlikely to get a signal in BHP because it's not the sort of stock that moves quickly enough for my system. I had a lot less money back then too. I think the sort of dollars you have has an impact on how you trade. So daily, you've got to get in and out in a day. With weekly, if you don't do it today you can do it tomorrow, so you've got a little bit more time to build a position in a stock.

Nick: And less reliance on slippage being a drag on the account?

Steve: Yes. I always average things—or randomise those sorts of things.

Nick: Randomising when you're testing? Something like: rather than getting a signal and buying on the Monday, what happens if I buy on the Tuesday? Is it going to make a big difference to the bottom line?

Steve: Yes. Or buy it at a random price some time during the week.

Nick: And doing that didn't make a great deal of difference to the bottom line?

Steve: Usually you're better off buying on the Monday, but it wasn't enough that you'd worry. But if I'd have a meeting on Monday at 10 o'clock as the market opened and I had to go out and buy, it was hard. I had a ticker that gave you live share prices. I had it for six months and then I said, "No, this is not for me, this does not work." What do you do with that information?

Nick: Too much noise.

Steve: Exactly. I went through the full cycle, trying to trade on fundamentals—I don't know what strategy I had. It was probably the turning point to getting into system trading.

Nick: The strategy back in 2002, do you still measure momentum the same way today? Or do you measure it differently?

Steve: I developed the system in 2002; I ran it through to 2009. I had others, but there was one core system that I ran for seven years. Yes, the strategies I'm using now are very similar to the strategies I was using in 2002.

Nick: Can you tell us what it's based on?

Steve: It's a simple rate of change—nothing more than it's gone up x% over x-weeks or months, or however long you wish to choose.

Nick: Alan Hull's strategy, Active Investing, for example, uses a rate of change indicator—a year-on-year type indicator. Is that the kind of strategy?

Steve: Yes—very similar strategies but I found Alan only after I'd developed the system for myself. I don't think Alan had a big impact but what I did like about Alan was he was using similar timeframes.

Nick: For seven years you used weekly data. How were those seven years in terms of performance? It was a pretty good run in the market?

Steve: It was a good run, I mean let's face it, 2002 to 2007...

Nick: Doesn't get much better.

Steve: It was good. I think obviously the exit was very useful for getting out of stocks. One of the things that has changed my trading style, because of my other business interests, is I've got more money. When trading a weekly system there were stocks I couldn't buy enough of over a couple of days. Whereas with the monthly system I can buy some today and I can buy some tomorrow. I could buy four or five times on some of the smaller, faster moving stocks.

Nick: How many positions do you run at once?

Steve: I wouldn't go much past 20. I use a 1% risk strategy, or 1.5% on one of them and 1% on another. I trade a super fund and I trade an investment company that I also set up.

Nick: When you were trading the weekly system, what was your average hold time?

Steve: It was just under a year, on average probably 200 days or so. The monthly's not that much longer. I use an ATR[45] trailing stop so instead of multiplying it by two or three I might multiply it by one or one-and-a- half.

Nick: Was there any pyramiding of positions once you got into them or you just let it run?

---

45 Average True Range

Steve: I tested the pyramid and I didn't have much luck with it. Also, if it's any good you might as well buy it all upfront in one hit. It just seemed a bit complex and you'd end up getting a small amount of some stock and then you'd add some more on and I'm better off just buying the lump—buy it all and ride it out.

Nick: During that period of time trading the weeklies you were obviously researching other things which is why you went to the monthly. But were there any tweaks you made to the strategy?

Steve: No. Once I wrote the system, if I was going to change it, it became a new system. So I stuck to the original system for that long and I didn't touch it.

Nick: For seven years?

Steve: Yes.

Nick: Wow.

Steve: That's not bad is it?

Nick: That's great. It's rare to find someone who can stick with a strategy for that long.

Steve: If I had some other idea that became another system. Actually, at one stage, I was probably trading about four systems. Then I thought, "No. This is crazy because they're all similar systems for a start." So now I've got one system for the super fund and one system for my other account and that's it.

Nick: So the four systems were more or less doing the same kind of thing, yet they're all momentum based strategies?

Steve: Yes.

Nick: And all longer term?

Steve: Yes. Always been momentum based. I don't short stocks, I don't trade on margin—it's all cash. That probably stops me from losing too much because if you're trading on 1% margin you could come a cropper pretty quick.

Nick: If you only trade long what happened in 2008?

Steve: I went to cash although I had a bit of a drawdown: about 15% to 16% drawdown before going to cash. The market dropped for a while then I got some more signals. Actually there was a good little run in there.

Nick: Yes, mid-2008, from June or July 2008.

Steve: Actually one of my best trades was just last year. I had Mesoblast (MSB), I gained 500% on one trade which really makes a year. I put $200,000 into one stock and you walk away with over $1 million out of it.

Nick: Nice.

Steve: The rest of the year I was slightly up, but that one big trade makes the year, which I think is a little bit the way the momentum trades work. You get a lot of ones that might get 50% or 60% or even 100%. But just occasionally something will come along and give you a 200% or 300% or 500%. It's just a matter of how long you can stick with it and how quickly the system kicks you out.

Nick: Going back to 2008, was that a discretionary call to go to cash?

Steve: No, no.

Nick: That's built into your system?

Steve: Yes. It's got exits and it had an Index Filter. So the index turned off and then I just got sell signals.

Nick: Where did you learn about this Index Filter? The reason I ask is that I was at a trader's expo recently and one of the speakers was talking about a market filter. The comment was that this was a very secret instrument that no one knows about—only professional traders know about it. And here I am speaking to someone that's never worked in the business and they're talking about an Index Filter. So I'm intrigued as to where you got that idea from?

Steve: Back in 2002 the thought was if the markets going up we [our discussion group] said, "What if we only buy shares when the market's moving in the right direction?"

Nick: It's a logical step isn't it?

Steve: Yes. It's a logical step and it's a matter of do you use the All Ordinaries or the Small Ordinaries or a specific sector? I tested the All Ordinaries, the Small Ordinaries and possibly some of the sectors as Index Filters and yes, included them in that system. Not all my systems have Index Filters. The two I'm trading now—one has, one hasn't. I find with an Index Filter you trade less. Maybe you don't make quite as much, but you don't go through quite as much ups and downs. The Index Filter really smooths things out.

Nick: This Index Filter, the actual mechanism—is that something like your rate of change indicator or different?

Steve: Yes—it's like a one week rate of change. Look at the last week, look at this week, if it's up this week then the filter could go green and you'd get buys. It's a fairly short term filter rather than one of these longer ones with a six month moving average. With the monthlies it doesn't seem to matter much—you can have a short term one or long term—they seem to work pretty well with the monthlies.

Nick: And it's just keeping you on the right side of the market?

Steve: Yes, although as I say, I do trade a system without an Index Filter.

Nick: Back to 2008 when you went to cash, how long were you in cash for?

Steve: It was probably six months before I got some signals. At the moment I'm mainly cash.

Nick: When you're in cash do you get the urge to do something or you just sit there and follow the system?

Steve: No, I'm happy to put it in a bank account and get 5%.

Nick: So there's no urge to design another system to get trigger-happy and you're quite happy to just sit with your system and be patient?

Steve: Yes.

Nick: You've mentioned before that you buy $200,000 worth of stock—that's obviously a fairly sizable portfolio that you've got running. Is that something that was built up over time?

Steve: I've got two accounts. One's a super fund that I trade for my brother and a couple of others. The other [account] is my own and I've been shovelling money into that. One of the tricky things when you're adding a large sum of money is how do you position size? I got some really nice business contracts back in 2005 so I had all this money in '06 and '07 and I was shovelling that into the market when it corrected. So that made it hard for me [to size positions]. Whereas the super fund, I feel more comfortable actually trading because I'm not getting those big lumps of money.

Nick: When you had a big deposit into your account, what did you do with existing positions? Did you just leave them as were or did you add the money to those existing positions?

Steve: No. I would start calculating how much money was coming in during the next six months or next year and I would position size based on the future inflows. So in other words instead of say using 1% risk I was using 1.5% or 2% risk and would position size based on having that money already. I was taking more risk in essence knowing that new capital was coming in down the track. Otherwise I end up with these little positions running forward. You're sitting there and you've got $100,000 worth of some stock and you probably should have $300,000. But it's tricky; it's probably one of the things I really struggled with.

Nick: It's a common question I get from some of the financial planning companies that I consult to. When they have their clients adding money they're asking, "How do we add this extra money in there?"

Steve: If you know you've got a fairly steady stream of money flowing in then you can sort of front run it. It's the only way that I can think of anyway. That's what I'm trying at the moment.

Nick: How long does it take for your system to get involved in the market because it's obviously looking for some bigger movements?

Steve: On the one without the Index Filter I've got six possible trades. So I take at least the first four this month. I rank them and just take the first four in order. I bought three of those four, or most of them. It's the fourth one that I haven't actually looked at yet because it's only early in the month. I've got a bit of time, so I'll pull the next one up next week and have a look. So there's a little bit of discretion.

Nick: Right, I was going to say.

Steve: I could have three or I could have four each month, but in general my aim is to have at least four stocks in any one month. So if you look at it that way, if we got a good market it could take three or four months to get sixteen positions.

Nick: I understand.

Steve: But actually five positions in a month is not bad. I rank them on turnover because the one that comes up first is going to be the one that's easiest to buy. The one that's at the bottom it might come up and, say, you can only buy $9,000 worth of that stock—so that's discounted straight away.

Nick: So do your systems have any filter on them for volume and turnover?

Steve: Only a ranking, but my rule is I won't take less than a $30,000 position.

Nick: So your discretion really comes into ranking them according to their turnover or liquidity?

Steve: Yes. With the old system I had I might get seven signals then I'd just have to pick some out of it and buy them. I didn't really have a strategy but I probably wouldn't take them all in the week.

Nick: It didn't bother you that you didn't take them all?

Steve: Well it did, that's why I added the ranking system. The aim now is to take those first four signals.

Nick: And that's the maximum you'll take in any given month? What happens if you get 10 signals in a month?

Steve: I've tested it with one, two, three, four, five, six, seven, eight, nine, and ten. In general the more signals you take, the better it is. But four's a comfortable number to buy for me and five would be okay.

Nick: With your testing, did you do Monte Carlo simulations?

Steve: Yes.

Nick: When you're looking at system performance, what do you personally look for?

Steve: Obviously it's got to make money. I tend to look at the equity curve to see if that looks pretty straight, not too lumpy—although monthly systems can have a bit of up and down in them. I step through trades to see how I'd feel with them. In summary it's got to make decent profits, not too much drawdown, and a reasonable equity curve—although the last three or four years has been tricky.

Nick: When you talk about good returns, what's a benchmark for you?

Steve: On a system I'd want it to be 20% plus on a non-compounded basis. Now whether you achieve that's another thing of course.

Nick: In the real world?

Steve: Yes, because there's always the future and you don't know what that holds.

Nick: So 20% non-compounded return?

Steve: Yes, that's a pretty good target. There's a certain science to it all but at the end of the day you've got to look and work through all the trades. You say, "If I actually traded these, how would I feel there? How would I feel when I've just had 10 straight losses?" It's something nowadays that I don't even think about, but it can happen.

Nick: Absolutely. It's easy to plug it into the computer and go away and not think that through, isn't it?

Steve: Absolutely. The beauty of system testing is you can look at 10 years in a minute and then go trade it, not realising that for two years it was doing nothing.

Nick: We've talked returns, what about drawdowns?

Steve: I'm not so fussed about drawdowns anymore—it's going to happen. By having the correction in 2007/8 it actually gave us data to look at drawdowns, the same with the dot com bust. You look at it and understand how the system performed in that period. A lot of people say it was terrible but I think it's actually quite useful to have. The more exposure we have to different circumstances in the market, the stronger we can make our systems, which is probably another reason to go to longer term. Most people would struggle with the idea of waiting a month to get out of something that's tanking. But often they drop in just one day or one week—so it didn't make much difference.

Nick: So in your opinion an objective function would be a personal choice, rather than a specific mathematical number—because everybody's different?

Steve: Yes. If I have to have something I usually look at return. It's as close as I get to a good objective function. But then I've got to look at drawdown and I'll look at the equity curve and I'll look at the period. How did it perform in 2007? 2008? 2009? I don't think I do anything clever. I think there are a lot of people out there that probably can write these sorts of systems if they want to.

Nick: I think a lot of people would be surprised that some of the greatest traders on the planet have very simple strategies. One of the big trend followers we talk about in this book can actually write the code on the back of an envelope. That is a key component—keeping it simple. It doesn't have to be complex.

Steve: If you make it complex then you've got to check all your code and make sure you haven't made a mistake.

Nick: Why do you think people gravitate towards more complex systems? At least they go that way to start with, they might reverse and go back the other way eventually, but why do you think they do that to start with?

Steve: Roy Larsen, that I spoke of earlier, I think he just likes to code. Some of the systems I've seen have been seven pages in length. I think he just enjoys doing it, quite frankly. I'm not saying complex systems don't work, they probably do, but you've got a lot of code to check. Often in a system you might have five or six lines of core code and the rest is just making the chart look pretty.

Nick: If it's simple strategies that make money, which you obviously believe, why can't people follow them?

Steve: I think it really helps to do the testing yourself. I've tried to help people trade. There's a guy that works with my brother and manages a super fund. He'll buy, but he always struggles on the sell, although sometimes that's made him money. He's held off selling for a month or more.

Nick: But that's reinforced the error though?

Steve: Yes, that's right. Then when 2008 came along, he was a bit slow.

Nick: And that cost him a lot…

Steve: Yes. Just follow the system, it's easier. You don't have to second guess or think—you just sell them. I don't even look at whether I've made or lost money on a trade. I might glance at it, but it's amazing how much I forget. That's the beauty of systems trading—forget the fundamentals. It could be two lizards crawling up a wall and you're betting on which one's going to crawl fastest or something weird like that. You don't have to know what they do.

Nick: So it's not about falling in love with the stock. When you exit it's just a tool?

Steve: That's right; the company itself really means nothing.

Nick: What about if you're holding a stock that becomes a take-over target whilst you're holding it. Do you have a rule that you follow?

Steve: Quite often I'll watch it and I'll just get out of it before the take-over comes through because your money can sit there for some time. You know you're not going to get a lot of upside out of it for three months unless another bidder comes in and that never seems to happen. So usually I'll get out.

Nick: Again, that's a bit of a discretionary call, but needed.

Steve: Yes, but what do you do? It's just sitting there doing nothing.

Nick: The rule we use is very similar. We give it two weeks, if there's no counter-offer in two weeks we exit the position. As you rightly say, the stock can sit there for three or four months, you may as well put that money to work somewhere else.

Steve: Exactly.

Nick: At the moment the markets have moved a little bit off the recent lows—do you have any positions on at the moment?

Steve: Yes. I've got two positions in my personal account that I've held for a little while and they're up quite nicely—about 37%. Then in the super fund I've got five or six positions. I'm buying three this month but I'll probably add another one to make it four for the month.

Nick: Due to market conditions since you turned this monthly system on have you ever been fully invested?

Steve: I've come close but not fully—around the 80% mark. It's been a pretty up and down sort of market.

Nick: When you back test how far back do you go?

Steve: I'll step through from January 1, 1999 and test up to 2008. It's actually very interesting to look at when you step through it on a month-to-month basis. Start a month later and step it through to see the impact on the results. The starting time that someone gets into the market can have an impact on a trading system. If you're unlucky and you got in at the peak in 2007/8, you probably wouldn't be real happy.

I'm helping a friend with his super fund. He started at the beginning of this year and he's had a bit of drawdown. I told him you're going to lose money in the first six months or year of start-up on a long term system like this because you'll just be selling the losers. It's the ones you hang on to that hopefully bring you rewards. So those first trades you sell will generally be losing trades.

Nick: How did he take that?

Steve: He lost a lot back in 2008 with a financial advisor when the market dropped. He's actually got investments in there that he can't sell—some sort of managed fund where you couldn't actually take your money out.

Nick: Right, they've been locked.

Steve: Yes, and you know, it's pretty frustrating to see your investments drop so much and you're not able to get out. Some just went broke. Advisors tend to tell clients to buy yet they don't tell them when to sell. They're more interested in keeping the money in their pockets or in the managed fund rather than want to make money for the client. I wouldn't touch a managed fund myself.

Nick: What do you think are the biggest hurdles that you have to face?

Steve: Just following the system, even now. I can be a bit slow or a bit slack. Where I could get in on Monday, I might get in on Wednesday or Thursday although ideally I should get in reasonably quickly early in the month. The other hurdle is if I think too much about the amount of money at stake, so I try to think of it as Monopoly money. The fear of losing can freak some people out. You've just got to jump in there and go for it.

Nick: Why didn't it freak you out?

Steve: If I lost all the money I had in the market it would be a bit of a disaster but that's unlikely to happen. I think if you haven't developed the system yourself you've really got to have a lot of education about what you're doing. You can't just hand a system to a person and tell them to run it on the weekend or at the end of the month and follow the signals blindly. You need to really hold people's hand. I've been helping someone this year and every month he'll send me his signals and needs to know if they're right before he makes the trade.

Nick: Just go ahead and do it.

Steve: Yes.

Nick: So the psychological part of the journey, you could say, is what most people would find very difficult?

Steve: Yes. If you haven't tested the system yourself, if you haven't done Monte Carlo simulations and you don't understand what it is, then it's a black box. You're putting your faith in something that you don't understand. The other interesting thing is that many people want to trade but they don't want to learn to write systems. Only one person that has approached me actually asked me to show them how to write a system.

Nick: Why do you think that is?

Steve: I think you've got to have a certain aptitude or desire.

Nick: Do they think maybe a system is a bit 'smoke and mirrors' or they don't believe it. The only way to make money is to do what Warren Buffett does?

Steve: Maybe. I know a professor at Sydney University. He said, "...you can't make money in the market the way you make money in the market." That's exactly how he said it.

Nick: And what did you say?

Steve: Whatever!

Nick: When did this happen?

Steve: This was a while back. He puts his money into property. I told him he was a smart guy that he could write formulas and trade shares but he's an economist. He's convinced by the Efficient Market

Theory and says you might get 6% or 7% if you're lucky. He doesn't have the attitude that you can beat the markets and he can't get past that. Then there are other people who just don't have the time or the desire. I think you've got to be a certain sort of person to want to write a trading system, to go buy the software and learn it.

Nick: You mentioned this other friend of yours who's just started out. Did he buy AmiBroker and learn how to code it himself?

Steve: It took him about three years. He had come to me and said he'd lost a whole pile of money in his super fund and he'd rather manage it himself. I told him to buy AmiBroker, get a data supplier and then I gave him a system. I sat down with him to take him through how it works, how you run the scans and generate the signals. I even sat with him on the first few trades.

Nick: What would your daily routine be?

Steve: Monthly.

Nick: Of course—monthly routine. So is that on the first day of the month?

Steve: Yes. So if it's a Thursday I download all the data on the Wednesday night and then you run the scan and then you buy on the Monday, Tuesday, Wednesday or Thursday until you've got all the stocks you need.

Nick: What happens if there's a significant intra-month decline like the Japanese earthquake? Do you have to wait for the month to close before you close a position out, or it can be stopped out at intra-month?

Steve: No, at the end of the month.

Nick: End of month only. So the month has to close?

Steve: Yes.

Nick: And then you'll exit a position.

Steve: Yes.

Nick: So nothing intra-month at all?

Steve: Otherwise I might as well go back to daily or weekly because of the timeframe. The nice thing about monthly is I can go away for one week or two weeks and it's no big deal.

Nick: That's a common question I get when people go away and what they should do with their positions. I guess it's one of those situations when using a monthly system you wouldn't have this problem.

Steve: Right, it's as much lifestyle as anything. It's not a big deal for me in terms of getting in and getting out of the market at a specific time either. The other benefit is that I can take my time to get in and out so volume doesn't become as big a problem.

Nick: Do you look at any other third party information such as news services or anything like that?

Steve: Not to trade with. I'll look at what's happening in the US overnight and the rest of the world.

Nick: How close are your real time results to your test results?

Steve: Not as good. If you run a Monte Carlo test there's always that range of outcomes so I'd fall in there somewhere. Worst case or best case—I'm in there somewhere. Last year was a great year in the super fund because I picked up that MesoBlast and 500%. I probably had some 200% and 300% gains in the past.

Nick: Over the last five or six years what do you think your annualised return was?

Steve: I know I've had some years better than 40%. You can have a year where you lose money, like in 2008, but then you'll have a really nice year. The last 5 years have been pretty tough. In the super fund that I run the returns have been quite lumpy, ranging from 16% down to over 40% up. Since 2003 I have had one really bad year, one year just below breakeven, and all the other years in the black. Quite a few years have been in excess of 20%

Nick: And a losing year is something that you accept?

Steve: Yes, you have to. You haven't got much choice have you?

Nick: No.

Steve: The other thing is you're not in it for just one year. It's something that I'll do for the rest of my life. If I have a bad year I'm sure there's going to be another good year sometime in the future. Unless the markets are going to go down forever from here.

Nick: But even then, you know, there can be some outstanding years. Have you ever gone back and had a look at what happened in the '30s and early '40s?

Steve: No, I haven't, but I can only assume that there were some good years in there somewhere.

Nick: Absolutely.

Steve: I think the big problem we have is where something big happens on a single day and, just like that, a 50% drop.

Nick: Like an '87 crash?

Steve: Yes. It can happen and there's a reasonable chance in '87 those systems would have been fully invested. I don't know how I'd handle it. I'd probably be very philosophical and say, "...ah look, that's the market". Then just keep going.

Nick: I was trading in '87 and I can tell you there was nothing you could do because you woke up and the market had gapped 25% so it didn't matter.

Steve: Yes and what can you do?

Nick: It would be an interesting question to see if that could happen in modern days because of the 24 hour markets. But I think you're right—anything can happen.

Steve: Exactly, and that's the other thing—it's all good to look at the stats in the world, there's always going to be outliers, the Black Swan event. That's why it's nice to have a few of these events in recent times to test. I'd call 2008 a bit of a Black Swan and the dot com was also very interesting.

Nick: Have you ever overridden your strategy?

Steve: No. I may have been slack and not closed out the position entirely by the Friday, when I was trading weekly, but I get really quite agitated if I don't follow the system. If you don't follow it then what are you doing? You're lost, you've got nothing. That's why I get frustrated with people who don't sell when they think it's good. What happens if the stock keeps dropping?

Nick: So you consider reinforcement of errors quite a bad thing?

Steve: Yes.

Nick: Because you get away with it once so you think you're going to get away with it another time and that's when the damage is done.

Steve: Yes. Also some people think they're better than the system and that's just scary. When you've tested hundreds of systems you know the market's not going to give you a free ride. You're going to get burnt seriously at some stage. Not following the system is like closing your eyes and wandering around in the dark—it just makes no sense. I'm sure there have been very rare occasions but it's an exception, not the rule. We're human.

Nick: So where to from here? You're just going to keep trading the system?

Steve: Yes, just keep trading.

Nick: Do you think you'll make any changes?

Steve: No, not at the moment. I actually haven't done any system testing for myself for over a year. I did change an Index Filter for someone else. I spent probably four hours back testing and just changed one parameter. Actually people do learn—there's another friend I've got who's been trading a system for about four years now and he went through 2008. He was a bit slack but now he follows the system. I think that's great—it's a hard way to learn, but...

Nick: You've got to learn it.

Steve: Absolutely.

Nick: My experience is you can tell people all these kinds of things, but until they've actually experienced it for themselves they're not going to take it on board. Once they experience it then they get the lesson.

Steve: Exactly.

Interview with Craig Francis

Craig is the founder and Director of a boutique financial services firm. Looking out for the best interests of the firm's clients and intimately aware of the short comings of standard financial products, Craig embarked on a new strategy approach using momentum investing for the firm's clients direct share portfolios. Not only did this differentiate his firm completely from his competitors, it also provided his clients with a product they could easily relate to and feel comfortable with.

Nick: Can you explain the type of business you own.

Craig: We operate a holistic financial services firm. We manage our clients' complete financial advisory affairs—business, accounting, tax, superannuation, investments, insurance, financing and estate planning. Previously we were solely a chartered accounting practice, but we've diversified into other areas now.

We saw there was a real need to offer a point of difference in the market.

Nick: Why did you see that need?

Craig: We noticed a deterioration in our clients' overall wealth and the loss of confidence our clients were experiencing from advisors in the financial planning industry.

Nick: Did this stem from the events of 2008 or do you think it started beforehand?

Craig: It's been bubbling away for a long time. There were periods during the 2003–2007 bull market where substantial gains were made, however the clients' portfolios were not reflective of that.

Nick: Why do you think that is?

Craig: Fundamental errors in the way their portfolios had been constructed. The standard theory and practice of asset-based allocation and Buy and Hold strategies are, and were, flawed, in my opinion.

Nick: So what did you do?

Craig: We moved the firm away from Buy and Hold we looked at the other opportunities we could make available to clients. We looked at how the client had their investments structured, assessed their existing investments and then showed clients other options which are available.

Nick: What options did you put forward that were different from what's already out there?

Craig: We looked at a direct share strategy which was based purely on momentum and trend analysis. We also took a risk-based analysis of the client rather than asset-based analysis; how much risk are they prepared to take versus how much risk they should take if they want to achieve a certain goal for their retirement—whatever date that may be. So instead of just assessing the risk they're prepared to take through risk profiling, we show them what they really need to take to achieve their goals in retirement. We then allow the client to decide whether they increase their savings towards investment, make lifestyle adjustments now or in retirement or increase their risk appetite in order to achieve their goal. We review this regularly for the client, dialling the risk down or increasing it as their life circumstances change from year to year.

Nick: Do you find people tend to be more risk seeking or more risk averse?

Craig: Every client's different and it really depends on their age. A lot of people have been burnt through their investments, particularly in the stock market, and more recently in the property market as well. People seem to mention the stock market a lot more because they can physically see the value of their investment each and every day. They're more likely to take a conservative approach particularly with some clear exit points if the market turns down sharply.

Nick: There are a lot of different opportunities out there; what led you to go down the route of using a momentum strategy?

Craig: The rules and discipline which are applied to the strategy. We have set rules which we follow religiously; we are able to test it back throughout history and can get a very accurate measure on what the returns could have been. I think that's your best guide when it comes to investing—most investment decisions are based on history as no one can predict the future.

As the rules of the strategy are very strict, if we apply them going forward we should be able to achieve gains and limit losses from the momentum of share price movements. It's very easy to convey this concept to clients as well—this is how we do it and this is why we do it. Clients understand there's a very clear exit strategy whereas with a Buy and Hold strategy, they've got an entry point, but they've got no exit point. Having an exit strategy is a very important element to have.

Nick: Do you think clients react positively to knowing there's an exit strategy and that they're not going to hold a stock that drops from $100 to $5?

Craig: Absolutely—it's key. They know they can get through the turbulence and limit the downside.

Nick: When you bring a client on board do you actually show them the buy and sell signals on the computer?

Craig: Yes, we go through it in detail. We don't show them the specifics of the strategy, but we do give them an overall concept of what triggers a buy, what triggers a sell and so on.

Nick: How do you assess which stocks for which client?

Craig: We base the clients' portfolio on their risk appetite, so with a lower risk tolerance we only look at the ASX100, versus a client that's got a higher risk tolerance where we look at the ASX300. Their risk tolerance will determine how many trades and how long they hold them for.

Nick: Do you have clients that come to you and say, I want to be aggressive, I want to trade smaller stuff?

Craig: No, we stick to our risk profile rules of not investing outside the ASX300. However, we do have a separate strategy for more aggressive traders.

Nick: Do you ever use any discretion?

Craig: No. In the testing period we played with the strategy, but we got burned.

Nick: So the strategy did better than what you thought you could do?

Craig: Yes, 100 per cent. It's a good lesson, but everyone's got to learn that lesson for themselves. You've got to trust the strategy and stick to it. I feel most people like to think they can beat the strategy and that's the general perception in the market, but you can't. If you've got set rules you stick to them, it removes the emotion. It's not a matter of having the best set of rules; it's a matter of consistently following those rules over the longer term.

Nick: How long do you encourage your clients to stay involved with the strategy?

Craig: Minimum two to three years.

Nick: Have any of your clients moved fully away from their other direct share market investments and into this portfolio?

Craig: Yes—the majority of clients.

Nick: This is a solid point of differentiation between you and your competitors—if you walk into most financial planning offices with this idea 9 out of 10 would probably just laugh you back out the door again.

Craig: No, not all. I've actually shown this to other planners and accountants and they absolutely love it. They love the rules that go with it; they see a real point of difference. Most proactive advisors are very embracing of this strategy.

Nick: Does the strategy operate on daily data or weekly data?

Craig: We use weekly data so the beauty of the strategy is we only place trades once a week. That way it leaves us four days a week, or even longer, to manage the client's portfolio and all the other areas of advice. We don't get phone calls—clients know what's happening. They're very relaxed with the strategy although we spent a lot of time educating them in the beginning especially to change those preconceived emotions that they had with previous advisors and their own investment strategies. They understand that when the market starts to move up, we'll start to move into it with appropriate stocks. If it's going down, they know that we'll exit the stocks when they're signalled to exit. If the market has been trending down for a while they know that we'll be in cash. As recently as six months ago we were 100 per cent cash.

Nick: How long does it take the strategy to get invested again once the market starts to pick up?

Craig: It needs to show clear signs of the market trending up, but also individual stocks trending up—so that can be over a period of a number of weeks.

Nick: Do any of your clients use gearing?

Craig: We steer away from gearing—it's internal office policy. When we're assessing a client's risk profile we determine whether gearing's appropriate or not but we tend not to employ that strategy.

Nick: Going forward, do you envisage further research with the strategy or adding other strategies in there?

Craig: We're quite happy with the strategy as it is but there may be tweaks that we employ down the track, depending on the size that we get to. We see that we could move the market in certain stocks, particularly the smaller ASX 300 stocks so that might mean that we tweak the strategy or start using different trading days.

Nick: So you'd buy some Monday morning, then buy some Monday afternoon perhaps?

Craig: Or ideally we'd like to use VWAP[46] which enables us to fill the order throughout the day. Or we might have slightly different rules within the strategy such as portfolios dedicated to particular sub-industries.

Nick: So trading in different universes?

Craig: Yes.

Nick: So it's possible you might have a client come to you and say, I just want to trade metals and mining stocks?

Craig: Yes, although we'd have to analyse the strategy and do our testing but we could quite possibly look at that.

---

46 Volume Weighted Average Price

Nick: So your clients have had a good uptake of the strategy?

Craig: Yes, it's been great. One of our key philosophies is the education process in the beginning. It's not extensive, but it's just changing that mind-set. I'm pretty happy with the strategy although we've had very turbulent times over the last two years. Considering what the markets have done, we've still been able to collect our performance fees which are a fair indication that it's performing better than what the market is doing.

Nick: What do you base your outperformance on?

Craig: If a client's in ASX100 we benchmark it against the ASX100, if they're in the 300, we benchmark it against the 300.

Stephen Marshall

Lessons from a Veteran Investor

Experience is an asset that can't be bought—only earned. It's extremely rare to come across a broker with 46 years of practical investment experience and hands-on application who is still open to new concepts. My brief conversation with someone of Stephen's wisdom was very rewarding. I was also impressed to see that his 'Elderly Statesman' attitudes of respect and integrity in business have been duly passed on to the younger brokers in his office. He may have been around for a long time but he's acutely attuned to new ideas that are beneficial to his clients. After the events of 2008 Stephen was quick to put into place some new processes which he kindly discusses with us here.

Stephen: Back in 1964 I was working for CSR which happened to be in the same street as the Sydney Stock Exchange. At the time a number of us came under the tutelage of an older gentleman who just happened to be technical analyst and it was he who introduced me to the stock market. This was when the nickel boom started to fire. I made a lot of money and I lost a whole lot.

Nick: What was his technical analysis based on?

Stephen: It was very basic analysis and I've moved on since then.

Nick: You are now part of a large firm's regional stockbroking office. Traditionally stockbrokers are aligned to fundamentals and technicals are more or less ignored. What do you do that is different?

Stephen: About 8 or 9 years ago one of my clients was subscribing to a newsletter called Stockradar and said he wanted to trade according to the selections that came up in the newsletter. That's how I was introduced to Richard Lie and I've subscribed to his Stockradar service ever since.

After 2007 we were asking ourselves questions such as, "Could we have handled the impact of the GFC better with our clients?" So working with Richard we came up with a momentum portfolio. We did some back testing on his figures—he covers the ASX200. Richard has a Trend Intensity Indicator and we determined to buy only stocks that had a Trend Intensity of 7 or higher. We then apply other criteria such a company's financials using Stock Doctor.

Nick: Stock Doctor being a fundamental overlay?

Stephen: Yes, then we also look at our own in-house research—if the stock is covered. We look for good fundamentals from Stock Doctor, a Buy or Accumulate recommendation from our own research people and an entry from Stockradar. We call this the Alpha Portfolio—it's our momentum portfolio. So for example, if a client has $1 million to invest, $200,000 could be earmarked to go to the Alpha Portfolio, $800,000 to be invested based on fundamentals.

Interestingly quite a number of clients say they've always known that they should have stop losses in place so they become quite keen to go ahead with this portfolio—usually because they haven't got the time or the discipline to run stop losses themselves. We get all the data on a Sunday night, Monday morning we determine which stocks meet the criteria for buying or selling and depending on this lining up with our own internal research recommendations we appropriately advise our clients.

Nick: So it's a weekly system.

Stephen: Yes. Theoretically we get rid of all the noise in between. Any that breach our stop losses get dropped on the Monday and any that meet our criteria move in on Monday.

Nick: How many positions do you generally hold?

Stephen: The maximum we've had is 28 but at the moment we're just holding 3 stocks.

Nick: Using these criteria, how long do you tend to hold a position for?

Stephen: Once the stock is bought it'll stay there so long as it hasn't broken its stop loss—we have a rising or trailing stop loss running behind the stock. In terms of time it can be longer term. Iluka is a good example. We bought on July 19th 2010 at $5.34 and exited in early August 2011 around $15.00—so that was just over a year holding time. We had 24 increases in the stop loss over that period. Iluka went to $18 or so then broke our stop loss and we exited.

Nick: During much of that time Iluka was actually bucking the trend of the broader market.

Stephen: Yes. Interestingly when we entered it there were very few analysts wanting anything to do with Iluka. It was difficult to find any positive research on it at all.

There are always occasions where a stock will surprise; back in 2003 when Jubilee Mines was around $1.70, for example. We sorted the top 200 by PEs[47]. We looked at the recommendations by Investor Web, our own research and Stock Doctor and then looked at the yields. The stock that jumped out at me was Jubilee Mines—so we started buying them.

I remember a technical analyst at the time said if it got to $2.30 it'd be pretty good. Well we eventually sold out at $23. No one could foresee what was happening with the nickel price. When we entered the nickel price was about $8,000 a ton and it went to $30,000 a ton.

Nick: But it just goes to show, the market will go where it wants to go.

Stephen: Exactly, and you just follow along for the ride; but it is good to have a methodology to ensure you don't miss the bus.

Nick: Richard Lie's Trend Intensity is a momentum-type indicator, isn't it?

Stephen: Yes—momentum.

---

47 Price to Earnings ratios

Nick: So you put this Alpha Portfolio into place in 2007?

Stephen: By the time we got it through compliance, through management and all that sort of thing our first trades were in September 2008.

Nick: Did your internal research department or your quant department have reservations or were they happy for you to move ahead?

Stephen: I put it to our management on the basis that the Alpha Portfolio would be peripheral to normal investing and we are not suggesting people put all their money into it.

Nick: The Alpha Portfolio has some subjective and discretionary inputs. How do you interpret those?

Stephen: We've determined what we want to look at.

Nick: But even so, with this fundamental overlay you can't go back historically and test that, can you?

Stephen: No. We could go back and test what we've done and compare it to, say, if we'd just followed Stockradar.

Nick: That's an interesting point, have you done that?

Stephen: We're doing it right now actually.

Nick: How many transactions a year would the Alpha Portfolio average?

Stephen: In the last 12 months we realised 12 profitable trades, 22 losses and we have 4 unrealised.

Nick: How does your stop loss work?

Stephen: We work with Richard's data with stop losses.

Nick: So when his Trend Intensity index turns down you exit?

Stephen: Yes.

Nick: How's your performance been?

Stephen: We got a lot of whipsaw earlier this year but we'd done very well up until about September 2009—we were running at round 20% but it depends when clients entered. One client returned 21.28% for the 12 months ended 30th June 2011. Another client who invested $700,000—his return was 9.79% compared with the All Ordinaries which was 7.1% and the Accumulation Index which was 11.2%. So that client underperformed the Accumulation Index. There was a smaller account with $200,000 that returned 11.9%—so just above the Accumulation Index. You're going to have short term periods where you'll underperform or outperform and that depends on when the client starts.

Nick: Just coming back to the fundamentals versus the technicals, you've said you'll only buy stocks when your research department is saying buy or accumulate.

Stephen: That's one of the things that we look at. It might be a Hold.

Nick: What if your research department puts a sell on a stock?

Stephen: Then we don't buy it.

Nick: How do other brokers in the firm view this strategy?

Stephen: Our Newcastle office had a new manager come on board and she visited our office, wanted to operate the same way and also learned about the Alpha Portfolio. They've now established the same sort of portfolio but named it the Momentum Portfolio. Again, they don't sell it as the only way for you to invest, but rather to supplement your portfolio.

Nick: It gives you a point of differentiation from almost every other broker, doesn't it?

Stephen: It does indeed. But clients like it as well because of the comfort of stop losses. I've got a pharmacist client who is very conservative. He says, "Stephen, I can just rest. I know my money's in Alpha and I don't worry about it because I know you've got stop losses and I go to bed with no worries at all."

Nick: If the market goes into a sustained downtrend like we saw in 2008, does the portfolio turn off?

Stephen: Yes. We've only got three positions right now so that's telling you that you really should be almost 95% cash. You're fairly heavily weighted in cash at the moment?

Nick: We have been 100% or 95% cash from April until just recently. Personally I'm now 45% invested and 55% cash. So just in the last few weeks we've started picking up a bit, but that's probably a little bit more aggressive than what you're doing here. We're trading a little bit further out as well. You're sticking with the top 200?

Stephen: Yes.

Nick: How do your clients take it if you're sitting in cash?

Stephen: They're comfortable. We have an arrangement where if they're in cash the management fee is 0.25% of funds under management. It goes up when they're invested.

Nick: When you're sitting in cash do you ever have any clients ring up and say, can we do something?

Stephen: No. Remember they still have exposure with their other 80%.

Nick: The great thing with the Alpha Portfolio is you don't have to worry about market noise and uncertainty—it'll tell you what to do.

Stephen: Exactly. As my pharmacist client says, "I don't worry, Stephen, because I know you'll be out, that's good for me. I don't have to be worrying about what the market is doing." He said, "I want to be making money, but I know I'm going to be protected." That's the selling point. What we say to people is we'll run with the gains and we'll cut our losses.

Nick: Do you educate your clients or give them an information sheet to get them prepared?

Stephen: We give them that sort of information when they're coming on board, then every Monday and every Friday I send out an email advising what are buys and what stocks need to be exited. From time to time we'll throw in some other material about technical trading. We are constantly in contact with the client.

Nick: You're holding three stocks at the moment with a high level of cash. How long would it take you to get invested if the market really started to pick up?

Stephen: We try and limit it to have no more than two new entries every week.

Nick: And you just trade the top 200?

Stephen: Yes.

Nick: And if you get an aggressive client that comes in and says I want to be more aggressive with it, can you go beyond the ASX200?

Stephen: We won't, no.

Nick: Do you trade on client's behalf or do you actually ring them on the Monday morning and say, okay, we've got to buy this or sell that?

Stephen: We can phone, email or SMS.

Nick: Would you change the Alpha Portfolio through further research and investigation?

Stephen: It's quite possible. Always learning.

Nick: Does it ever end?

Stephen: I don't think so, because if it does I think you're dead.

Nick: How do you deal with a client that says they don't want to do a particular trade?

Stephen: Never had it. They understand and trust the advice. That's the point we make clear—if you want to benefit, you have to trust the advice. I have had clients who've backed off for a while especially when we were getting whipsawed but then come back in again. That's human nature.

Nick: With the fundamentals, what are you specifically looking at?

Stephen: We assess what our firm's analysts think and what Stock Doctor thinks. Do the financials look good? Have they borrowed a lot? What's their financial strength? Although knowing human nature, just because a stock has a weak balance sheet is not going to stop it from running higher—there could be some other blue sky trigger that's really attracting people.

Nick: So you consider the markets are strongly driven by sentiment rather than the fundamentals.

Stephen: Yes.

Nick: You mentioned Iluka before and as we saw it went a long way beyond what could be claimed to be reasonable—both upside and downside.

Stephen: Yes. I remember Antimony Nickel in the late '60s at about 10c that went to $3. Poseidon ran from 30c to $280 and all the way back to nothing.

Nick: We see a few of these stocks that had pretty spectacular rises and falls such as Compass Resources.

Stephen: Yes. Using a momentum approach will allow you to get out because as investor sentiment turns the stock also turns down and signals you to exit.

Nick: That was one of the big problems with Macquarie Bank back in 2007/2008—they had incredible earnings growth over prior years. The stock hit $98 and the valuations were up at $120 and $130.

Stephen: Yes—that is right.

Nick: Then by the time the lag of earnings came through the stock was back down around $15 or $20.

Stephen: Yes. It was amazing. Even our banking analyst who was rated number one year after year by his peers and had worked for Macquarie previously was bullish on Macquarie at the time. It was a stock that was just going to take on the world.

Nick: Here you've got a banking analyst, an analyst that only looks at banks, he knows them inside out, and his valuation for Macquarie, a bank he knows well having once been a part of the team there, is well above the market price. What does that say? Is there more to markets than fundamental analysis?

Stephen: Absolutely. I think it depends what sort of a person you are. Personally, with my investments, I like to have control and know the reason for doing something.

Nick: Would you agree that fundamentals are more of a crutch, if you like, to be involved in the market?

Stephen: You could use that word. As I grow older managing my own superannuation, if technically it says out, I'm out; I'm not going to ask any questions. It's peace of mind.

Nick: That's saying something; how long have you been in the markets?

Stephen: Started in 1964, so 46 years. It's been interesting. One thing I've learnt is you can't account for blue sky mentality—you don't know why something's running. Everyone seems to price things, including the analysts, as though they're going to stay at high levels. History always says that if a stock goes up from here to here, then a whole lot of people will come in and support it. When I lived in Alice Springs avocados were $3.50 each. So everyone on the Coast started planting avocados—they were everywhere. Now they give them away for 20c each.

Nick: The 'greater fool theory' effectively?

Stephen: Yes, that's right. The extraordinary thing is that a lot of people thought that because they put their money into the Superfund, they had to invest it in shares, which they didn't have to do at all of course. There are some horrific stories of people putting a lump sum straight into their super and then being told to invest it straight away, which they didn't have to do. As a stockbroker I've always had the philosophy that I want to be able to walk down the street and not cross over to the other side because I can see somebody coming along that I gave poor advice to.

Nick: What other lessons have you learned?

Stephen: Like many things, 80% of your profits come from 20% of your trades. The same as in many community organisations where 20% of the people do 80% of the work, so on and so forth.

Nick: It's the need to therefore get through that 80%—lots of small losing trades, and a lot of small winners. You need to push through that feeling that, gee—we're not making a great deal of progress here. Then all of a sudden, wham—out comes one or two Ilukas, or Lynas and away you go.

Stephen: Exactly right—they're the saviours those outliers—they're supposed to be there. They're the ones to make the Alpha for you.

Nick: And over time you'll get a lot more of those.

Stephen: Yes.

Nick: From 2008 until now—late 2011—it has been some of the most frustrating periods in the market. My research shows that the last time we saw this kind of price action was in the early '90s—very similar range bound backwards and forwards price action. If your clients are living through this or staying with it through this, that's got to be a good sign that they're there for the longer term.

Stephen: I've not had one client who has been unhappy that they've gone into the Alpha Portfolio. Overall clients are there for the long term. I read about a famous trader who said, "Man's a funny thing; he buys a stock expecting it to go up. When it does go up he won't sell it because he thinks it'll go higher. When it goes down he won't sell it because he thinks it'll go up again". Momentum investing gets rid of all that mentality.

SECTION 4

Overcoming Yourself

In the initial stages of this book it was suggested that to be a successful investor or trader you must:

- Find a strategy that works
- Validate it
- Do it

A major point of difference between success and failure, between professional and amateur, is how you do it, or more specifically whether or not you can actually do it. This book has given you quantitative rules to follow—a process to follow. We've discussed strategies and validated them. However, what about actually doing it? To 'do it' means how we think and act in various situations. The key to succeeding in the investment arena are the behavioural or qualitative traits that can't actually be taught. These traits must come from within and be developed over time with ongoing and concerted discipline.

An investor learning to recognise and implement quantitative and qualitative traits is similar to that of a teenager learning to drive a car. The quantitative traits are definable and repeatable; turn the wheel left to steer the vehicle left, foot on the brake to slow or stop, indicate when turning and drive on the left side of the road (in Australia). All these are teachable.

But what about feeling the flow of traffic and being aware of impending danger, looking far enough ahead for possible hazards, lane position and driving in others people's blind spot or recognising fatigue and failing judgment? These are the qualitative traits that can't be taught. They are learned over time and from experience.

When it comes to investing it's one thing to know that your account value may decline by 20%, yet it's another to actually stomach it in real terms. How do you teach someone that it's not only acceptable to lose money, it's imperative to success? We know it's highly probable that a string of losing trades will occur, but to feel 8 or 10 losses in a row when you're at the controls will plant serious doubts in your mind. How you think and act during this losing streak is the make or break moment. Believe it or not, sitting in cash for periods of time can be difficult for a lot of people. It's human nature to want to act but in theory we know it makes complete sense to stay sidelined when a sustained downtrend is in place. How do you teach patience?

Quantitative can be taught. Qualitative on the other hand must be developed and development takes time, effort and practice. It is highly unlikely you can read a book or attend a weekend seminar and turn up on Monday morning as a professional trader or investor. In fact many of the hurdles we face come from within and the journey to success is not a straight line, as many sales people would have us believe.

FIGURE 88: Investing Success

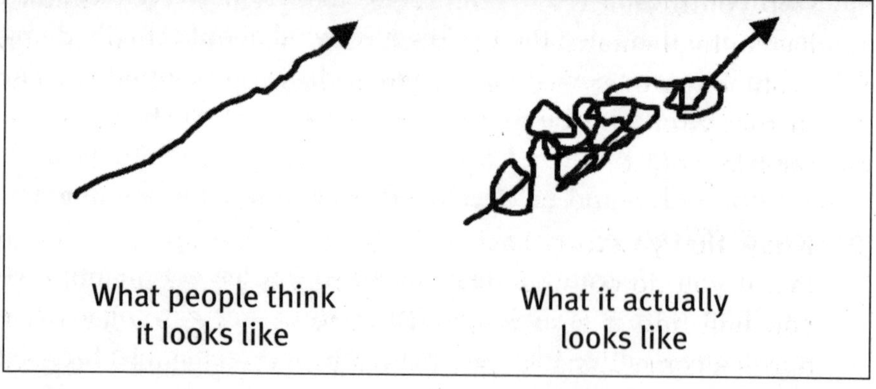

When faced with everyday decisions and hurdles we understand what is required in order to overcome or complete them. But when it comes to investing we're rarely aware of what hurdles actually lay ahead and how to deal with them psychologically. When faced with unknown or unexpected disruptions we tend to deviate from our plan in order to alleviate the uncomfortable feelings. Our emotions, fear, greed, uncertainty and our need to be right, all step in and hinder progress. This deviation is known as the Beginner's Cycle and is why we tend to accumulate a myriad of investing books and continue to sign up for the weekend seminars and courses. The problem is that these weekend 'warrior' seminars can't teach you how to lose money, yet losing money is an important part of success.

"The best loser is the long term winner." **Art Simpson**

Here are a few tips and tricks to help you remain objective. The more aware you are of your thought process, the better prepared you can be to overcome negative emotions when they occur.

1. **Surrender yourself to the market.** Try this exercise for a week: before the market opens each day write down (a) if you think the market will close the day higher or lower, and (b) by how much it will move up or down. By the end of the week you should realise that you can't predict the direction of the market and from that you can extrapolate that you can't predict the outcome of a specific trade. Regardless of what you want, the market is going to do what the market is going to do, so just let it. Focusing on a future event that you cannot control will only stop you from acting in the present moment. If your strategy has a mathematical edge then it's that edge that creates profitability over the longer term, not your predictive powers. Just let your strategy and positions evolve. Everything else is senseless noise.

2. **Know that you truly have an edge.** It can't be stressed enough that if you do not understand why profits are generated, then you will find it extremely difficult to stay the journey when hurdles come along. If you have a proven edge all you need

to do when markets get tough is execute the signals rather than make difficult decisions under stress. Remember that an edge is the mathematical outcome of the buying and selling process, specifically the knowledge that generated profits will outweigh losses and costs. Momentum investors create their edge by riding trends that move in the desired direction and cut positions that don't move in our favour. This concept ensures that the average win is substantially larger than the average loss and even with a strategy that has a win rate of less than 40% a positive edge can still be made. Whilst we can backtest and simulate our edge using computer software, it's more important to truly understand it conceptually. Once you have true confidence in your system then you will find it substantially easier to participate in the market.

3. **Next 1000 trades.** We occasionally hear about a trader making one great trade that 'made them'. But for each of these success stories there are hundreds of people that have come unstuck from a single bad trade. Great traders know this game is not a sprint or a lottery. It's a long distance event based on our strong underlying mathematical edge and, as a result, no single trade should make or break us. 'Next 1000 trades' is an important reminder that our edge comes from a great number of trades rather than a lucky one or two. It's also a reminder that any small sample of trades within that bigger picture is insignificant. Always be cognizant that it's the big picture that is important—not the next week, month or even year. Some of the world's best traders not only have losing months but they do have losing years as well. They look beyond the short term because they know the law of large numbers will ensure their edge is exploited eventually. There is no point in 'trying' momentum investing for a few months to see how it goes. It needs to be a long term commitment.

4. **Rome wasn't built in a day**. There is no such thing as an overnight success in any endeavour, especially high performance events where emotion plays such an important role. In this

day and age our culture has a need for constant activity and immediate gratification. When it comes to investing however the prevailing market conditions will dictate when activity or inaction is required. Good times and bad times are part and parcel of investing. Sow the seeds during the good times yet play strong defense when the bad times come along. A strong defense does not mean a change of tactics or strategy. Do not be swayed by noise from others that a new strategy is needed. Chasing performance is a loser's game. Let the market come to you rather than force yourself on the market.

"Success in the stock market requires patience. So few people succeed in the market because they have no patience.[48]"

Jesse Livermore

5. **Don't relate work ethic to profitability.** Sustained trends do not occur all of the time, but over the longer term they occur often enough to generate above average returns for those that are patient. However, in the interim there are times we simply go through the motions even though there will be no reward or payment for that effort. The market doesn't have a set pay day like your employer does, even though you're working to place orders and manage positions. Rather than focus on the wanted outcome, it's best to work through the correct processes that will eventually lead to the desired goal. The market will reward you when it's ready—all you need to do is be there for it.

6. **Be a manager of bad trades rather than attempt to pursue good trades.** You cannot control the market, which intrinsically means you cannot control the outcome of a single trade nor can you know ahead of time whether a trade will be profitable or not. What you can control is how large any loss will be. Over the longer term you can skew the numbers, your mathematical edge, in your favour by limiting losses and allowing the profits to run. Failing to manage a losing trade adequately will work against your edge. After a losing streak, or during a drawdown,

---

48 *Reminiscences of a Stock Operator* by Edwin Lefevre. Wiley & Sons, 1994

the urge to take a quick profit can be very strong. You need to do the opposite of what seems natural at this time. Follow your system's rules. Don't second guess.

7. **Forget the balance of your account**. You don't check the value of your home every day but you know that over the longer term it is likely to appreciate. The same is true when using a momentum strategy that has a long term positive expectancy. Your strategy's edge, coupled with the law of large numbers, is all that matters on a day-to-day basis. Profitability takes time to develop and during that time your account value tends to move up and down. Looking at it every day won't speed that process up but it can cause you to ride an emotional roller coaster that can detract from the end game.

8. **You'll never make a big profit taking a small profit**. The large money is made capturing the large swings therefore you need to allow the trailing stop room to move so the larger trend can continue. A natural by-product of this is that on occasion large open profits can be given back, creating the urge to take profits quicker next time. Cutting a profit short adversely impacts on the win/loss ratio and therefore the systems expectancy.

9. **Don't be a dick for a tick**. On many occasions a stock may dip after it's bought on momentum. This can induce the user to finesse the entry next time around in the hope of getting a slightly better price. The risk, however, is missing out on a substantial trend and profit if the stock fails to dip back to the discretionary buy level. Being more concerned about picking up a few cents on the initial entry opens the door to missing a massive trend. You simply can't afford to miss a large trend.

10. **Don't give up your day job.** It seems to be the goal of every aspiring trader but the reality is much different. Making trading or investing your only source of income will place financial pressure on you and your family. Trading can also be a very lonely endeavour, creating psychological issues. Momentum investing is not a quick road to riches. Nothing good ever is.

What it will do is build a nest egg over the long term a lot faster than a Buy & Hold strategy. Momentum investing is also low stress and low maintenance. Rather than trade for a living, run a momentum strategy in the background and go out and do the things you love to do or are good at.

APPENDIX

Common Misconceptions

Every strategy, regardless of style, has a flaw of some kind, somewhere. Some are serious, others not so. A strategy that is not accepted as traditional thinking tends to come under greater scrutiny than those considered acceptable by 'the herd'. Scrutiny can be blinded by confirmation bias or the tendency for people to favour information that confirms their beliefs regardless of evidence to the contrary. Whilst momentum investing is still considered a 'fringe' strategy or method I am not a vocal proponent of converting the non-believers.

There are however numerous misconceptions surrounding momentum investing that should be addressed here.

1. *Trends don't last forever and if a stock becomes too popular it will reverse, leading to a sharp decline from which you can lose a lot of money.*

It is true that trends don't last forever. Being reactive rather than predictive, a momentum investor will hop off the trend as it starts to reverse. Secondly, there is no evidence that sharp declines always occur after a sustained trend terminates. There are certainly some situations where a sharp reversal will occur, usually following a parabolic rise, but this does not automatically transpire into sharp losses. Some stocks slowly roll over after a period of distribution before they decline; that is, investors gradually sell off the stock and price moves sideways before a decline occurs. A key reason why so many people, professional or otherwise, lost so much money during 2008 was not because of a sharp selloff. It was a slow decline over the course of 15 months and the reason why damage was inflicted was because many assumed it was simply a 'dip' in the ongoing up trend. That dip was essentially a stealth downtrend. The irony of this misconception is that a momentum investor is being singled out from any other investor holding the same stock but for different reasons. Indeed, holding a stock that reverses sharply will cause losses regardless of the reason it is being held. If that reversal is the start of a sustained decline, a momentum investor will fare somewhat better than investors who continue to hold the stock, waiting for strength to re-establish itself.

2. *You will always be at risk of timing a buy incorrectly and end up losing money.*

Firstly, nobody can predict the future and as nobody can predict the future it stands to reason that everyone, regardless of their style of investing, will be at risk of timing errors. One only needs to look at the numerous fund managers who lost between 30% and 50% of capital during 2008 to appreciate that even their strenuous application of fundamental analysis was burdened by poor timing. As discussed earlier in this book, buying weakness suggested further weakness was more than likely. Timing a purchase and being wrong is not a risk. Staying wrong with a bad investment is the risk. Being unwilling to accept that your investment is wrong, or allowing your ego to dictate decision making, can lead to catastrophic losses and it's those losses that drag long-term performance down.

Secondly, the implication that decisions must be consistently correct in order to generate a profit, or at least right more often than not, has been shown to be inaccurate. An investor with a 50% win rate still has a high positive expectancy and can therefore generate decent returns over the long term. Indeed, our real time examples from 2006 through 2011 only had a win rate of 43% yet produced a 95% total return.

3. *High turnover leading to expensive fees.*

Momentum investing will certainly have a higher turnover (generate more trades) than long-term investing, but high turnover is a relative term. Many very effective momentum strategies can outperform the market with around 30 transactions per year, not hundreds. Secondly, the cost of transacting business is extremely cheap and getting cheaper every year. Making 30 transactions a year can cost as little as 0.25% of capital which is a minor drag on an account. If a person chooses to pay higher commissions and indulge in expensive broker-operated platforms then drag will rise but will still remain well within acceptable boundaries. Drag will become a more pronounced cost if a strategy executes more than 100 transactions a year. The slow lowering of commissions will enable smaller account holders to gain some traction with this style. There are several brokers now operating in Australia that have commission rates of less than $10 per transaction without any other fees.

4. *Time intensive.*

A fully systematic momentum strategy, once built and tested, takes substantially less time to execute than one using fundamental decisions. Software packages allow markets to be dutifully scanned, opportunities signalled and orders placed within a brief period of time. When sustained trends are in place and an account is fully invested, or alternatively fully committed to cash, then no effort or time is required. Remember that as no discretion is used with many of these strategies, thinking time or exhaustive on-going research time is limited.

To prove this point, I timed my daily activities relating to my momentum strategy:

Task	Time Taken
Download data*	3 mins 7 secs
Open AmiBroker. Scan market. Generate signals.	2 mins 57 secs
Calculate position size	0 mins 15 secs
Login to broker platform. Place order.	1 mins 24 secs
Total elapsed time:	7 mins 43 secs

**Premium Data by Norgate Investor Services. www.premiumdata.net.au*

5. *Momentum investing only works in bull markets.*

Correct, but so does every other traditional long-only strategy looking for growth. The following table conclusively shows that in 2008 the majority of managed funds, all of which are arguably fundamentally driven, suffered substantial losses.

MAJOR FUND MANAGER PERFORMANCE 2008	
The Ten Best	**1Yr %**
Advance Wholesale Imputation	-29.43%
Investors Mutual Wholesale—Industrial Shares	-29.56%
Advance Sharemarket—Wholesale	-29.60%
Maple-Brown Abbott Australia Equity	-30.46%
Investors Mutual Wholesale—Australian Shares	-30.62%
Advance Alleron Australian Equity Growth Wholesale	-30.46%
Aviva Investors Prof Elite Opportunities	-30.86%
Integrity Australian Share	-31.18%
Goldman Sachs JBWere Australian Equities Wholesale	-31.88%
EQT-Flagship Fund (Common Fund No.2)	-32.66%
Benchmark: S&P/ASX200 Accumulation Index	-38.44%
The Ten Worst	**1Yr %**
Challenger Select Australian Shares	-53.8%
PM Capital—Australian Opportunities	-48.71%
Colonial First State FC—Arcadian Wholesale Australian	-46.09%
Challenger Wholesale Australian Share	-44.41%
AUI-Platypus Australian Equities Trust—Wholesale	-44.36%
Invesco Wholesale Australian Share	-43.55%
Perennial Growth Shares	-42.65%
Colonial First State Wholesale PM Capital Aust. Shares	-42.61%
Orion Wholesale Australian Shares	-42.43%
Barclays Man Investment—Australian Shares	-41.72%
Benchmark: S&P/ASX200 Accumulation Index	-38.44%
	Source: Morningstar

Figure 55: The best and worst fund managers in 2008.

The key ingredient to the success of any strategy is in its long term implementation, and momentum investing is no different. You do not become a momentum investor for a week, a month or even a year. It should be a commitment over the longer term.

6. *Momentum strategies have high tax implications.*

Buying and selling within a 12-month timeframe will incur a higher tax liability. Whilst some positions will extend beyond 12 months, the likely holding period will fall between 6 and 10 months. However, the decision to use a strategy should firstly be made from a capital growth perspective and not a taxation perspective. A simple analogy is a company spending on advertising—if the benefits outweigh the costs of doing so, then an advertising campaign is worthwhile. If the benefits are minimal, if any, then it would be smart not to advertise. The same is true for active investing. If the risk adjusted rewards are strongly beneficial then it would make sense to proceed. Also, the use of structures such as self-managed super funds (SMSFs) or trusts can cut down tax drag quite substantially. It is important to discuss the tax implications with your accountant and get professional advice on the structure that is right for your circumstances.

Further Reading and References

By Nick Radge

www.nickradge.com

Nick Radge's momentum strategy, the Growth Portfolio, is available via subscription for Do-It-Yourself investors or via individually managed accounts for people who don't have the time or inclination to manage their own investments. Nick Radge uses the Growth Portfolio signals to manage his own superannuation fund.

www.thechartist.com.au

Nick Radge is Head of Research & Trading at The Chartist. The Chartist provides in-depth technical research and analysis to help you make more informed investment and trading decisions, as well as offering several trading strategies for both short and longer term traders.

The Growth Portfolio, discussed in *Unholy Grails,* is available at both The Chartist and NickRadge.com.

By Other Providers

www.trendfollowing.com
Michael Covel's site, arguably the world's leading source of trend following research and education.

www.AmiBrokercoding.com
Brett Winton is one of Australia's premier AmiBroker programmers and was instrumental in producing the code used in this book.

www.premiumdata.net
Serious investors use only quality data that can be relied upon to be clean and accurate. Nick Radge uses and recommends Norgate Investor Services, supplier of Premium Data, for all his trading and investment strategies.

www.AmiBroker.com
There are many technical software packages on the market. Some are simple, others more complicated and some extremely expensive. In terms of value for money AmiBroker is hard to beat as a simulation and ongoing position management platform.

Nick Radge does not receive endorsement or referral fees for the products listed above. This information is based on the products Nick chooses to use to operate his own trading and investment strategies and research.

Glossary

Active Investing—Buying and selling instruments with the intention of outperforming a benchmark.

ASX—Australian Securities Exchange.

Bear Market—A sustained downward price trend, usually defined as being greater than 20%.

Benchmark—A comparative figure used to measure relative performance.

Broker Consensus—The opinion of analysts on the future value and financial metrics of a company.

Buy & Hold—The purchase of an instrument with the intention of never selling it.

Bull Market—A sustained upward price trend, usually defined as being greater than 20%.

CAGR—Compound Average Growth Rate. The annual growth rate of an investment over a period of time.

Call Option—A derivative that gives you the right, but not the obligation, to own an underlying instrument at some stage in the future.

Cash—Current assets that can be accessed immediately and deemed no or low risk.

Dividend—A sum of money paid to company shareholders from earnings.

Discretionary—Using personal judgment to make buy and sell decisions.

Dividend Adjusted—The amended share price calculated after dividends have been taken into account.

Drawdown—A decline in account equity from a peak to a trough.

Earnings Growth—The annual growth rate of a company's earnings.

Edge—The mathematical outcome of the buying and selling process.

Expectancy—The amount of money on average we can expect to make for every dollar risked.

Expectancy Curve—A graphical representation of the win/loss ratio plotted against the winning percentage.

Herd—The thoughts and actions of the majority who tend to react collectively.

Index Filter—A filtering technique that defines the trend of an underlying index.

Long—To have bought, or currently own, an instrument.

MAR Ratio—Annual return divided by maximum drawdown.

Maximum Drawdown—The largest peak to trough decline of account equity over the life of the strategy.

Momentum—The consistent progress of price in a particular direction.

Momentum Investing—Interchangeable with Trend Following. The act of buying high to sell higher or selling low to buy lower.

Monte Carlo Simulation—A method of statistical sampling used to measure probability from broad or random outcomes.

Moving Average—The unweighted mean of a series of data points, usually the closing price, over a period of time.

Open Position—An investment that has not yet been closed.

Optimisation—An attempt to find the best input value from a set of alternatives in order to maximize profits and/or minimize risk.

Outperform—A rating used by brokers or analysts that suggests the performance of a company's share price will exceed the performance of the benchmark.

Position—To own an instrument or investment.

Price to Earnings Ratio—Measure of price paid for a share compared to the net profit earned by the company.

Price to Book Ratio—Ratio used to compare the book value of a company against its current share price.

Qualitative—Unable to be measured with numerical results.

Quantitative—Being measured or quantified or containing objective properties through empirical investigation.

Range—Sustained sideways price movement with no visible trend.

Robust Strategy—Persistence of a system's characteristic behaviour under conditions of uncertainty.

Sharpe Ratio—A risk adjusted measure of return calculated by subtracting the risk free rate from a portfolio return and dividing by the standard deviation of annual returns.

Simulation—The imitation or modeling of an investment or trading strategy to better understand its behaviour.

Slippage—The difference between the theoretical price and the actual achieved price.

Standard Deviation—The measure of a strategy's volatility of annual returns.

Strategy—Interchangeable with System. A set of rules or investment plan that may include an entry, exit and risk management components.

Survivorship Bias—The error of overlooking elements of a strategy that existed in the past that no longer exist.

Systematic—Investing rules that can be hard-coded into a computer which in turn generate buy and sell signals.

Trading Range—Sustained sideways price movement with no visible trend.

Trailing Stop—An order that follows behind an open position that, when executed, will lock in open profits.

Trend—A sustained movement in price either up or down.

Trend Following—Interchangeable with Momentum Investing. To follow a trend rather than predict a future price movement.

Underwater Equity—A graphical representation of drawdowns.

Universe—A group of candidates (or investment products) to which a strategy can be applied.

Volatility—A measure of price variation.

Win/Loss Ratio—The average win divided by the average loss.

www.nickradge.com
www.thechartist.com.au

info@nickradge.com